*Lyrical Symbols and
Narrative Transformations*

Essays in Honor of Ralph Freedman

Ralph Freedman

Lyrical Symbols and Narrative Transformations

Essays in Honor of Ralph Freedman

Edited by
Kathleen L. Komar
and
Ross Shideler

CAMDEN HOUSE

Copyright © 1998 by
CAMDEN HOUSE, INC.

"Foucault and Najibullah"
©1997 by Gayatri Chakravorty Spivak

Published by Camden House, Inc.
Drawer 2025

Columbia, SC 29202 USA
Printed on acid-free paper.
Binding materials are chosen for strength and
durability.

All rights reserved,
including the right of reproduction
in whole or in part in electronic or any other form.
All rights to this publication will be vigorously defended.

Printed in the United States of America

ISBN 1-57113-120-5

Library of Congress Cataloging-in-Publication Data

Lyrical symbols and narrative transformations : essays in honor of
   Ralph Freedman / edited by Kathleen L. Komar and Ross Shideler.
     p.   cm.
Includes bibliographical references and index.
ISBN 1-57113-120-5 (alk. paper)
   1. Freedman, Ralph, 1920–   . 2. Literature, Comparative.
I. Komar, Kathleen L. II. Shideler, Ross. III. Freedman, Ralph,
1920–   .
PN863.L97   1997
809--dc21   97–25500
                                                                    CIP

   Quotations from "Alien Territory" from *Good Bones and Simple Murders,* by Margaret Atwood copyright ©1983, 1992, 1994, by O. W. Toad Ltd. A Nan A. Talese Book. Used by permission of Doubleday, a division of Bantam Doubleday Dell Publishing Group, Inc.
   Excerpts from *Morning in the Burned House* copyright ©1995 by Margaret Atwood. Reprinted by permission of Houghton Mifflin Company. All rights reserved.
   Excerpts from *Selected Poems: Poems Selected and New 1976–1986* by Margaret Atwood copyright ©1987 by Margaret Atwood. Reprinted by permission of Houghton Mifflin Company. All rights reserved.
      "Book 8: A Day for Songs and Contests," from *The Odyssey* by Homer, translated by Robert Fagles, translation copyright ©1996 by Robert Fagles. Used by permission of Viking Penguin, a division of Penguin Books USA Inc.

   Frontispiece photo of Ralph Freedman by Charles Huguley, Atlanta, Georgia.

Contents

Acknowledgments	ix
Tabula Gratulatoria	x
Introduction	1

Part I: Lyrical Symbols

Helen Sword
   Lyric Transformation and the Poetics of
   Gender in Rilke's *Sonnets to Orpheus*
	9

Thomas Kovach
   Rilke's "Die Insel der Sirenen" and the
   Music of Silence
	24

Robert Fagles, Translator
   Homer: *The Odyssey*
   Book Eight: A Day for Songs and Contests
	33

Anna Tavis
   Rilke, Dostoyevsky and Tolstoy:
   The Unpublished Chapter
	51

Katherine Callen King
   Antigone's Lyric Heart: Marguerite Yourcenar's
   Revision of Sophocles' *Antigone*
	64

Ellen Waldinger
   "That come before the swallow dares"
   (Thinking about Leonardo's *St Anne Cartoon*)
	81

David Lenson *Ptyx*: The Metaphysics of the Symbol	94

Part II: Narrative Transformations

Anca Vlasopolos
  Free-Floating Marginals and Contagious 115
  Degeneracy in the London and Paris of the
  Mid and Late Nineteenth Century

Ross Shideler
  Hardy, Darwin, *Tess* and the Father's Changing Name 132

Jonathan Freedman
  Mania and the Middlebrow: The Case of *Trilby* 149

Kathleen L. Komar
  Whatever Happened to the Lyrical Novel? 172
  Madness and the Lyrical in Bessie Head's *A
  Question of Power* and Ingeborg Bachmann's *Malina*

Martine Watson Brownley
  Atwood on Women, War, and History: 186
  "The Loneliness of the Military Historian"

Lore Metzger
  Atwood's *Robber Bride*: At the Borders of 204
  Feminist Narrative

Gayatri Chakravorty Spivak
  Foucault and Najibullah 218

In Memoriam: Lore Metzger 1925–1997 237

Ralph Freedman: Professional Life and Publications 241

Index 247

Acknowledgments

We would like to thank the institutions and individuals who provided special support for this volume including: The Department of English at Emory University; The Department of Comparative Literature at Princeton University, Robert Hollander, Chair; The Program in Comparative Literature at the University of California, Los Angeles, Katherine King, Chair; The Department of Germanic Languages at the University of California, Los Angeles, Ehrhard Bahr, Chair; Lore Metzger, Emory University; Barry Munitz, Chancellor of the California State University; Joseph A. and Sophie H. Komar; and Byron H. Shideler. We would also like to acknowledge the Academic Senate of UCLA for its support for the editorial work on this volume.

To all the many colleagues who appear in the *Tabula Gratulatoria*, we send our appreciation for your encouragement and kind words.

And finally, we express our gratitude to Bill Phelan for his precise and patient copy editing work without which we would not have survived.

Tabula Gratulatoria

Elizabeth Abel	University of California, Berkeley
William Abernathy	Collegiate School, New York
Emily Apter	University of California, Los Angeles
Claudia Brodsky Lacour	Princeton University
Clarence Brown	Princeton University
Victor Brombert	Princeton University
Martine Watson Brownley	Emory University
Wai Wah Chin	New York
Volker Dürr	Northwestern University
Robert Fagles	Princeton University
Jonathan Freedman	University of Michigan
Ann Gaylin	Yale University
Rachel Hadas	Rutgers University
Beverly Haviland	State University of New York, Stony Brook
Luc Herman	University of Antwerp
Marilyn Kerst	Washington, D.C.
Katherine Callen King	University of California, Los Angeles
Kathleen L. Komar	University of California, Los Angeles
Thomas Kovach	University of Arizona
Murray Krieger	University of California, Irvine
Alexandra Reed Lajoux	President, Alexis & Co.
David Lenson	University of Massachusetts, Amherst
Jinny & Earl Miner	Princeton University
Jane Newman	University of California, Irvine
Marjorie Perloff	Stanford University
Juliet G. & Richard H. Popkin	University of California, Los Angeles
Richard Rorty	University of Virginia
Patricia A. Rosenmeyer	Yale University
Albert Rossi	University of Trento, Italy
Merle Ruberg	Paris, France
George C. Schoolfield	Yale University
Ross Shideler	University of California, Los Angeles
Naomi Sokoloff	University of Washington, Seattle
Albert Sonnenfeld	University of Southern California
Gayatri Chakravorty Spivak	Columbia University
Garth St. Omer	University of California, Santa Barbara

Helen Sword	Indiana University
Carol A. Szymanski	Princeton University
Anna Tavis	Fairfield University
Lewis E. Thayne	Mount Holyoke College
Anthony Vidler	University of California, Los Angeles
Anca Vlasopolos	Wayne State University
Ellen Waldinger	Independent Writer
Florence Weinberg	Trinity University
Theodore Ziolkowski	Princeton University

Special Contributors

Lore Metzger, Emory University
Barry Munitz, Ralph's former student & Chancellor of the California State University
Joseph A. & Sophie H. Komar, from a mother and father to a *Doktorvater*
Byron H. Shideler

The Department of English at Emory University
The Department of Comparative Literature at Princeton University, Robert Hollander, Chair
The Program in Comparative Literature at the University of California, Los Angeles, Katherine Callen King, Chair
The Department of Germanic Languages at the University of California, Los Angeles, Ehrhard Bahr, Chair

Introduction

In 1963 Ralph Freedman's *The Lyrical Novel* elegantly broke open narrative and genre boundaries. His rethinking of generic categories and his expansion of the interplay between lyric and narrative spread around the world. One of our current faculty, who read *The Lyrical Novel* in Korean, told us of its influence on Asian students during the late 1960s and 70s, thus demonstrating its groundbreaking importance within in a very wide sphere. Ralph has published much more than that volume, of course, as *Hermann Hesse: Pilgrim of Crisis* (1979), and most recently *Life of a Poet: Rainer Maria Rilke* (1996) as well as his early novel *Divided* (1948) and current novel-in-progress, "The Mark of the Tooth," demonstrate. But we have chosen to focus this volume thematically toward the framework established by *The Lyrical Novel*, as well as by Ralph's later work on Rainer Maria Rilke.

Beginning with essays on Rilke, the collection focuses on nineteenth- and twentieth-century European and North American poetry and prose, but it turns to the *Odyssey* and other classical texts to suggest and to analyze the role of aesthetic symbols and narratives in the process of personal and social transformation. Moving out from the European and into a broader world context, the volume's final essay brings together Kipling's *Kim*, Foucault, and current events in Afghanistan, to discuss literacy and the post-colonial states. These studies examine issues of aesthetic transformations related to those outlined by Ralph Freedman — transformations that encompass revisions of one genre by another, of classical by modern texts, and of gendered perspectives by new critical insights. The authors explore the ways in which historical, cultural, and aesthetic contexts interact with and help to shape and reshape modern literary texts.

The first seven essays emphasize Rilke's opus and the rich ancient and modern traditions and poetic works that illuminate textual interactions between the lyrical, the classical, and the symbolic. The second group of essays present different perspectives on the philosophically and politically transformative capacities of literature, in both a positive and negative sense, during the past one hundred and fifty years.

Part I of the volume, "Lyrical Symbols," begins with Helen Sword's essay, the first of a series on Rilke and his work, which introduces the motif of the lyric as transformative and symbolic. Her study of Rilke's *Sonnets to Orpheus* adds a complex new dimension to our understanding of his poetics of gender. Beginning with Rilke's limited vision of women, Sword sees in these famous sonnets the role of Eurydice, shaped in part by the notebooks of the dying young Wera Knoop, as first actively transformative, and then finally as a way of listening, "at once fleeting and eternal."

Using Homer's *Odyssey* as a foundational text for Rilke's "The Isle of Sirens," Thomas Kovach argues next that Rilke, as part of the transition from his early to his late poetry, turns away from a vision of the Sirens' threatening music and toward music as a means of empowering his art. Contrasting *The Odyssey* and Rilke, Kovach shows how Rilke's effort results in a recognition of music's sacred and creative functions, an affirmation of the identity between music and silence.

Continuing the volume's mix of classical and modern and helping to elucidate the discussion of Homer in Kovach's essay, Robert Fagles generously provides Book Eight — Odysseus' joyous, yet melancholy stay among the Phaeacians — of his masterful new translation of *The Odyssey*. Fagles's contribution provides a fitting celebration of his long-time colleague and friend, Ralph Freedman, who is himself a creative teller of famous lives. Hearing the song "the famous harper sang" describing his own exploits, Odysseus serves as a model for the personal intensity, yet intertextual and social power of lyric and narrative that Freedman saw in lyrical novels and which we discover in the essays that follow.

Returning to Rilke, Anna Tavis turns to *The Notebooks of Malte Laurids Brigge* and shows us the influence of the Russian novelists Dostoyevsky and Tolstoy — in the presence of the "double," in scenes of death, and in Rilke's obsession with writing. Katherine Callen King combines and illuminates both classical and modern texts when she first analyzes the problematic representation of female gender in Sophocles' *Antigone*, then contrasts it with two prose poems by the modern French author Marguerite Yourcenar. King demonstrates that Yourcenar's revisions of classical themes in her "Antigone ou le choix" and "Apollon tragique" reflect not only events in her personal life, but represent a "celebration of love and a critique of the male culture that was threatening Europe with fascism."

Ellen Waldinger also takes up the theme of love, as she ponders the relation of love, painting, and poetry to the fullness of life. She asks what the classical Leonardo and the modern Cézanne knew about perspective and its connection to the moment, to identity. Contemplating a collage of poems by Baudelaire, Rimbaud, Blake, Dickinson and others, Waldinger decides, finally, that "Leonardo's painting shows that Grace which overwhelms death, even of children. To know such Grace is surely to praise." Similarly looking for meaning in what at times seems the inexplicable, David Lenson ventures from medieval allegory to Coleridge's Fancy and Poe's Secondary Imagination. To begin his lucid explication of "alternative representation," he offers the layers of the emblem, "whether inlaid upon the phenomena or upon the surface of a textual representation," as a means of understanding Gérard de Nerval's "transcendental signifying." Through readings of poems by Baudelaire, Lenson leads us to Mallarmé's ptyx and an art which salvages "consciousness from the categories of time and space."

Part II of the volume uses the notion of "Narrative Transformations" as its guiding principle, but several of these essays suggest the difficulty of social change by discussing texts with narratives seemingly pushing toward progressive change and simultaneously portraying cultural resistance to it. Identifying one aspect of this vacillation in the nineteenth century, Anca Vlasopolos examines the discourse of "contagious degeneracy" as a means of representing "the undesirable within biological determinism." For her examples of the medicalizations of discourse, she discusses the city in French authors such as Emile Augier and Alexandre Dumas (fils), then continues with Dickens's *Bleak House* and returns to France and Baudelaire and Zola as the final exemplars of literary representations of contagion, degeneracy, and marginalization.

Marginalized by both history and family, Tess in Hardy's *Tess of the d'Urbervilles* is sent out to profit from her family's name, but ends up the victim of that patriarchal heritage. Ross Shideler's essay relates Tess's allegorical quest to Freedman's work, then discusses the novel in terms of Darwin's questioning of the divine father and Jacques Lacan's "Name-of-the-Father." Shideler argues that *Tess*'s narrative development hinges on a triangular intersection of the absence of a divine father, the weakness of a family father and the rise and fall of a strong woman.

If Vlasopolos and Shideler deal with the complicated discourse that underlay the transition from the nineteenth to the twentieth century, Jonathan Freedman shows how George Du Maurier's near turn-of-the-century novel *Trilby* portrayed the appropriation of cultural status through Svengali and Trilby and simultaneously served as a model for the developing middlebrow public to appropriate what it perceived as high culture. Freedman uses the novel to suggest how Trilby mania was "part of what Adorno and Horkheimer would call the 'culture industry.'" But he also explores and clarifies the duality of the novel and the response it evoked, and he concludes with a persuasive comparison of twentieth-century manias that quickly become demonizations.

Returning to *The Lyrical Novel*, Kathleen L. Komar considers it as a theoretical text to assist contemporary women writers in locating a new lyrical space within the context of narrative; such a space would make room for other forms of knowing besides the rational. Komar examines works by South African writer Bessie Head and Austrian Ingeborg Bachmann to reveal both similarities of structure and the use of madness as a lyrical expression of the possibility of a different kind of understanding. *The Lyrical Novel*, Komar suggests, might serve contemporary feminist critics as a fruitful theoretical ground to provide new ways of thinking about texts by women.

The next two essays by Martine Brownley and Lore Metzger take up the Canadian writer Margaret Atwood's revising and questioning of fundamental human institutions and values. Brownley focuses on an early dramatic monologue, "The Loneliness of the Military Historian," and its relation to Atwood's novel *The Robber Bride*, as a means of discussing Atwood's preoccupation with "the study of human aggression" and war. Brownley points out Atwood's use of an incongruous female military historian to "problematize the relationship of women to war." Juxtaposing that female figure to a male academic historian in Atwood's *The Handmaid's Tale* allows Brownley to identify Atwood's evolving attitude toward militarism as well as the rigorous standards she implicitly proposes for historians and critics.

In her last essay, Lore Metzger probes Atwood's *The Robber Bride*'s complex representation of women as both victims and victimizers as well as her questioning of the authenticity and the moral value of both fiction and history. Focusing on Tony, the female historian, and the classic femme fatale, Zenia, Metzger wonders why Atwood "gives center stage to this destructive female figure," but proposes that doing so allows Atwood to destabilize "our certainties about good and evil." Metzger argues that Atwood's novel "places the personal and warfare not in opposition (women as victims of war), but in apposition (the personal as war)." As for literature, Tony's fictional construct of "definitive moments" which become *The Robber Bride* is "a morally dubious enterprise," but one which raises flags "on the long march to chaos."

In its raising of such flags, we see literature as traversing genre and gender boundaries, as having the capacity for transformation, and our closing essay calls for a specific transition. Gayatri Chakravorty Spivak moves from Foucault's *Discipline and Punish* and the hanging of Najibullah, the last Communist President in Afghanistan, to propose alternative Development, an ab-use of the Enlightenment. Concerned that "not much will change for the woman at the bottom," Spivak proposes that "If we are gender-sensitive, we must be able to imagine the very long haul, and think of constituting the future subject for academic freedom for a much-delayed opening of access to the university." As an example, she suggests "the *pouvoir/savoir* of the rural girl-child in literacy," and argues that "so-called New Social Movements must build up an alternative internationality that will stand behind the state."

With this emphasis of the real transformative power of literature in the world, we come full circle, back to the life and literary and critical accomplishments of the man we celebrate in this volume. Ralph Freedman's remarkable career and legacy are reviewed in the short closing essay of this volume, which outlines both his academic achievements and his contributions as mentor to future generations of comparatists. Before that piece, there appears a brief homage, which we asked Ralph to write, to his longtime companion, Lore Metzger, who battled cancer while completing her essay for this book and whose influence on Ralph and on us pervades this volume.

Ross Shideler
Kathleen L. Komar

Part I:

Lyrical Symbols

HELEN SWORD

Lyric Transformation and the Poetics of Gender in Rilke's *Sonnets to Orpheus*

Rainer Maria Rilke's *Die Sonette an Orpheus* (1923) (*Sonnets to Orpheus*, 1942), as the dedication on the title page reminds us, were composed to and about a mythical man but for a real woman: "Geschrieben als ein Grab-Mal für Wera Ouckama Knoop" (Written as a grave-monument for Wera Ouckama Knoop).[1] Two years after her death from leukemia at the age of nineteen, Wera, a young family friend whom Rilke had barely known, mysteriously came to haunt the poet's imagination; although she appears, unnamed, in only a handful of the *Sonnets*, her ghostly presence, as Rilke told her mother, "beherrscht und bewegt" (commands and impels) the cycle as a whole.[2] In invoking and celebrating Orpheus throughout the *Sonnets*, Rilke eventually takes on the poetic and metamorphic powers of the demigod he praises; Wera, meanwhile, becomes a double for Eurydice, Orpheus' lost bride. Orpheus' mandate throughout the *Sonnets* is clear: he is both a symbol and an agent of transformation, reconciling through language such seemingly irreconcilable oppositions as life and death, presence and absence, motion and stasis, transience and permanence, fragmentation and wholeness, humanity and divinity. Eurydice's role, however, is a more elusive one. On the one hand, she personifies the silence and mystery of a deathly underworld persistently and problematically coded by Rilke as female; her symbolic potency is thus subordinate to that of Orpheus, who passes easily in and out of the subterranean darkness from which she, in contrast, is allowed no escape. Yet on the other hand, through her identification with Wera, Eurydice possesses a range of artistic accomplishments — dance, music, drawing — unavailable even to the powerful Orphic poet. She, too, then, is a master of creative transformations, albeit of a different kind; if Rilke/Orpheus controls the Word, Wera/Eurydice inhabits the realm of the senses, embodying a corporeal dynamism that the male poet can describe but never fully experience.

Wera/Eurydice's ambivalent status in the *Sonnets to Orpheus* reflects Rilke's own lifelong ambivalence toward women, both in real-life relationships and as poetic symbols. In a famous 1904 letter, Rilke described artistic creativity as an essentially feminine act: "Es ist so natürlich für mich, *Mädchen und Frauen zu verstehen*; das tiefste Erleben des Schaffenden ist weiblich — denn es ist empfangendes und gebärendes Erleben" (It is so natural for me *to understand girls and women*; the deepest experience of creativity is feminine — for it is a receptive and birth-giving experience).[3] Although he often praised femininity, however, Rilke's poetry also contains many passages privileging a specifically masculine form of artistry and linking the forces of poetic creativity with the inseminating, phallic energies of stereotypical maleness instead. Moreover, even his most sincere and envious celebrations of the feminine are often troubling in their associations of women with self-sacrifice, loss, and death. Kathleen L. Komar notes that "While women may find the privileged image flattering — as, no doubt, Rilke's many patronesses did — it is disturbing that woman's position is defined by absence, deprivation or renunciation, and inescapable limitation."[4]

In his eloquent new biography of Rilke, Ralph Freedman ascribes Rilke's "sexual dialectic" — his shifting, often paradoxical definitions of sexuality and creative power as either male or female — to the "androgynous nature" of his vision; in much of his mature poetry, Freedman suggests, Rilke imagistically affirms his own earlier speculation, in a 1903 letter, that "vielleicht sind die Geschlechter verwandter, als man meint" (perhaps the sexes are more closely akin than one thinks).[5] I have argued elsewhere that Rilke's purported idealization of women all too often masks a hidden masculinist bias; the Eurydice of the *Sonnets to Orpheus*, for instance, serves as a potent symbol of death's presence in life, yet she lacks the transformative powers of her poet-husband, who can pass effortlessly between the realms of the living and the dead while she remains locked in the underworld.[6] In this essay, however, I want to complicate my own previous reading of Eurydice in light of Freedman's recent work, exploring in greater detail the vexed and often contradictory nature of Rilke's poetics of gender. While I do not mean to argue, as Freedman does, that Rilke is a poet of "androgynous" sensibilities — he seldom strays very far from fairly conventional sexual stereotyping, and his identification in the *Sonnets* is almost entirely with Orpheus — I will show how he achieves, through the figure of Eurydice, a kind of symbolic androgyny, erecting gendered oppositions only to subvert and deconstruct them.

In his 1904 poem "Orpheus. Eurydike. Hermes," Rilke portrays Eurydice as the embodiment of pure feminine mystery, "voll von ihrem grossen Tode" (full of her great death), like a woman heavy with child.[7] She has been utterly emptied of subjectivity and agency, reduced to an element of nature:

> Sie war schon aufgelöst wie langes Haar
> und hingegeben wie gefallner Regen
> und ausgeteilt wie hundertfacher Vorrat.

> [She was already loosened like long hair
> and given forth like fallen rain
> and shared out like a hundredfold provision.]

Yet she continues to possess, even in her dissolution, an underworldly power and authority far superior to that of her archetypal poet-husband, whom Rilke portrays as a figure of weakness and confusion, "stumm und ungeduldig" (mute and impatient), neither the enchanting poet-singer nor the resolute hero of legend. By the end of the poem, in fact, Eurydice has become so independent of Orpheus, so filled with and fulfilled by death, that she fails even to notice Orpheus' famous turn:

> Und als plötzlich jäh
> der Gott sie anhielt und mit Schmerz im Ausruf
> die Worte sprach: Er hat sich umgewendet — ,
> begriff sie nichts und sagte leise: *Wer?*
>
> [And when suddenly
> the god [Hermes] stopped her and with pain in his cry
> spoke the words: He has turned around — ,
> she understood nothing and said softly: *Who?*]

Instead, she executes a dismissive turn of her own, descending back toward the darkness of the underworld that, in Rilke's view, so richly empowers her. Orpheus, meanwhile, having failed to capture her essence or comprehend her mystery, fades to a far away, faceless figure by the entrance gates: "irgend jemand, dessen Angesicht / nicht zu erkennen war" (someone or other, whose countenance / could not be recognized).

Thus "Orpheus. Eurydike. Hermes" communicates, above all, the male poet's deep envy of Eurydice, his thwarted desire to partake of the secrets of her dark realm. Nearly two decades later in the *Sonnets to Orpheus*, however, Rilke portrays Orpheus in a very different light; now he has become a successful intercessor between life and death who draws his poetic power from his ability to inhabit and integrate opposing worlds: "Ist er ein Hiesiger? Nein, aus beiden / Reichen erwuchs seine weite Natur" (Is he from here? No, from both / realms his wide nature grew).[8] Transformation — the act of turning, once a sign of Orpheus' irresolution and futile longing — is celebrated, instead, as the supreme poetic gesture:

> Wolle die Wandlung. O sei für die Flamme begeistert,
> drin sich ein Ding dir entzieht, das mit Verwandlung prunkt;
> jener entwerfende Geist, welcher das Irdische meistert,
> liebt in dem Schwung der Figur nichts wie den wendenden Punkt.
>
> (2:12)

> [Will transformation. O be inspired for the flame
> in which a Thing eludes you, resplendent with change;
> that spirit of creation, which masters what is earthly,
> loves in the figure's swing nothing more than the turning point.]

Yet while Rilke's Orpheus now passes effortlessly between death and life, the *Sonnets*' Eurydice remains locked in her role of archetypal female, a creature of passivity and death, permanently consigned to the realm of inviolable Otherness that Rilke himself, Orpheus-like, has finally achieved the power to sing:

> Sei immer tot in Eurydike . . . .
> Hier, unter Schwindenden, sei, im Reiche der Neige,
> sei ein klingendes Glas, das sich im Klang schon zerschlug.
>
> (2:13)

> [Be forever dead in Eurydice . . . .
> Here, amidst vanishing ones, be, in the realm of decline,
> be a ringing glass that shattered even as it rang.]

Eurydice is still Orpheus' inspiration, "den unendlichen Grund deiner innigen Schwingung" (the infinite source of your intimate vibration). All women, in fact, as Rilke indicates in a series of "Gegen-strophen" originally intended as part of the Fifth Duino Elegy, can be seen as endlessly duplicated versions of Eurydice, forever turning back toward the underworld while the male poet climbs upward toward the light:

> Blumen des tieferen Erdreichs,
> von allen Wurzeln geliebte,
> ihr, der Eurydike Schwestern,
> immer voll heiliger Umkehr
> hinter dem steigenden Mann.[9]

> [Flowers of the deeper realm,
> beloved of all roots,
> you, Eurydice's sisters,
> forever full of holy turning
> behind the ascending man.]

In contrast to the self-sufficient bride of "Orpheus. Eurydike. Hermes," then, who by the end of the poem is clearly "jenes Mannes Eigentums night mehr" (no longer that man's possession), the Eurydice of the *Sonnets* represents a comprehensible, attainable ideal; by invoking and thereby possessing her, the Orphic poet acknowledges and celebrates the presence of death in his own life. Charles Segal sees her as "a part of Orpheus himself, . . . those deep springs of his knowledge that extend down into the realm of the dead in a mysterious unity with all being."[10] Stephen Mitchell, similarly, calls her

> absolute receptivity.... When she falls (or, more exactly, rises) asleep in the poet's ear, she returns into the vivid being at the core of us.... Like the rose which Rilke later chose for his epitaph, this inner woman is pure Self, the delight of being nobody under so many eyelids.[11]

As I will demonstrate, however, the *Sonnets*' Eurydice is in fact a far more complex, actively transformative, and vividly embodied figure than abstractions such as Segal's or Mitchell's might imply. Rilke's identification of Eurydice with Wera, a real (albeit highly idealized) young woman, elevates her from a one-dimensional symbol of silence, death, and femininity — in Mitchell's account, both a receptive "nobody" and a part of the male poet's "pure Self" — to a potent artist whose metamorphic capacities complement and perhaps even rival Orpheus' own.

Rilke had met Wera Knoop only a few times in her short life; but the journal that she kept during the final months of that life, sent to Rilke by her mother shortly before he began writing the *Sonnets*, struck a powerful resonance in this poet who had always idealized both youth and early death. As Ralph Freedman notes, Wera's diary "opened Rilke's eyes to the realities of suffering and death endured in a life he knew: to the palpable anguish of an actual 'youthfully dead.'"[12] Later, Rilke provided his own eloquent summary of Wera's tragic decline:

> Dieses schöne Kind, das erst zu tanzen anfing und, bei allen, die sie damals sahen, Aufsehen erregte, durch die ihrem Körper und Gemüt eingeborene Kunst der Bewegung und Wandlung, — erklärte ihrer Mutter unvermutet, daß sie nicht länger tanzen könne oder wolle . . . ; (das war eben am Ausgang des Kindseins) ihr Körper veränderte sich seltsam, wurde, ohne seine schöne östliche Gestaltung zu verlieren, seltsam schwer und massiv . . . (was schon der Anfang der geheimnisvollen Drüsen-Erkrankung war, die dann so rasch den Tod herbeiführen sollte) . . . In der Zeit, die ihr noch blieb, trieb Wera Musik, schließlich zeichnete sie nur noch — , als ob sich der versagte Tanz immer leiser, immer diskreter noch aus ihr ausgäbe . . . .

> [This beautiful child, who had just begun to dance and attracted the attention of everyone who saw her, by the art of movement and transformation which was innate in her body and spirit — unexpectedly declared to her mother that she no longer could or would dance (this happened just at the end of childhood). Her body changed, grew strangely heavy and massive, without losing its beautiful Slavic features; this was already the beginning of the mysterious glandular disease that later was to bring death so quickly. During the time that remained to her, Vera devoted herself to music; finally she only drew — as if the denied dance came forth from her ever more quietly, ever more discreetly.][13]

Wera's battle with leukemia — slow, painful, and no doubt terrifying in the physical changes wrought by the disease — becomes here, in Rilke's lyrical narrative, a metaphorical journey through the non-verbal arts, from dance to music to drawing, each mode of expression issuing from her disfigured body "more discreetly" than the last. In the *Sonnets*, similarly, Rilke will depict both dance and drawing as essential components of Eurydice's identity, the media by means of which she undertakes her transformations of imminent absence into physical substance.

The first poem of the *Sonnets to Orpheus* opens with phallic ascent and poetic transcendence, described in a series of grammatical ejaculations announcing Orpheus' dramatic arrival: "Da stieg ein Baum. O reine Übersteigung! / O Orpheus singt! O hoher Baum im Ohr!" (A tree ascended there. O pure transcendence! / O Orpheus sings! O tall tree in the ear! [1:1]). The second sonnet, in contrast, seems to begin in mid-sentence, even before Wera/Eurydice, "almost a girl" (but not quite?), has been fully formed by the poet's voice:

> Und fast ein Mädchen wars und ging hervor
> aus diesem einigen Glück von Sang und Leier
> und glänzte klar durch ihre Frühlingsschleier
> und machte sich ein Bett in meinem Ohr.
>
> (1:2)
>
> [And it was almost a girl and came to be
> from this united joy of song and lyre
> and shone forth clearly through her veils of spring
> and made herself a bed inside my ear.]

Eurydice spends most of the sonnet sleeping, bedded down in the poet's ear: "Und schlief in mir. Und alles war ihr Schlaf.... Sie schlief die Welt.... Sieh, sie erstand und schlief" (And slept in me. And her sleep was everything.... She slept the world.... See, she arose and slept). Then, at the end of the poem, she fades away in a series of question marks and ellipses, mere shadows of the emphatic exclamation points that heralded Orpheus' arrival in the previous sonnet:

> Wo ist ihr Tod? O, wirst du dies Motiv
> erfinden noch, eh sich dein Lied verzehrte?
> Wo sinkt sie hin aus mir?... Ein Mädchen fast....
>
> [Where is her death? O, will you yet invent
> this theme before your song consumes itself?
> Where does she sink to from me?... A girl almost....]

She will appear again in only a few more of the sonnet cycle's fifty-five poems, "resurfacing," as Stephen Mitchell puts it, "in the loveliest and most tactful way."[14] Mitchell's description of Eurydice's "tactful" manifestations in the *Son-

nets echoes Rilke's account of Wera's "ever more discreet" descent into death; both the mythical Eurydice and the historical Wera are praised for their delicacy, subtlety, and grace rather than for their poetic presence or metamorphic power.

Yet although the unconscious Eurydice of Sonnet 1:2, formed from Orpheus' "song and lyre," is clearly a creation of, perhaps even a part of, the male poet inside whose head she silently reclines, it is, paradoxically, her passive sleep that awakens the poet to the world of sensual experience:

> Und alles war ihr Schlaf.
> Die Bäume, die ich je bewundert, diese
> fühlbare Ferne, die gefühlte Wiese
> und jedes Staunen, das mich selbst betraf.
>
> [And her sleep was everything.
> The trees I had once admired, this
> tangible distance, the meadow I'd felt
> and every amazement that touched me.]

Indeed, as the poet's gateway to nature, Eurydice mediates his experience not only of the "tangible distance," the "felt" meadow, and the "veils of spring" but also of "the trees I had once admired," including, presumably, the one that rose in the previous sonnet to announce Orpheus' song: "A tree ascended there. O pure transcendence!" That tree in turn recalls a number of earlier poems — the final section of the *Stundenbuch* (1905) (*The Book of Hours*, 1961) and the opening lines of the Third Duino Elegy (1912) come most readily to mind — in which Rilke similarly depicts poetic transcendence as a physical act strongly linked to male sexuality.

In particular, as Ralph Freedman notes, the "tall tree in the ear" of Sonnet 1:1 echoes Rilke's "representation of male desire ... in the sexually explicit phallic poems of 1915," a group of seven metaphorically inventive if erotically unsubtle fragments in which the poet variously describes the erect male member as "the full flower bud" on man's "limb of life" ("die volle Knospe seines Lebensgliedes"), a column erected in "pubic woodlands" ("die Säule ... in meinem Schamgehölze"), a stiff corpse ("meine steife Leiche"), a tower from whose cupola the poet launches "womb-dazzling rockets" ("schooßblendend[e] Raketen"), and an "image of a god" ("Gottesbild") standing "at the delicate crossroads under my clothing" ("am leisen Kreuzweg unter meinem Kleide").[15] Most significantly for the *Sonnets*, two of the seven poems specifically portray the phallus as a tree that comes to life only through the ministrations of a female lover, associated here with summer and elsewhere with other aspects of nature as well:

> Du hast mir, Sommer, der du plötzlich bist,
> zum jähen Baum den Samen aufgezogen.

      . . . .
Nun hob er sich und wächst zum Firmament,
ein Spiegelbild das neben Bäumen steht.
O stürz ihn, daß er, umgedreht
in deinen Schooß, den Gegen-Himmel kennt,
in den er wirklich bäumt und wirklich ragt.

[You, who are suddenly summer, have drawn
semen up into the irascible tree.
      . . . .
Now it arises and grows to the firmament,
a mirror image standing beside trees.
O plunge it down, so that, inverted
in your vagina, it will know the counter-heaven
in which it can truly tower, truly tree.][16]

          aus meinem Körper hebt
ein neuer Baum die überfüllte Krone
und ragt nach dir: denn sieh, was ist er ohne
den Sommer, der in deinem Schooße schwebt.

          [from my body
a new tree raises its overfilled crown,
towering toward you; for look, what is it without
the summer that hovers in your womb?]

While the "irascible tree" and the "new tree" described in these two poems bear only a cursory resemblance to the "tall tree in the ear" of Sonnet 1:1, they provide an important reminder of Rilke's penchant, apparent even in some of his most profound and delicate verse, for thinly disguised sexual metaphors. Indeed, in light of such explicit intertexts, it would be difficult *not* to interpret Rilke's "tall tree in the ear" as, among other things, a phallic symbol that emphatically links Orpheus' physical, poetic, and spiritual transcendence with male sexuality — a sexuality dependent, to be sure, on the ministrations of a silent, passive, yet compliant female partner.

    As I have already noted, however, such a reading is complicated in subsequent sonnets by metaphorical associations of Wera/Eurydice, too, with the trees that symbolize Orpheus' phallic ascent into song. Throughout the first part of the *Sonnets* such associations are made only obliquely, if at all; women, including Wera, are frequently linked to the natural world, but mostly to flowers, fruits, and springtime rather than specifically with trees. In Sonnet 1:25, for instance, Rilke calls Wera "eine Blume, von der ich den Namen nicht weiß" (a flower whose name I don't know), praising the "natürlichen Frühling" (natural springtime) of her blood. In several poems at the beginning of the *Sonnets*' second part, similarly, the poet reinforces familiar gender stereotypes by metaphorically likening women to flowers, which gently exude "Warmes der Mädchen, wie Beichten" (the warmth of girls, like confessions [2:7]) and stretch open their "Muskel des unendlichen Empfangs, / manchmal *so* von Fülle übermannter" (muscle of infinite receptivity, / sometimes *so* overpowered by abundance [2:5]).[17] And in Sonnet 1:15 he exhorts a group of "warm" and "mute" girls to dance "den Geschmack der erfahrenen Frucht" (the taste of the experienced fruit):

> Tanzt die Orange. Wer kann sie vergessen,
> wie sie, ertrinkend in sich, sich wehrt
> wider ihr Süßsein. Ihr habt sie besessen.
> Sie hat sich köstlich zu euch bekehrt.
>
> [Dance the orange. Who can forget it,
> how, drowning in itself, it struggles
> against its own sweetness. You have possessed it.
> Deliciously, it has converted to you.]

In Sonnet 1:13, however, Rilke offers a more morbid fruit/female association, asserting that fruit "spricht Tod / und Leben in den Mund" (speaks / death and life into the mouth) when it explodes into flavor at the very moment of its physical dissolution.

The constellation of images invoked in the poems cited above — death, female creativity, and fruit, all united in the figure of Wera, the dancer — recalls two earlier poems in which Rilke similarly likens women both to fruit and to the underworld in which all living things have their roots: "Orpheus. Eurydike. Hermes," in which dead Eurydice is suffused "wie eine Frucht von Süßigkeit und Dunkel" (like a fruit with sweetness and darkness); and the haunting 1909 poem "Requiem für eine Freundin" (Requiem for a Friend), in which the painter Paula Modersohn-Becker, recently dead from complications following childbirth, is remembered for her physical and artistic empathy with fruits: "Denn Das verstandest du: die vollen Früchte.... Und sahst dich selbst zuletzt wie eine Frucht" (For that one thing you understood: ripe fruits.... And finally you saw yourself as a fruit).[18] These poems reinforce Rilke's association, throughout the first part and much of the second part of the *Sonnets*, of young dead women such as Wera and Eurydice with the ripe fruits — dark, sweet, and silent — that passively fall from the "tall tree" that represents the male poet's song.

Towards the end of the *Sonnets*, however, Rilke suddenly loosens up the gendering of his metaphors; fruit, formerly female, and trees, formerly male, become potent images of all human experience, male and female alike. Sonnet

2:12, for instance, begins with the Orphic exhortation, "Wolle die Wandlung" (Will transformation); by the end of the poem, however, metamorphosis has become the province not only of the male poet but also of a female figure, Daphne: "Und die verwandelte Daphne / will, seit sie lorbeern fühlt, daß du dich wandelst in Wind" (And the transfigured Daphne, / since she feels like laurel, wants you to turn into wind). It is important to remember, of course, that the mythical Daphne was turned to a laurel tree when Apollo, the god of poetry, tried to rape her; thus her female creativity and transformative power are intertextually linked to her role as quarry and victim. All the same, Rilke's neologistic use of the word "lorbeern" — an adverb or adjective, formed from the noun "*Lorbeer*," that might best be translated as "laurelly" or "laurelish" — suggests that his Daphne personifies a linguistic playfulness and freedom very different from the kind of physical and poetic transformation willed by Orpheus or forced by Apollo. And his direct exhortation to the reader — "Daphne . . . wants *you* to turn into wind" (my emphasis) — suggests that Daphne's metamorphosis can serve as a positive example to men as well as to women.

In Sonnet 2:18, similarly, the figures of Daphne, changed into a tree, and of Wera, Rilke's idealized young dancer, come together in a single arboreal image, a "Baum aus Bewegung" (tree made of motion) achieved through the art of dance:

> Tänzerin: o du Verlegung
> alles Vergehens in Gang: wie brachtest du's dar.
> Und der Wirbel am Schluß, dieser Baum aus Bewegung,
> nahm er nicht ganz in Besitz das erschwungene Jahr?
>
> Blühte nicht, daß ihn dein Schwingen von vorhin umschwärme,
> plötzlich sein Wipfel von Stille? Und über ihr,
> war sie nicht Sonne, war sie nicht Sommer, die Wärme,
> diese unzählige Wärme aus dir?
>
> Aber er trug auch, er trug, dein Baum der Ekstase.
> Sind sie nicht seine ruhigen Früchte: der Krug,
> reifend gestreift, und die gereiftere Vase?
>
> Und in den Bildern: ist nicht die Zeichnung geblieben,
> die deiner Braue dunkler Zug
> rasch an die Wandung der eigenen Wendung geschrieben?
>
> [Dancer: oh you displacement
> of all transience into movement: how you offered it there.
> And the whirl at the end, this tree made of motion,
> did it not fully possess the accomplished year?

Did not its top branches, so that your previous swaying might swarm
    around them,
suddenly bloom with stillness? And above them, too,
was it not sunshine, was it not summer, the warmth,
this immeasurable warmth out of you?

But it bore too, it bore, your tree of ecstasy.
Are not these its tranquil fruits: the pitcher,
streaked with ripeness, and the even more ripened vase?

And in the pictures: does not the drawing remain
that your eyebrow's dark stroke
swiftly inscribed on the surface of its own turning?]

Much as he earlier made a static noun (*Lorbeer*) into a neologistic adverb (*lorbeern*) connoting movement and change, Rilke here makes the language of his sonnet undergo semantic shifts that mimic the dancer's transformations of motion into substance: verbs become solidified as nouns (*Verlegung, Vergehen, Gang, Bewegung, Zeichnung, Zug, Wandung, Wendung*); opposing principles of stability and change are represented, paradoxically, by nearly identical-sounding words (*Wandung* signifies the wall of a vase or other vessel, whereas *Wendung* means "turning"); and Rilke's very use of the word *Wandung*, an unusual and unexpected noun that might easily be misread as the more familiar *Wandlung* (transformation), further underscores the precariousness relationship between form and substance, between signifier and signified. Thus this poem about the physical transformations brought by a female dancer turns out also to be an unabashed celebration of the male poet's powers of linguistic metamorphosis.

    At the same time, however, the dancer sonnet finally transforms the phallic tree of Sonnet 1:1 from a symbol of specifically male transcendence into an emblem of female artistic achievement as well. In the final lines of the sonnet, Wera's "tree made of motion" in turn bears as its "fruit" a vase on which she draws, with the stroke of her whirling eyebrow, a lasting picture of her own ephemeral movement. This striking poetic image, which turns dance and drawing into a single gesture, reminds us both that the *Sonnets* themselves were inspired by a drawing (an Italian Renaissance sketch of Orpheus) and that Wera, at the end of her life, abandoned dance for drawing: "schließlich zeichnete sie nur noch —, als ob sich der versagte Tanz immer leiser, immer diskreter noch aus ihr ausgäbe . . . ." (finally she only drew — as if the denied dance came forth from her ever more quietly, ever more discreetly). But the poem moves far beyond Rilke's earlier associations of Wera either with Eurydice's archetypal fulfillment in death or, at best, with the pure, fruitlike physicality of dance; instead, it underlines the complexity and subtle grace of her transformation from mortal body into immortal artist.

In its celebration of the dancer and the dance, Sonnet 2:18 reflects the influence both of Paul Valéry's "L'Ame et la danse," which Rilke had read only a few weeks before he composed the *Sonnets*, and of John Keats's "Ode on a Grecian Urn"; like the lovers in Keats's ode, frozen within yet forever memorialized by the urn's static surface, Rilke's dancer is caught in the eternal paradox of art.[19] But the poem's most startling intertextual resonances are with Rilke's own poetry, and particularly with the two "phallic hymns" of 1915, quoted earlier, in which he described his penis first as an "irascible tree" and then as a "new tree" raising its "overfilled crown" towards the "summer" of his lover's vagina/womb. Now, however, it is the female dancer whose "treetop" ("Wipfel") suddenly "bloom[s] with stillness," exuding the "immeasurable warmth" of summer; male and female images alike, in other words, are subsumed in Rilke's description of her dance. Even the "tranquil fruits" borne by the dancer's "tree of ecstasy" belie Rilke's previous gendering of fruits as female and of females as fruit; these symbolic fruits, the "pitcher / streaked with ripeness and the even more ripened vase," serve not as metaphors for women's passivity and gravitas but rather as tactile, enduring monuments to the dancer's otherwise ephemeral art.

The dancer of Sonnet 2:18, then, is a drastically different figure both from the unconscious Eurydice, "almost a girl," who sleeps her way through Sonnet 1:2 and from the stilled, tragic Wera of Sonnet 1:15: "Tänzerin erst, die plötzlich, den Körper voll Zögern, / anhielt, als göß man ihr Jungsein in Erz" (At first a dancer, until suddenly, her body full of hesitation, / she stopped, as though her youth had been cast in bronze). Nor is this young woman "forever dead in Eurydice . . . a ringing glass that shattered even as it rang," as Rilke exhorts Wera (and his readers?) to be in Sonnet 2:13. Instead she is vital, creative, and forever alive, a potent agent of transformation, as much an artist of the body as Orpheus is an artist of words. When Rilke describes her as a tree, it is not because her roots stretch down to the underworld but because her body blooms upward into life. The tree metaphor is not, of course, entirely unproblematic; in consigning her to a realm of pure physicality, Rilke, so deeply moved by the real Wera Knoop's diary, denies his poetic Wera the gift and power of language. All the same, by imagistically linking her both with the phallic "tall tree in the ear" that heralds Orpheus' arrival in Sonnet 1:1 and with the ancient oak that, in Sonnet 1:17, produces Orpheus' lyre, Rilke accomplishes what is perhaps his own most impressive act of poetic transformation, bridging and even transcending the ancient symbolic opposition of male and female.

Wera/Eurydice makes one final appearance in the *Sonnets to Orpheus*, in Sonnet 2:28, the penultimate poem of the cycle:

> O komm und geh. Du, fast noch Kind, ergänze
> für einen Augenblick die Tanzfigur
> zum reinen Sternbild einer jener Tänze,
> darin wir die dumpf ordnende Natur
>
> vergänglich übertreffen. Denn sie regte
> sich völlig hörend nur, da Orpheus sang.
>
> [O come and go. You, almost still a child,
> fill out the dance-figure for just an instant
> into the pure constellation of
> one of those dances in which dull ordering Nature
>
> is fleetingly surpassed. For Nature stirred
> to total hearing only when Orpheus sang.]

Though "almost still a child," Wera is at last allowed, like Orpheus, to "come and go" between the worlds of the dead and the living, surpassing "dull ordering Nature" through the transformative powers of her dance. Her most important role in the poem, however, is not as a performing artist but rather as Orpheus' most perceptive and sensitive listener: "Du wußtest noch die Stelle, wo die Leier / sich tönend hob — ; die unerhörte Mitte" (You knew still the place where the lyre / arose resounding — ; the unheard, unheard-of center). Although she is no longer "forever dead in Eurydice," forever confined to the underworld, Wera still inhabits and embodies that "unerhörte Mitte" from which Orpheus' lyre rises like a tree to charm all of Nature: the "unheard, unheard-of center," silent and unspeakable, that represents the death at the core of every life, the woman at the core of the male poet's being.

In Sonnet 2:29, the final poem of the *Sonnets*, Rilke makes no mention at all of Eurydice, praising instead the transformative and linguistic potency of the Orphic poet: "zu der stillen Erde sag: Ich rinne. / Zu dem raschen Wasser sprich: Ich bin" (to the silent earth say: I'm flowing. / To the rushing water say: I am). In the next-to-last sonnet, however, he pauses a moment to acknowledge the act not of speaking but of listening. In particular, he celebrates Wera's way of listening with her whole body, her ability to transform Orpheus' songs about transformation into something at once physical and unearthly, at once fleeting and eternal: the "pure constellation" of dance. Without an audience, we are reminded, even the most eloquent poet is voiceless, like the proverbial tree that falls in a forest where there is no one around to hear.

Indiana University

Notes

[1] All translations, unless otherwise noted, are my own.

[2] Rainer Maria Rilke, letter to Gertrud Ouckama Knoop, 7 February 1922. (*Briefe*, [Frankfurt am Main: Insel, 1950], 3:740).

[3] Rilke, letter "to a young girl," 20 November 1904. (*Briefe*, 1:104).

[4] Kathleen L. Komar, "The Mediating Muse: Of Men, Women and the Feminine in the Work of Rainer Maria Rilke," *Germanic Review* 64.3 (1989): 129.

[5] Ralph Freedman, *Life of a Poet: Rainer Maria Rilke* (New York: Farrar, Straus, and Giroux, 1996), 193; Rilke, letter to Franz Xaver Kappus, 16 July 1903 (*Briefe*, 1:55).

[6] See my *Engendering Inspiration: Visionary Strategies in Rilke, Lawrence, and H.D.* (Ann Arbor: U of Michigan P, 1995), especially chapters one ("Rainer Maria Rilke and the Poetics of Femininity") and four ("Orpheus, Eurydice, and the Poetics of the Turn"), from which the first few pages of my argument are largely drawn.

[7] Rilke, *Sämtliche Werke* (Frankfurt am Main: Insel, 1987) 1:542–45. All translations, unless otherwise noted, are my own.

[8] Sonnet 1:6. Quotations from *The Sonnets to Orpheus* (Rilke, *Sämtliche Werke*, 1: 727–71) will be cited throughout this essay by part and sequence number, as above, rather than by page number.

[9] *Sämtliche Werke*, 2:137.

[10] Segal, *Orpheus: The Myth of the Poet* (Baltimore: Johns Hopkins UP, 1989), 143.

[11] Mitchell, introduction to Rainer Maria Rilke, *The Sonnets to Orpheus* (New York: Simon and Schuster, 1985), 9.

[12] Freedman, 481.

[13] Letter to Countess Margot Sizzo-Noris-Crouy, 12 April 1923 (*Briefe*, 3:829–30); all ellipses are Rilke's. Translation Mitchell, 160.

[14] Mitchell, 9.

[15] *Sämtliche Werke*, 2:435–38.

[16] Rilke's verb *bäumen* literally means "to rear" or "to prance" but also puns on the noun *Baum*, meaning "tree." With the phrase "truly tree," in which "tree" can be read either as a noun or a neologistic verb, I have opted to preserve Rilke's tree pun at the expense of his equestrian image. The noun *Schooß*, which appears in both poems quoted here, poses perennial difficulties for translators; although it means both "lap" and "womb," Rilke frequently uses it to denote the place between the two, namely the vagina. Given the sexually explicit nature of these poems, such a clinical, non-euphemistic translation seems perfectly appropriate.

[17] Another Rilkean pun here: *übermannt* (overpowered) literally means "overmanned": overpowered by a man or, in the case of these flowers, by "das polyphone / Licht der lauten Himmel" (the polyphonous / light of the sonorous heavens), i.e., the auditory, visual, and spiritual enlightenment provided by Orpheus.

[18] *Sämtliche Werke*, 1:649.

[19] Rilke had read Keats's poetry, in German translation, in 1911. See Ingeborg Schnack, *Rainer Maria Rilke: Chronik seines Lebens und seines Werkes* (Frankfurt am Main: Insel, 1975), 380.

THOMAS KOVACH

Rilke's "Die Insel der Sirenen" and the Music of Silence
For Ralph Freedman

"Die Insel der Sirenen" (The Isle of the Sirens), written in July and August of 1907 and first published as the fifth poem in *Der neuen Gedichte anderer Teil* (1908) (*New Poems: The Other Part*, 1964),[1] is the only poem in this cycle, standing so conspicuously under the sign of the visual arts, which takes the power of music as its central theme. The poem makes reference in both its title and its opening lines to Homer's *Odyssey*, a work which provides the context in which, I will argue here, the poem can best be read. Odysseus, who has been shipwrecked on the land of the Phaeacians, is rescued and treated to their hospitality, which includes being regaled by the bard Demodocus, who sings tales of the Olympian gods. At dinner afterward, Odysseus pays tribute to the bard in the following words:

> "From all who walk the earth our bards deserve esteem and awe, for the Muse herself has taught them paths of song. She loves the breed of harpers."[2]

The word in ancient Greek which Fagles translates first as "bards" and then as "harpers" is *aiodos*, plural *aiodoi*. The word is variously translated as "singer" (Lattimore), "poet" (Fitzgerald), "bards/minstrel fraternity" (Rieu), "minstrels" (Rouse), "bards/harpers" (Palmer and Fagles). The ambiguity of the translations points to the well-known fact that our separation between poet and singer, poetry and music, did not exist in ancient Greece, where both lyric and epic poetry were sung rather than recited.

Following this tribute, the hero requests a song of the Achaeans' exploits in Troy, including his own. His response to this song is a striking evocation of the power of music:

> That was the song the famous harper [*aiodos*] sang
> but great Odysseus melted into tears,
> running down from his eyes to wet his cheeks . . .
> as a woman weeps, her arms flung round her darling husband,
> a man who fell in battle, fighting for town and townsmen,

> trying to beat the day of doom from home and children.
> Seeing the man go down, dying, gasping for breath,
> she clings for dear life, screams and shrills —
> but the victors, just behind her,
> digging spear-butt into her back and shoulders,
> drag her off in bondage, yoked to hard labor, pain,
> and the most heartbreaking torment wastes her cheeks.
>
> (208)

Through Demodocus' song, the warrior and sacker of cities is placed in the role of the victim, the widowed Trojan women being led off to slavery.

The idea of music as a dangerous force which saps one's vital energies was a familiar one to the young poet from Prague. It appears in the 1899 poem "Musik" from *Das Buch der Bilder* (1902) (*The Book of Images*, 1991) (1: 379–80), in the letter to Lou Andreas-Salomé of 8 August 1903, in which he rails against music as "dieser Gegensatz der Kunst" (this antithesis of art) (58), and even as late as the 1910 novel, *Die Aufzeichnungen des Malte Laurids Brigge* (*The Notebooks of Malte Laurids Brigge*, 1949) (6: 824).

In Homer, the same art which reduces the hero to tears can empower him as well. When the assembled Phaeacians observe Odysseus' tears, they urge him to identify himself and tell his story, which he then proceeds to do in the tale of his wanderings following the fall of Troy, a narrative which occupies Books 9 through 12 and constitutes the most famous portion of the epic. The power of his "art" is confirmed in Book 11, as the hero recounts his journey to the land of the dead. In the only break during this entire four-book narrative, the royal household praises him, culminating in these words from King Alcinous:

> "But you,
> what grace you give your words, and what good sense within!
> You have told your story with all a singer's skill,
> the miseries you endured, your great Achaeans too."
>
> (261)

It might be argued that it is in part the musical skill of the "man skilled in all ways of contending" that helps him win over the Phaeacians and earn his final passage home. And we are reminded most unforgettably of Odysseus' role as musician, as creator of order out of chaos, in Book 21 when he strings his bow in preparation for the slaughter of the suitors who have been destroying his home:

> like an expert singer skilled at lyre and song —
> who strains a string to a new peg with ease,
> making the pliant sheep-gut fast at either end —
> so with his virtuoso ease Odysseus strung his mighty bow.

> Quickly his right hand plucked the string to test its pitch
> and under his touch it sang out clear and sharp as a swallow's cry.
>
> (437)

Though the "musicianship" here is metaphorical, the passage remains a powerful affirmation of the musician as an exemplar of power and mastery. As I will argue, Rilke in the course of his career sought to master the power of music in a way which empowers his art; the same poet who as a young man warns of the dangers of music pays tribute to the poet-musician Orpheus at the pinnacle of his career.

And yet, it is in Book 12, during his narrative of the fabulous voyages, that Odysseus narrates the episode on which Rilke's poem is based, one which seems clearly to emphasize the destructive power of music. The enchantress Circe warns the hero:

> 'First you will raise the island of the Sirens,
> those creatures who spellbind any man alive,
> whoever comes their way. Whoever draws too close,
> off guard, and catches the Sirens' voices in the air —
> no sailing home for him, no wife rising to meet him,
> no happy children beaming up at their father's face.
> The high, thrilling song of the Sirens will transfix him,
> lolling there in their meadow, round them heaps of corpses,
> rotting away, rags of skin shriveling on their bones . . . '
>
> (272–73)

She advises Odysseus to stop his shipmates' ears with wax so that they cannot be tempted, and then to have them lash him to the mast "so you can hear the Sirens' song to your heart's content." He does as he is told, and then we hear the following account:

> We were just off shore as far as a man's shout can carry,
> scudding close, when the Sirens sensed at once a ship
> was racing past and burst into their high, thrilling song:
> 'Come closer, famous Odysseus — Achaea's pride and glory —
> moor your ship on our coast so you can hear our song!
> Never has any sailor passed our shores in his black craft
> until he has heard the honeyed voices pouring from our lips,
> and once he hears to his heart's content sails on, a wiser man.
> We know all the pains the Achaeans and Trojans once endured
> on the spreading plain of Troy when the gods willed it so —
> all that comes to pass on the fertile earth, we know it all!'
>
> So they sent their ravishing voices out across the air
> and the heart inside me throbbed to listen longer.

> I signaled the crew with frowns to set me free —
> they flung themselves at the oars and rowed on harder,
> Perimedes and Eurylochus springing up at once
> to bind me faster with rope on chafing rope.
> But once we'd left the Sirens fading in our wake,
> once we could hear their song no more, their urgent call —
> my steadfast crew was quick to remove the wax I'd used
> to seal their ears and loosed the bonds that lashed me.
>
> (277)

Without this constraint, Odysseus would presumably be destroyed by the music, as were so many men before him. And yet it is worth noting that Circe urges him, and he chooses, to find a way of experiencing this music for the "joy" it will bring, rather than avoiding it by stopping his own ears. If it can be asserted in general that the experiences which Odysseus undergoes give this sacker of cities the greater mastery required for the creation and re-establishment of order — the task that awaits him in his homecoming — it is perhaps not too much of a stretch to argue that this musical experience is part of the training that enables him to appear as the master musician in the famous simile of Book 21 quoted above.

With this thought in mind, let us turn once more to the young Rilke, who in 1907, as he continued to work on the poems which were to constitute the two volumes of the *Neue Gedichte*, still was struggling, as he would at least until 1922, for the mastery which he later identified with the poet/musician Orpheus.

Here is how "Die Insel der Sirenen" begins:

> Wenn er denen, die ihm gastlich waren,
> spät, nach ihrem Tage noch, da sie
> fragten nach den Fahrten und Gefahren,
> still berichtete: er wußte nie,
>
> wie sie schrecken und mit welchem jähen
> Wort sie wenden, daß sie so wie er
> in dem blau gestillten Inselmeer
> die Vergoldung jener Inseln sähen;
>
> deren Anblick macht, daß die Gefahr
> umschlägt; denn nun ist sie nicht im Tosen
> und im Wüten, wo sie früher war.
>
> [When for them who were his hosts,
> late, after their day was done, when they

>   asked about his journeys and dangers,
>   he quietly reported: he never knew
>
>   how to scare them and with what sudden
>   word to turn them, so that they, just as he did,
>   in the bluely quieted sea of islands
>   would see the goldening of those isles
>
>   the sight of which causes the danger
>   to reverse itself; for now it is not in storming
>   and in raging, where it always was.]

The poem's first stanza makes it clear that the reference is to Odysseus' narration to his Phaeacian hosts, but the picture we get from this poem is almost the antithesis of the confident mastery displayed by Homer's hero. This is apparent in the halting and labored syntax of the stanza, and the phrase "spät, nach ihrem Tage noch" (late, after their day was done), which suggests the hero's weariness after his travails at sea. This is expressed most clearly when he confesses his inability to communicate his experience, in the phrase "er wußte nie" (he never knew), which receives special emphasis by being set off at the end of the first stanza. His narrative is "still," quiet, suggesting the near absence of sound, although the rich assonance and internal near-rhyme of the line "fragten nach den Fahrten und Gefahren" (asked about his journeys and dangers) gives the lie to this claim of austere stillness, suggesting a kind of evasiveness, a denial of the music which constitutes both the mode and the theme of this story.

This conjecture is supported by the curious fact that in trying to convey an experience of the power of music, the speaker in the second stanza seems most concerned with conveying his *visual* impressions: "daß sie so wie er/in dem *blau* gestillten Inselmeer/die *Vergoldung* jener Inseln *sähen*//deren *Anblick* macht, daß die Gefahr umschlägt" (so that they, just as he did/in the *bluely* quieted sea of islands/would see the *goldening* of those isles//the *sight* of which causes the danger/to reverse itself) (my emphasis). There is a strange tension in this stanza between the atmosphere of placidity, evoked in visual images, and the hero's stated intention to "scare" his listeners, to "turn" them with a sudden word, which suggests a violent auditory stimulus. The word "Vergoldung" (which I have translated as "goldening," but which has a range of potential meanings from "gilding" to "beautifying" or "enhancing") evokes the serenity of the sunset bringing a golden hue to the sea, but also, more radically, the sea's transformation into a timeless metal, reminiscent of Yeats's Byzantium poems. One is reminded of the poet's fervid embrace of Rodin's sculpture as a haven from the chaotic flux of the poet's inner life. Also worth noting is the fact that the island of Homer's epic and of this poem's title has in this stanza become a group, indeed a "sea" of islands ("Inselmeer," "jener Inseln").

In the third stanza, the speaker evokes the specific danger associated with these islands. In Homer, the danger is one of seductive song, in contrast to loud and violent monsters such as the Cyclops; if one can block out the sound (as do the sailors with their ears stopped with wax), one is safe. With Rilke, things are more complex. First of all, what is at issue is a reversal in the nature of this danger (the verb "umschlägt" [reverses] of course exemplifies the motif of "Umschlag" [reversal] which Judith Ryan has shown to be central to Rilke's work of the middle period);[3] and it is precisely the *sight* of these islands that causes this reversal. This suggestion of a transformation in the nature of danger is absent in Homer; instead, Odysseus' narrative displays a pattern of alternation between savage monsters (Cyclops, the cannibalistic Laestrygonians, Scylla and Charybdis), seductive sirens (including Circe and Calypso), and what in Homer is the greatest danger of all: that arising from the human propensity to foolhardiness and overreaching (Ciconians, Aeolus, the Oxen of the Sun). Rilke, in contrast, focuses on the change from the danger represented in the "loud" imagery of storming and raging, the traditional source of danger ("wo sie früher war" [where it was earlier]), to a new and literally "unheard of" danger:

> Lautlos kommt sie über die Matrosen,
>
> welche wissen, daß es dort auf jenen
> goldnen Inseln manchmal singt — ,
> und sich blindlings in die Ruder lehnen,
> wie umringt
>
> von der Stille, die die ganze Weite
> in sich hat und an die Ohren weht,
> so als wäre ihre andre Seite
> der Gesang, dem keiner widersteht.
>
> [Without a sound it comes over the sailors,
>
> who know that there on those
> golden isles sometimes there is singing — ,
> and blindly put their weight into their oars
> as if surrounded
>
> by the silence, which the whole expanse
> has within itself and which blows on the ears,
> as if its other side were
> the song which no one can resist.]

The "sie" (it) in line 12 clearly refers to the danger of line 9, which lies no longer in storming and raging, but instead comes over the sailors without a sound. Homer's sailors avoid the danger by blocking off the physical sound, but the threat here is more insidious; the sailors indeed know the danger of the singing, which is vaguely alluded to in the impersonal construction ("daß es dort auf jenen/goldnen Inseln manchmal singt" [that there on those/ golden isles sometimes there is singing]). Heinz Politzer has pointed out the curious way in which this singing is robbed of all concreteness: the "es singt" (there is singing) replaces the actual sirens, a group of islands replaces one particular island, and the "manchmal" (sometimes) further adds to the air of tentativeness.[4]

The sailors, knowing of the danger, lean "blindly" into their oars. On a literal level, this suggests their panic and determination to escape the danger at all costs. But on another level, there is a curious poetic justice enacted here. We have already noted, in the first half of the poem, the curious avoidance of auditory images in favor of the visual. But here, the sailors' avoidance of the sirens' music has made them insensible to the visual as well, literally "blind." It is not just that the danger here is in seductive sound rather than in the loud and violent; the danger is not only quiet, it is literally "lautlos," without a sound.

The danger is in fact precisely the silence, "Stille," which is named in line 13 and enacted in the truncated line which precedes it at the end of the third stanza. The silence surrounds the sailors, is contained in the vast expanse around them, it blows against their ears, just as a heard music (to use Keats's phrase) would do. In spite of the sailors' avoidance of song, the silence reaches them as would actual song, and it is precisely this fact that justifies the final subjunctive statement: as if the other side of this silence were the song which no one can resist.

This is the first of Rilke's music poems in which this image of the "other side" appears, as it does later in the 1917 poem "An die Musik" (To Music), though Beda Allemann points out that the similar image of music viewed in a mirror appears in the poem "Der Duft" (The Scent), which was originally intended for the *Neue Gedichte*.[5] Rilke uses this image on two occasions in a lengthy letter to Princess Marie von Thurn und Taxis-Hohenlohe written from Toledo on 17 November 1912. Referring to a book he is reading by Fabre d'Olivet, he speaks initially of "das Stumme in der Musik, . . . ihre mathematische Rückseite" (What is mute in music, . . . its mathematical reverse side) and later speaks of the notion

> daß nicht allein das *Hörbare* in der Musik entscheidend sei, denn es kann etwas angenehm zu hören sein, ohne daß es *wahr* sei . . . . mir würde es verständlich sein, daß man in den Mysterien eingeweiht wurde in die *Rückseite der Musik*, in die selige Zahl, die sich dort teilt und wieder zusammennimmt und aus unendlichen Vielfachen in die Einheit zurückfällt . . . . (375–76)
>
> [that it is not only what is *audible* in music which is decisive, for something can be pleasant to hear without being *true* . . . . it would be comprehensible to me

that in the mystery religions a person was initiated into the *reverse side of music*, into the sacred number which is divided there and united once more, and which falls back from infinite diversity into oneness . . . .]

Here, as in our poem, this "other side" or "reverse side" of music is equated with silence. In the 1912 letter and in Rilke's later work, this recognition that the other side of music is silence is a major stepping-stone toward a relationship to music in which the destructive temptation is secondary to a recognition of music's sacred and creative function. But in this poem, the image is not yet free of threat. In the hypothetical suggestion that the other side of the silence surrounding the sailors is the song which none can resist or withstand (the German "widerstehen" has both meanings, implying both seductive pleasure and destructive force), the poet seems to be affirming that the menace inheres within the silence as well, and thus (as we have already noted) that one cannot escape the danger by blocking out the physical sound.

Still, this conception represents a major change from the 1899 poem "Musik"; in that earlier poem, "Schweigen," or "silence," is evoked as a kind of antidote to the destructive power of music, and it is clearly viewed as the antithesis of music. In affirming the essential identity of music and silence, the poet has taken a major step on the path that leads to the *Sonette an Orpheus* (1923) (*Sonnets to Orpheus*, 1942). Another feature of the poem which strikingly anticipates the mystical nature of his later conception of music is the fact that the two agents on whom Homer's narrative focuses the most — Odysseus and the sirens — are both virtually eliminated by Rilke. The hero appears in his guise as narrator after the fact, but apparently it is only the sailors who are subject to the danger. Likewise, as has already been pointed out, the sirens vanish to make way for the impersonal singing on the islands. Finally, one could argue that the "disappearance" of Odysseus the hero in the poem is a tribute to Odysseus the *aiodos* or poet/musician, who despite his earlier disclaimer *does* effectively evoke the menacing effect of the dispersed and silent Siren song. And so for the poet who, at the time this poem was written, was still clinging to the reassuring concreteness of the visual arts, this poem brings him a step closer to mastering the art of Orpheus.

The University of Arizona

Notes

[1] All references to Rilke's poetry and prose fiction are cited by volume and page number from the standard edition, Rainer Maria Rilke, *Sämtliche Werke*, (Frankfurt am Main: Insel, 1955–66). References to the letters are from Rainer Maria Rilke, *Briefe*, (Frankfurt am Main: Insel, 1950). All translations from the German are my own.

[2] *Homer: The Odyssey*, trans. Robert Fagles, intro. Bernard Knox (New York: Viking, 1996), Book 8, 206–07.

[3] Judith Ryan, *Umschlag und Verwandlung: Poetische Struktur und Dichtungstheorie in R. M. Rilkes Lyrik der Mittleren Periode (1907–1914)* (Munich: Winkler, 1972), 36–38.

[4] Heinz Politzer, *Das Schweigen der Sirenen: Studien zur deutschen und österreichischen Literatur* (Stuttgart: J. B. Metzler, 1968), 39.

[5] Beda Allemann, *Zeit und Figur beim späten Rilke. Ein Beitrag zur Poetik des modernen Geistes* (Pfullingen: Neske, 1961), 165.

* * * * *

I would like to thank Ralph Freedman, who gave me valuable advice on my first essay on the subject of Rilke and music, more years ago than I care to remember, and also my University of Arizona colleague Prof. Marilyn Skinner for her help with Homeric Greek.

ROBERT FAGLES, Translator

Homer: *The Odyssey*
Book Eight: A Day for Songs and Contests

When young Dawn with her rose-red fingers shone once more
royal Alcinous, hallowed island king, rose from bed
and great Odysseus, raider of cities, rose too.
Poised in his majesty, Alcinous led the way
to Phaeacia's meeting grounds, built for all
beside the harbored ships. Both men sat down
on the polished stone benches side-by-side
as Athena started roaming up and down the town,
in build and voice the wise Alcinous' herald,
furthering plans for Odysseus' journey home   10
and stopped beside each citizen, urged them all,
"Come this way, you lords and captains of Phaeacia,
come to the meeting grounds and learn about the stranger!
A new arrival! Here at our wise king's palace now,
he's here from roving the ocean, driven far off course —
he looks like a deathless god!"

                                Rousing their zeal,
their curiosity, each and every man, and soon enough
the assembly seats were filled with people thronging,
gazing in wonder at the seasoned man of war . . .
Over Odysseus' head and shoulders now   20
Athena poured a marvelous splendor, yes,
making him taller, more massive to all eyes,
so Phaeacians might regard the man with kindness,
awe and respect as well, and he might win through
the many trials they'd pose to test the hero's strength.
Once they'd grouped, crowding the meeting grounds,
Alcinous rose and addressed his island people:
"Hear me, lords and captains of Phaeacia,

hear what the heart inside me has to say.
This stranger here, our guest — 30
I don't know who he is, or whether he comes
from sunrise lands or the western lands of evening,
but he has come in his wanderings to my palace;
he pleads for passage, begs we guarantee it.
So now, as in years gone by, let us press on
and grant him escort. No one, I tell you, no one
who comes to *my* house will languish long here,
heartsick for convoy home.

                              Come, my people!
Haul a black ship down to the bright sea,
rigged for her maiden voyage — 40
enlist a crew of fifty-two young sailors,
the best in town, who've proved their strength before.
Let all hands lash their oars to the thwarts then disembark,
come to my house and fall in for a banquet, quickly.
I'll lay on a princely feast for all. So,
these are the orders I issue to our crews.
For the rest, you sceptered princes here,
you come to my royal halls so we can give
this stranger a hero's welcome in our palace —
no one here refuse. Call in the inspired bard 50
Demodocus. God has given the man the gift of song,
to him beyond all others, the power to please,
however the spirit stirs him on to sing."

   With those commands Alcinous led the way
and a file of sceptered princes took his lead,
while the herald went to find the gifted bard.
And the fifty-two young sailors, duly chosen,
briskly following orders,
went down to the shore of the barren salt sea.
And once they reached the ship at the surf's edge, 60
first they hauled the craft into deeper water,
stepped the mast amidships, canvas brailed,
made oars fast in the leather oarlock straps,
moored her riding high on the swell, then disembarked
and made their way to wise Alcinous' high-roofed halls.
There colonnades and courts and rooms were overflowing
with crowds, a mounting host of people young and old.

The king slaughtered a dozen sheep to feed his guests,
eight boars with shining tusks and a pair of shambling oxen.
These they skinned and dressed, and then laid out a feast   70
to fill the heart with savor.

                             In came the herald now,
leading along the faithful bard the Muse adored
above all others, true, but her gifts were mixed
with good and evil both: she stripped him of sight
but gave the man the power of stirring, rapturous song.
Pontonous brought the bard a silver-studded chair,
right amid the feasters, leaning it up against
a central column — hung his high clear lyre
on a peg above his head and showed him how
to reach up with his hands and lift it down.   80
And the herald placed a table by his side
with a basket full of bread and cup of wine
for him to sip when his spirit craved refreshment.
All reached out for the good things that lay at hand
and when they'd put aside desire for food and drink,
the Muse inspired the bard
to sing the famous deeds of fighting heroes —
the song whose fame had reached the skies those days:
The Strife Between Odysseus and Achilles, Peleus' Son . . .
how once at the gods' flowing feast the captains clashed   90
in a savage war of words, while Agamemnon, lord of armies,
rejoiced at heart that Achaea's bravest men were battling so.
For this was the victory sign that Apollo prophesied
at his shrine in Pytho when Agamemnon strode across
the rocky threshold, asking the oracle for advice —
the start of the tidal waves of ruin tumbling down
on Troy's and Achaea's forces, both at once,
thanks to the will of Zeus who rules the world.

    That was the song the famous harper sang
but Odysseus, clutching his flaring sea-blue cape   100
in both powerful hands, drew it over his head
and buried his handsome face,
ashamed his hosts might see him shedding tears.
Whenever the rapt bard would pause in the song,
he'd lift the cape from his head, wipe off his tears
and hoisting his double-handled cup, pour it out to the gods.

But soon as the bard would start again, impelled to sing
by Phaeacia's lords, who reveled in his tale,
again Odysseus hid his face and wept.
His weeping went unmarked by all the others;   110
only Alcinous, sitting close beside him,
noticed his guest's tears,
heard the groan in the man's labored breathing
and said at once to the master mariners around him,
"Hear me, my lords and captains of Phaeacia!
By now we've had our fill of food well-shared
and the lyre too, our loyal friend at banquets.
Now out we go again and test ourselves in contests,
games of every kind — so our guest can tell his friends,
when he reaches home, how far we excel the world   120
at boxing, wrestling, jumping, speed of foot."

   He forged ahead and the rest fell in behind.
The herald hung the ringing lyre back on its peg
and taking Demodocus by the hand, led him from the palace,
guiding him down the same path the island lords
had just pursued, keen to watch the contests.
They reached the meeting grounds
with throngs of people streaming in their trail
as a press of young champions rose for competition.
Topsail and Riptide rose, the helmsman Rowhard too   130
and Seaman and Sternman, Surf-at-the-Beach and Stroke-Oar,
Breaker and Bowsprit, Racing-the-Wind and Swing-Aboard
and Seagirt the son of Greatfleet, Shipwrightson
and the son of Launcher, Broadsea, rose up too,
a match for murderous Ares, death to men —
in looks and build the best of all Phaeacians
after gallant Laodamas, the Captain of the People.
Laodamas rose with two more sons of great Alcinous,
Halius bred to the sea and Clytoneus famed for ships.
And now the games began, the first event a footrace . . .   140
They toed the line —
                     and broke flat out from the start
with a fast pack flying down the field in a whirl of dust
and Clytoneus the prince outstripped them all by far,
flashing ahead the length two mules will plow a furrow
before he turned for home, leaving the pack behind
and raced to reach the crowds.

                              Next the wrestling,
grueling sport. They grappled, locked, and Broadsea,
pinning the strongest champions, won the bouts.
Next, in the jumping, Seagirt leapt and beat the field.
In the discus Rowhard up and outhurled them all by far.   150
And the king's good son Laodamas boxed them to their knees.
When all had enjoyed the games to their hearts' content
Alcinous' son Laodamas spurred them: "Come, my friends,
let's ask our guest if he knows the ropes of any sport.
He's no mean man, not with a build like that . . .
Look at his thighs, his legs, and what a pair of arms —
his massive neck, his big, rippling strength!
Nor is he past his prime,
just beaten down by one too many blows.
Nothing worse than the sea, I always say,   160
to crush a man, the strongest man alive."

   And Broadsea put in quickly,
"Well said, Laodamas, right to the point.
Go up to the fellow, challenge him yourself."

   On that cue, the noble prince strode up
before Odysseus, front and center, asking,
"Come, stranger, sir, won't you try your hand
at our contests now? If you have skill in any.
It's fit and proper for you to know your sports.
What greater glory attends a man, while he's alive,   170
than what he wins with his racing feet and striving hands?
Come and compete then, throw your cares to the wind!
It won't be long, your journey's not far off —
your ship's already hauled down to the sea,
your crew is set to sail."
                              "Laodamas,"
quick to the mark Odysseus countered sharply,
"why do you taunt me so with such a challenge?
Pains weigh on my spirit now, not your sports —
I've suffered much already, struggled hard.
But here I sit amid your assembly still,   180
starved for passage home, begging your king,
begging all your people."
                              "Oh I knew it!"
Broadsea broke in, mocking him to his face.

"I never took you for someone skilled in games,
the kind that real men play throughout the world.
Not a chance. You're some skipper of profiteers,
roving the high seas in his scudding craft,
reckoning up his freight with a keen eye out
for home-cargo, grabbing the gold he can!
You're no athlete. I see that."
                                With a dark glance   190
wily Odysseus shot back, "Indecent talk, my friend.
You, you're a reckless fool — I see *that*. So,
the gods don't hand out all their gifts at once,
not build and brains and flowing speech to all.
One man may fail to impress us with his looks
but a god can crown his words with beauty, charm,
and men look on with delight when he speaks out.
Never faltering, filled with winning self-control,
he shines forth at assembly grounds and people gaze
at him like a god when *he* walks through the streets.   200
Another man may look like a deathless one on high
but there's not a bit of grace to crown his words.
Just like you, my fine, handsome friend. Not even
a god could improve those lovely looks of yours
but the mind inside is worthless.
Your slander fans the anger in my heart.
I'm no stranger to sports — for all your taunts —
I've held my place in the front ranks, I tell you,
long as I could trust to my youth and striving hands.
But now I'm wrestled down by pain and hardship, look,   210
I've borne my share of struggles, cleaving my way
through wars of men and pounding waves at sea.
Nevertheless, despite so many blows
I'll give your games a whirl. Your insults
cut to the quick — you rouse my fighting blood!"

   Up he sprang, cloak and all, and seized a discus,
huge and heavy, more weighty by far than those
the Phaeacians used to hurl and test each other.
Wheeling round, he let loose with his great hand
and the stone whirred on — and down to ground they went,   220
those lords of the long oars and master mariners cringing
under the rock's onrush, soaring lightly out of his grip,
flying away past all the other marks, and Queen Athena,

built like a man, staked out the spot and cried
with a voice of triumph, "Even a blind man,
friend, could find your mark by groping round —
it's not mixed up in the crowd, it's far in front!
There's nothing to fear in *this* event —
no one can touch you, much less beat your distance!"

    At that the heart of the long-suffering hero laughed,   230
so glad to find a ready friend in the crowd that,
lighter in mood, he challenged all Phaeacia's best:
"Now go match *that*, you young pups, and straightaway
I'll hurl you another just as far, I swear, or even farther!
All the rest of you, anyone with the spine and spirit,
step right up and try me — you've incensed me so —
at boxing, wrestling, racing; nothing daunts me.
Any Phaeacian here except Laodamas himself.
The man's my host. Who would fight his friend?
He'd have to be good-for-nothing, senseless, yes,   240
to challenge his host and come to grips in games,
in a far-off land at that. He'd cut his own legs short.
But there are no others I'd deny or think beneath me —
I'll take on all contenders, gladly, test them head to head!
I'm not half bad in the world of games where men compete.
Well I know how to handle a fine polished bow,
first to hit my man in a swarm of enemies,
even with rows of comrades pressing near me,
taking aim with our shafts to hit our targets.
Philoctetes alone outshot me there at Troy   250
when ranks of Achaean archers bent their bows.
Of the rest I'd say that I outclass them all —
men who are still alive, who eat their bread on earth.
But I'd never vie with the men of days gone by,
not Heracles, not Eurytus of Oechalia – archers
who rivaled immortal powers with their bows.
That's why noble Eurytus died a sudden death:
no old age, creeping upon him in his halls . . .
Apollo shot him down, enraged that the man
had challenged *him*, the Archer God.
                                      As for spears,   260
I can fling a spear as far as the next man wings an arrow!
Only at sprinting I fear you'd leave me in the dust.
I've taken a shameful beating out on heavy seas,

no conditioning there on shipboard day by day.
My legs have lost their spring."

    He finished. All stood silent, hushed.
Only Alcinous found a way to answer. "Stranger,
friend — nothing you say among us seems ungracious.
You simply want to display the gifts you're born with,
stung that a youngster marched up to you in the games,   270
mocking, ridiculing your prowess as no one would
who had some sense of fit and proper speech.
But come now, hear me out,
so you can tell our story to other lords
as you sit and feast in your own halls someday,
your own wife and your children by your side,
remembering there our island prowess here:
what skills great Zeus has given *us* as well,
down all the years from our fathers' days till now.
We're hardly world-class boxers or wrestlers, I admit,   280
but we can race like the wind, we're champion sailors too,
and always dear to our hearts, the feast, the lyre and dance
and changes of fresh clothes, our warm baths and beds.
So come — all you Phaeacian masters of the dance —
now dance away! So our guest can tell his friends,
when he reaches home, how far we excel the world
in sailing, nimble footwork, dance and song.
                                        Go, someone,
quickly, fetch Demodocus now his ringing lyre.
It must be hanging somewhere in the palace."

    At the king's word the herald sprang to his feet   290
and ran to fetch the ringing lyre from the house.
And stewards rose, nine in all, picked from the realm
to set the stage for contests: masters-at-arms who
leveled the dancing-floor to make a fine broad ring.
The herald returned and placed the vibrant lyre now
in Demodocus' hands, and the bard moved toward the center,
flanked by boys in the flush of youth, skilled dancers
who stamped the ground with marvelous pulsing steps
as Odysseus gazed at their flying, flashing feet,
his heart aglow with wonder.
                                  A rippling prelude —   300
now the bard struck up an irresistible song:

The Love of Ares and Aphrodite Crowned with Flowers . . .
how the two had first made love in Hephaestus' mansion,
all in secret. Ares had showered her with gifts
and showered Hephaestus' marriage bed with shame
but a messenger ran to tell the god of fire —
Helios, lord of the sun, who'd spied the couple
lost in each other's arms and making love.
Hephaestus, hearing the heart-wounding story,
bustled toward his forge, brooding on his revenge —   310
planted the huge anvil on its block and beat out chains,
not to be slipped or broken, all to pin the lovers on the spot.
This snare the Firegod forged, ablaze with his rage at War,
then limped to the room where the bed of love stood firm
and round the posts he poured the chains in a sweeping net
with streams of others flowing down from the roofbeam,
gossamer-fine as spider webs no man could see,
not even a blissful god —
the Smith had forged a masterwork of guile.
Once he'd spun that cunning trap around his bed   320
he feigned a trip to the well-built town of Lemnos,
dearest to him by far of all the towns on earth.
But the god of battle kept no blind man's watch.
As soon as he saw the Master Craftsman leave
he plied his golden reins, arrived at once
and entered the famous god of fire's mansion,
chafing with lust for Aphrodite crowned with flowers.
She'd just returned from her father's palace, mighty Zeus,
and now she sat in her rooms as Ares strode right in
and grasped her hand with a warm, seductive urging: 330
"Quick, my darling, come, let's go to bed
and lose ourselves in love! Your husband's away —
by now he must be off in the wilds of Lemnos,
consorting with his raucous Sintian friends."

                              So he pressed
and her heart raced with joy to sleep with War
and off they went to bed and down they lay —
and down around them came those cunning chains
of the crafty god of fire, showering down now
till the couple could not move a limb or lift a finger -
then they knew at last: there was no way out, not now.   340
But now the glorious crippled Smith was drawing near . . .

he'd turned around, miles short of the Lemnos coast
for the Sungod kept *his* watch and told Hephaestus all,
so back he rushed to his house, his heart consumed with anguish.
Halting there at the gates, seized with savage rage
he howled a terrible cry, imploring all the gods,
"Father Zeus, look here —
the rest of you happy gods who live forever —
here is a sight to make you laugh, revolt you too!
Just because I am crippled, Zeus's daughter Aphrodite   350
will always spurn me and love that devastating Ares,
just because of his stunning looks and racer's legs
while I am a weakling, lame from birth, and who's to blame?
Both my parents — who else? If only they'd never bred me!
Just look at the two lovers . . . crawled inside my bed,
locked in each other's arms — the sight makes me burn!
But I doubt they'll want to lie that way much longer,
not a moment more — mad as they are for each other.
No, they'll soon tire of bedding down together,
but then my cunning chains will bind them fast   360
till our Father pays my bride-gifts back in full,
all I handed *him* for that shameless bitch his daughter,
irresistible beauty — all unbridled too!"
                                        So Hephaestus wailed
as the gods came crowding up to his bronze-floored house.
Poseidon god of the earthquake came, and Hermes came,
the running god of luck, and the Archer, lord Apollo,
while modesty kept each goddess to her mansion.
The immortals, givers of all good things, stood at the gates,
and uncontrollable laughter burst from the happy gods
when they saw the god of fire's subtle, cunning work.   370
One would glance at his neighbor, laughing out,
"A bad day for adultery! Slow outstrips the Swift."

   "Look how limping Hephaestus conquers War,
quickest of all the gods who rule Olympus!"

"The cripple wins by craft."
                        "The adulterer,
he will pay the price!"
                        So the gods would banter
among themselves but lord Apollo goaded Hermes on:
"Tell me, Quicksilver, giver of all good things —

even with those unwieldy shackles wrapped around you,
how would you like to bed the golden Aphrodite?" 380

   "Oh Apollo, if only!" the giant-killer cried.
"Archer, bind me down with triple those endless chains!
Let all you gods look on, and all you goddesses too —
how I'd love to bed that golden Aphrodite!"

   A peal of laughter broke from the deathless ones
but not Poseidon, not a smile from him; he kept on
begging the famous Smith to loose the god of war,
pleading, his words flying, "Let him go!
I guarantee you Ares will pay the price,
whatever you ask, Hephaestus, 390
whatever's right in the eyes of all the gods."

   But the famous crippled Smith appealed in turn,
"God of the earthquake, please don't urge this on me.
A pledge for a worthless man is a worthless pledge indeed.
What if he slips out of his chains — his debts as well?
How could I shackle *you* while all the gods look on?"

   But the god of earthquakes reassured the Smith,
"Look, Hephaestus, if Ares scuttles off and away,
squirming out of his debt, I'll pay the fine myself."

   And the famous crippled Smith complied at last: 400
"Now *there*'s an offer I really can't refuse!"

   With all his force the god of fire loosed the chains
and the two lovers, free of the bonds that overwhelmed them so,
sprang up and away at once, and the Wargod sped to Thrace
while Love with her telltale laughter sped to Paphos,
Cyprus Isle, where her grove and scented altar stand.
There the Graces bathed and anointed her with oil,
ambrosial oil, the bloom that clings to the gods
who never die, and swathed her round in gowns
to stop the heart . . . an ecstasy — a vision. 410

   That was the song the famous harper sang
and Odysseus relished every note as the islanders,
the lords of the long oars and master mariners rejoiced.

Next the king asked Halius and Laodamas to dance,
the two alone, since none could match that pair.
So taking in hand a gleaming sea-blue ball,
made by the craftsman Polybus — arching back,
one prince would hurl it toward the shadowy clouds
as the other leaping high into the air would catch it
quickly, nimbly, before his feet hit ground again. 420
Once they'd vied at throwing the ball straight up,
they tossed it back and forth in a blur of hands
as they danced across the earth that feeds us all,
while boys around the ring stamped out the beat
and a splendid rhythmic, drumming sound arose,
and good Odysseus looked at his host, exclaiming,
"King Alcinous, shining among your island people,
you boasted Phaeacia's dancers are the best —
they prove your point — I watch and I'm amazed!"

   His praises cheered the hallowed island king 430
who spoke at once to the master mariners around him:
"Hear me, my lords and captains of Phaeacia,
our guest is a man of real taste, I'd say. Come,
let's give him the parting gifts a guest deserves.
There are twelve peers of the realm who rule our land,
thirteen, counting myself. Let each of us contribute
a fresh cloak and shirt and a bar of precious gold.
Gather the gifts together, hurry, so our guest
can have them all in hand when he goes to dine,
his spirit filled with joy. 440
As for Broadsea, let him make amends,
man-to-man, with his words as well as gifts.
His first remarks were hardly fit to hear."

   All assented and gave their own commands,
each noble sent a page to fetch his gifts.
And Broadsea volunteered in turn, obliging:
"Great Alcinous, shining among our island people,
of course I'll make amends to our newfound friend
as you request. I'll give the man this sword.
It's solid bronze and the hilt has silver studs, 450
the sheath around it ivory freshly carved.
Here's a gift our guest will value highly."

He placed the silver-studded sword in Odysseus' hands
with a burst of warm words: "Farewell, stranger, sir —
if any remark of mine gave you offense,
may stormwinds snatch it up and sweep it off!
May the gods grant *you* safe passage home to see your wife —
you've been so far from loved ones, suffered so!"

　　Tactful Odysseus answered him in kind:
"And a warm farewell to you, too, my friend.　　　　　　　　　　460
May the gods grant *you* good fortune —
may you never miss this sword, this gift you give
with such salutes. You've made amends in full."
　　　　　　　　　　　　　　　　　　　　　　With that
he slung the silver-studded sword across his shoulder.
As the sun sank, his glittering gifts arrived
and proud heralds bore them into the hall
where sons of King Alcinous took them over,
spread them out before their noble mother's feet —
a grand array of gifts. The king in all his majesty
led the rest of his peers inside, following in a file　　　　　　　　470
and down they sat on rows of high-backed chairs.
The king turned to the queen and urged her, "Come,
my dear, bring in an elegant chest, the best you have,
and lay inside it a fresh cloak and shirt, your own gifts.
Then heat a bronze cauldron over the fire, boil water,
so once our guest has bathed and reviewed his gifts —
all neatly stacked for sailing,
gifts our Phaeacian lords have brought him now —
he'll feast in peace and hear the harper's songs.
And I will give him this gorgeous golden cup of mine,　　　　　480
so he'll remember Alcinous all his days to come
when he pours libations out in his own house
to Father Zeus and the other gods on high."

　　And at that Arete told her serving-women,
"Set a great three-legged cauldron over the fire,
do it right away!"
　　　　　　　　And hoisting over the blaze
a cauldron, filling it brimful with bathing water,
they piled fresh logs beneath and lit them quickly.
The fire lapped at the vessel's belly, the water warmed.
Meanwhile the queen had a polished chest brought forth　　　490

from an inner room and laid the priceless gifts inside,
the clothes and gold the Phaeacian lords had brought,
and added her own gifts, a cloak and a fine shirt,
and gave her guest instructions quick and clear:
"Now look to the lid yourself and bind it fast
with a good tight knot, so no one can rob you
on your voyage — drifting into a sweet sleep
as the black ship sails you home."
                              Hearing that,
the storm-tossed man secured the lid straightway,
battened it fast with a swift, intricate knot   500
the lady Circe had taught him long ago.
And the housekeeper invited him at once
to climb into a waiting tub and bathe —
a hot, steaming bath . . .
what a welcome sight to Odysseus' eyes!
He'd been a stranger to comforts such as these
since he left the lovely-haired Calypso's house,
yet all those years he enjoyed such comforts there,
never-ending, as if he were a god . . . But now,
when maids had washed him, rubbed him down with oil   510
and drawn warm fleece and a shirt around his shoulders,
he stepped from the bath to join the nobles at their wine.
And there stood Nausicaa as he passed. Beside a column
that propped the sturdy roof she paused, endowed
by the gods with all her beauty, gazing at
Odysseus right before her eyes. Wonderstruck,
she hailed her guest with a winning flight of words:
"Farewell, my friend! And when you are at home,
home in your own land, remember me at times.
Mainly to me you owe the gift of life."   520

   Odysseus rose to the moment, deftly, gently:
"Nausicaa, daughter of generous King Alcinous,
may Zeus the Thunderer, Hera's husband, grant it so —
that I travel home and see the dawn of my return.
Even at home I'll pray to you as a deathless goddess
all my days to come. You saved my life, dear girl."

   And he went and took his seat beside the king.
By now they were serving out the portions, mixing wine,
and the herald soon approached, leading the faithful bard

Demodocus, prized by all the people — seated him in a chair   530
amid the feasters, leaning it against a central column.
At once alert Odysseus carved a strip of loin,
rich and crisp with fat, from the white-tusked boar
that still had much meat left, and called the herald over:
"Here, herald, take this choice cut to Demodocus
so he can eat his fill — with warm regards
from a man who knows what suffering is . . .
From all who walk the earth our bards deserve
esteem and awe, for the Muse herself has taught them
paths of song. She loves the breed of harpers."   540

   The herald placed the gift in Demodocus' hands
and the famous blind bard received it, overjoyed.
They reached for the good things that lay outspread
and when they'd put aside desire for food and drink,
Odysseus, master of many exploits, praised the singer:
"I respect you, Demodocus, more than any man alive —
surely the Muse has taught you, Zeus's daughter,
or god Apollo himself. How true to life,
all too true . . . you sing the Achaeans' fate,
all they did and suffered, all they soldiered through,   550
as if you were there yourself or heard from one who was.
But come now, shift your ground. Sing of the wooden horse
Epeus built with Athena's help, the cunning trap that
good Odysseus brought one day to the heights of Troy,
filled with fighting men who laid the city waste.
Sing *that* for me — true to life as it deserves —
and I will tell the world at once how freely
the Muse gave *you* the gods' own gift of song."

   Stirred now by the Muse, the bard launched out
in a fine blaze of song, starting at just the point   560
where the main Achaean force, setting their camps afire,
had boarded the oarswept ships and sailed for home
but famed Odysseus' men already crouched in hiding —
in the heart of Troy's assembly — dark in that horse
the Trojans dragged themselves to the city heights.
Now it stood there, looming . . .
and round its bulk the Trojans sat debating,
clashing, days on end. Three plans split their ranks:
either to hack open the hollow vault with ruthless bronze

or haul it up to the highest ridge and pitch it down the cliffs 570
or let it stand, a glorious offering made to pacify the gods —
and that, that final plan, was bound to win the day.
For Troy was fated to perish once the city lodged
inside her walls the monstrous wooden horse
where the prime of Argive power lay in wait
with death and slaughter bearing down on Troy.
And he sang how troops of Achaeans broke from cover,
streaming out of the horse's hollow flanks to plunder Troy —
he sang how left and right they ravaged the steep city,
sang how Odysseus marched right up to Deiphobus' house 580
like the god of war on attack with diehard Menelaus.
There, he sang, Odysseus fought the grimmest fight
he had ever braved but he won through at last,
thanks to Athena's superhuman power.

   That was the song the famous harper sang
but great Odysseus melted into tears,
running down from his eyes to wet his cheeks . . .
as a woman weeps, her arms flung round her darling husband,
a man who fell in battle, fighting for town and townsmen,
trying to beat the day of doom from home and children. 590
Seeing the man go down, dying, gasping for breath,
she clings for dear life, screams and shrills —
but the victors, just behind her,
digging spear-butts into her back and shoulders,
drag her off in bondage, yoked to hard labor, pain,
and the most heartbreaking torment wastes her cheeks.
So from Odysseus' eyes ran tears of heartbreak now.
But his weeping went unmarked by all the others;
only Alcinous, sitting close beside him,
noticed his guest's tears, 600
heard the groan in the man's labored breathing
and said at once to the master mariners around him,
"Hear me, my lords and captains of Phaeacia!
Let Demodocus rest his ringing lyre now —
this song he sings can hardly please us all.
Ever since our meal began and the stirring bard
launched his song, our guest has never paused
in his tears and throbbing sorrow.
Clearly grief has overpowered his heart.
Break off this song! Let us *all* enjoy ourselves, 610

the hosts and guest together. Much the warmer way.
All these things are performed for him, our honored guest,
the royal send-off here and gifts we give in love.
Treat your guest and suppliant like a brother:
anyone with a touch of sense knows that.
So don't be crafty now, my friend, don't hide
the truth I'm after. Fair is fair, speak out!
Come, tell us the name they call you there at home —
your mother, father, townsmen, neighbors round about.
Surely no man in the world is nameless, all told. 620
Born high, born low, soon as he sees the light
his parents always name him, once he's born.
And tell me your land, your people, your city too,
so our ships can sail you home — their wits will speed them there.
For we have no steersmen here among Phaeacia's crews
or steering-oars that guide your common craft.
Our ships know in a flash their mates' intentions,
know all ports of call and all the rich green fields.
With wings of the wind they cross the sea's huge gulfs,
shrouded in mist and cloud — no fear in the world of foundering, 630
fatal shipwreck.
           True, there's an old tale I heard
my father telling once. Nausithous used to say
that lord Poseidon was vexed with us because
we escorted all mankind and never came to grief.
He said that one day, as a well-built ship of ours
sailed home on the misty sea from such a convoy,
the god would crush it, yes,
and pile a huge mountain round about our port.
So the old king foretold . . . And as for the god,
he can do his worst or leave it quite undone, 640
whatever warms his heart.
           But come, my friend,
tell us your own story now, and tell it truly.
Where have your rovings forced you?
What lands of men have you seen, what sturdy towns,
what men themselves? Who were wild, savage, lawless?
Who were friendly to strangers, god-fearing men? Tell me,
why do you weep and grieve so sorely when you hear
the fate of the Argives, hear the fall of Troy?
That is the gods' work, spinning threads of death

through the lives of mortal men, 650
and all to make a song for those to come . . .
Did one of your kinsmen die before the walls of Troy,
some brave man — a son by marriage? father by marriage?
Next to our own blood kin, our nearest, dearest ties.
Or a friend perhaps, someone close to your heart,
staunch and loyal? No less dear than a brother,
the brother-in-arms who shares our inmost thoughts."

Princeton University

ANNA TAVIS

Rilke, Dostoyevsky and Tolstoy: The Unpublished Chapter

The idea of an essay on Rilke, Dostoyevsky and Tolstoy had evolved in the discussions between Ralph Freedman and me when we were working on our respective biographical studies of Rilke. Ralph was in the middle of his monumental biography *Life of a Poet*, and I had just started my dissertation (I enjoyed the research and dreaded the writing). In the course of this work, I struggled with the question of how Rilke's creative mind processed and assimilated Russian cultural material and how it became his own. This volume gives me the opportunity to revisit the dialogue with my teacher and conclude the unfinished chapter on Rilke's Russian connection.

Rilke Revisits Dostoyevsky

Gide once remarked, speaking of Dostoyevsky, that a literary genius always ran the risk of finding himself. He would write coldly and deliberately from then on, Gide suggested, trying to protect the self that he had found. Fearing inconsistency, which he dreads more than insincerity, he would imitate himself.[1] Gide touched in this observation on one of the most crucial differences between Dostoyevsky's and Rilke's creative minds. Even though art was their shared religion, Dostoyevsky was loyal to art as a religious idea while Rilke was faithful to art for its own sake. Dostoyevsky was seen as a prophet; Rilke became a visionary. When it came to Russia, he evolved from thinking in dependent stereotypes to psychologically complex ideas.

It is true that in his early career Rilke's creative genius contained many contradictions. What made him special, however, was the consistency with which he revisited the old places that he had once inhabited and reexamined them from his new location in time. What made him exceptional was the persistence with which he returned to people whom he had once loved. He worked hard at keeping continuity in his life by stringing interruptions together into a continuous pattern of returns. The story of the Prodigal Son, which concludes his autobiographical novel, *Die Aufzeichnungen des Malte Laurids Brigge* (1910) (*The

Notebooks of Malte Laurids Brigge, 1949), provides a metaphoric closure to Rilke's own life. "Dies alles noch einmal und nun wirklich auf sich zu nehmen, war der Grund, weshalb der Entfremdete heimkehrte" (To take all this once more, and this time really, upon himself — this was the reason he, the estranged, returned home).[2]

Rilke's interest in Dostoyevsky evolved very much according to the same pattern of returns. He first came across Dostoyevsky's work in the mid-1890s, at the recommendation of Jacob Wassermann, a fellow writer and a boarder at the same pension in Munich. After reading Dostoyevsky's novel *The Poor Folk*, Rilke wrote in his diary that he knew no other novel that could stand next to Dostoyevsky's first work. He even translated and intended to publish later his favorite scenes from the novel. Unfortunately, Rilke's translations were lost.

Rilke turned to Dostoyevsky in mid-career only when his fascination with the fairyland Russia of his youth was over and he needed to reexamine those episodes in his past that he had earlier overlooked, misinterpreted or simply neglected. On one occasion, he remembered that Dostoyevsky became important to him much later in life, only after he had already traveled to Russia and learned Dostoyevsky's native language. He read and reread *The Poor Folk* and prepared himself thoroughly to return to Dostoyevsky as a fellow writer.[3]

As much as Rilke deserves admiration for independently reworking dominant stereotypes into sophisticated personal images (specifically those of Russian culture and Russian literature), he followed the general Western European trend in rethinking cultural stereotypes, particularly as they applied to Russian culture.

In the first decade of the twentieth century, cultural and national idiosyncrasies of character were attributed to national and individual psychological makeup rather than traditional geographic, climatic and historical factors. The Russians and the Scandinavians had a very special role to play in the European rediscovery of the Soul. Tolstoy and Dostoyevsky, Ibsen and Jens Peter Jacobsen were seen by Western Europeans as articulators of a new psychological complexity. Questions about their stylistic limitations became irrelevant. The image of Russia as a barbaric semi-Eastern empire populated by largely unenlightened folk gave way to a vision of Russia as Europe's last spiritual sanctuary. In the words of Moller van den Bruck, Dostoyevsky's German admirer and commentator, "the Slavs alone were still capable of bringing back Jesus or Buddha once again."[4] A new view of Russia's messianic exceptionalism developed in the context of these religious associations. The new European agenda was to delve into the labyrinths of the inexplicable Russian psyche and to rekindle the extinguished Western European imagination through a powerful surge of elemental Russian sensibility.[5] Melchior de Vogue, the foremost Western Russophile, was among the first to register this shift in European thinking about Russia; in his preface to the first fundamental study of the Russian novel, *Le Roman Russe*, de Vogue wrote:

> We left it to a handful of orientalists to busy themselves with checking the writings of these Samaritans. We had a notion that a literature might exist in their midst, as in Persia or Arabia; we did not place much trust in it . . . .[6]

German Naturalists and their French fellow travelers discovered in Dostoyevsky's work a piece of social criticism, naturalistic in style and unpolished in execution. Refinements of style and perfection of form were matters of secondary importance in their judgment. Lou Andreas-Salomé, who became Rilke's mentor and companion on his Russian trips, also had an immediate and lasting influence on his perceptions. She emphasized the importance of the author's biography to a literary work and attempted to measure the depth of his psyche embedded in the text. There was little known of Dostoyevsky's private persona then, and his sketchy curriculum vitae was not dramatic enough to meet Andreas-Salomé's criteria for greatness. This situation began to shift in 1899 when Nina Hoffmann pioneered a comprehensive German-language biography of Dostoyevsky followed by a close reading of Dostoyevsky's works.

That Rilke learned to appreciate Dostoyevsky later than Tolstoy is in itself a revealing testimony of the deepening insight of his cultural vision and his desire to probe beneath cultural stereotypes.[7] Rilke found in Dostoyevsky's grim talent ("grausame Genie,") an objective genius who knew how to make individual destinies universal.

When in the late fall of 1907, Rilke responded to a questionnaire regarding the publication of the series "Books of Real Life," he named Dostoyevsky among the top ten writers on his list, and, still in mid-career, Rilke set out to answer Dostoyevsky's challenge addressed to the Europeans — "Why does Europe deny us independence, our own word?" — this professional connection can be indirectly traced to Rilke's textual assimilation of a Dostoyevskian subject. Even though much has been written about the affinities that exist between Rilke and Dostoyevsky, many subtle personal and textual connections pertaining to Rilke's Russian affinities still remain to be explained and explored. The old-fashioned critical method of looking for parallels and allusions works well on Dostoyevsky and Rilke's texts, because it lets us revisit obscure passages in the texts and focus on their similarities.

When Rilke's only novel, *The Notebooks of Malte Laurids Brigge*, was published in 1910. French reviewers were the first ones to notice thematic and stylistic parallels in Rilke's and Dostoyevsky's prose. After all, these similarities between Rilke's and Dostoyevsky's works were more than a mere circumstance of the two writers publishing for a deadline. Edmond Jaloux, a literary reviewer for the influential *Nouvelles Littéraires*, noted in his reaction to the novel that Malte's *Notebooks* could have been written by a Dostoyevskian character

("Notizen und Betrachtungen einer Figur Dostoewski's darstellen konnten, die dieser nicht ins Leben gerufen hatte" [Could represent notes and reflections of a Dostoyevsky figure, whom he had never called into being])[8] Emile Benveniste, an eminent journalist and critic, also remarked in the journal *Philosophies* that the psychological intensity of Rilke's descriptions was equal to Dostoyevsky's portrayals:

> wenn der Zufall ihm die — kaum uberwundenen oder schon gespaltenen — einander entgegengesetzten Krafte zeigt, auf die wir den Konflikt zurückzuführen versuchen, dann ist Rilke in seinem besonderen Element: er reicht dann an Dostojewski heran, wie an jener Stelle, in der er das Entsetzen eines Mannes beschreibt, in dem er einen Epileptiker ahnt, der bei vollem Bewusstsein das Herannäheren eines Anfalls fühlt . . . . (Betz, 67)

> [whenever chance shows him mutually conflicting forces (which he had scarcely overcome or already split apart) and with which we try to return to the conflict, then Rilke is really in his own element; then he reaches as high as Dostoyevsky, as in that passage in which he describes the terror of a man in whom he senses an epileptic, who, while fully conscious, anticipates the onset of a seizure.]

Rilke reserved for his protagonist, the artist Malte Laurids Brigge, the unwanted fate of his alter ego, whose eventual demise he himself was desperately trying to forestall. (It is appropriate to remember in this connection how often Dostoyevsky was accused of having the evil thoughts of his protagonists.) As long as the protagonists were given the right to live, they made demands on their creator's energy and time; they enveloped him in the lonely despair and the tedium of misery until their barely tangible connection with life was finally about to break.

> Aber der Andere, Untergegangene hat mich irgendwie abgenutzt, hat mit den Kräften und Gegenstanden meines Lebens den immensen Aufwand seines Untergangs betrieben, da ist nichts, was nicht in seinen Händen, in seinem Herzen war, er hat sich mit der Inständigkeit seiner Verzweiflung alles angeeignet, kaum scheint mir ein Ding neu, so entdeck ich auch schon den Bruch daran, die brüske Stelle, wo er sich abgerissen hat.[9]

> [But the Other, the diseased one, has used me up somehow. He appropriated the energy and circumstances of my life to play out the enormity of his own demise there is nothing that was not in his hands, in his heart. He took everything upon himself with the urgency of his despair. As for me, I could hardly see anything new but soon discovered a breaking point from which he tore himself away.]

The Double

Stylistically speaking, the "Doppelgänger" relationship between the creator and his protagonist was a dated technique already by the end of the nineteenth century. It was replaced by psychological portrayals in the form of autobiographical writing. In a sense, Rilke and Dostoyevsky were looking back towards early or mid-nineteenth-century Romanticism. The resurrection of a "double" in the relationship between author and protagonist provided an appropriate vehicle to communicate their respective messages.

One can see a parallel between Malte Laurids Brigge and a gallery of Dostoyevsky's psychological types. The foremost of these is Yakov Petrovich Golyadkin, the protagonist of Dostoyevsky's short novel *The Double*, who anticipates Malte in the pathos and grotesqueness of his situation. At another level, there is the story of Malte's two Petersburg neighbors, who lose track of time in the chaotic city of Paris. Finally and symbolically comes the historical cross-reference to Grishka Otrepyev, the sixteenth-century pretender to the Russian throne.

On the surface, there is nothing similar between Dostoyevsky's Golyadkin, a small functionary in St. Petersburg, and Rilke's Malte, a Bohemian artist in Paris. As the two authors develop their protagonists, Malte's story becomes an existential tragedy while Golyadkin's fate turns into a clinical farce. The underlying idea for doubling is an externalized identity crisis.

Golyadkin, a small functionary and Dostoyevsky's archetypal double, awakens one morning in the city of St.Petersburg to find himself haunted by his own double. The double's agenda is to get the best of everything that Golyadkin has owned in his life. In a few month's time, Golyadkin's job, his fiancée, and even his lazy man-servant Petrushka all go to his rival. The double occupies those spheres of life in which the protagonist or, as in Rilke's case, the author are having difficulties. Golyadkin, like Malte, is a writer, and the act of writing for both men is the only remaining connection with the world. Golyadkin finds that copying official papers at the office and writing and rewriting personal complaint letters are his only effective defenses against the fraudulent double. In a hand shaking with emotion, he scribbles the following missive to himself.

> My dear Sir, Yakov Petrovich,
>
> I should not take up my pen if my situation and your own action, my dear sir, had not forced me to do so. Believe me, necessity alone obliges me to enter into this explanation, and therefore I must first of all request you, my dear Sir, to regard this measure not as a deliberate attempt to insult you, but as the inevitable consequence of the circumstances which now link us together. Your obstinate desire, my dear sir, to insist on your own way and force yourself into the sphere of my practical life, however, oversteps all the boundaries set by common courtesy and simple social intercourse. "Well now, that's all right. The thing is done; it has even got as far as being put into writing. But who is

to blame? He is: he has driven a man to the necessity of demanding explanations in writing. And I'm in the right."[10]

Malte, too, responds to isolation by writing : "Ich habe etwas getan gegen die Furcht. Ich habe die ganze Nacht gesessen und geschrieben." (*Malte*, 19) (I have taken action against fear. I have sat all night and written. [*Notebooks*, 23]). Like Golyadkin, Malte writes for himself, and both characters find parallels in history. Uncannily, the simpleton Golyadkin and the refined Malte recall the haunting image of the same historical double: Grishka Otrepyev, the pretender to the Russian throne at the time of Boris Godunov. Even though Grishka's name is brought up in very different contexts, every time it appears in literary and historical texts, it effectively connects both protagonists with a long line of predecessors. Rilke was fascinated with the historical pretender, Otrepyev, as someone who lived the creation of his own life and death. The illusion of Otherness was so powerful for him that even on his deathbed, the pretender refused to acknowledge the falsity of his image; only his mother was able to recognize the pretender as her son.

Grishka Otrepyev's name flashes through Golyadkin's feverish mind at several decisive junctures in Dostoyevsky's text. Although Golyadkin does not have Malte's sophisticated tools for dealing with Otrepyev's psyche, he comes to a remarkably similar conclusion concerning the impostor's skills and fate:

> In his inmost heart he had formed a resolution, and in his inmost heart he swore to carry it out. To be honest, he did not yet know very well what steps to take, or rather he did not know at all; but it did not matter, it was nothing! 'In this day and age, my good sir, success does not come by imposture and impudence. No good will come of imposture and impudence, my good sir, they can only lead to downfall. Grishka Otrepyev deceiving the blind multitude, my good sir, was the only one who succeeded by imposture, and that not for long.' Notwithstanding this last circumstance, Mr. Golyadkin proposed to wait until such time as the mask fell from certain faces and something came to light.
>
> (*The Double*, 205–206)

As with Grishka Otrepyev, the double must die in order to restore the balance of reality. Thus, Dostoyevsky's Golyadkin fails to prevail over his double and is led away to the asylum in the final scene of the novel. Rilke, however, decides to sacrifice Malte, hoping for a long creative life for himself. But he shared with Andreas-Salomé the emptiness that he experienced with Malte's death:

> je weiter ich es zuende schrieb, desto stärker fühlte ich, daß es ein unbeschreiblicher Abschnitt sein würde, eine hohe Wasserscheide, wie ich mir immer sagte; aber nun erweist es sich, daß alles Gewässer nach der alten Seite abgeflossen ist und ich in eine Dürre hintergeh. (*Briefweschel*, 238)

[The closer to the end I got, the stronger I felt that it would be an indescribable loss, an important Watershed, as I have always told myself, but now I see that all waters flowed toward the old side and I remain in an arid place.]

Indeed, Malte Laurids Brigge's death became a watershed which prepared the author for the best writing he would ever do.

Writing as Religion in Rilke, Dostoyevsky and Tolstoy

For Rilke, as for Dostoyevsky, writing was always a way of life, a process, as well as the source, of living energy. Writing became for both writers an absorbing and almost religious commitment to life. They labored in literature with rolled up sleeves and with sweat on their brows, just as Tolstoy tilled his fields. They used the power of words to expose consciousness in their characters much as Tolstoy sought access to other minds in order to enlighten or control them with literature. Rilke and Dostoyevsky openly opposed Tolstoy's view of literature as the idle squandering of precious creative energies on idle entertainment.

Despite their obvious differences, Rilke and Dostoyevsky shared the view that writing facilitated the connection between the inner and the outer worlds. In Tolstoy, by contrast, literature was a means of deception; it did more harm than good. Thus, Tolstoy's Anna Karenina reads an English novel on her way to Moscow and subsequently meets Vronsky, her future lover. She tries her hand at writing books for children and in the process, she neglects her own daughter. Natasha Rostova similarly cannot live through a year of correspondence with her fiancée, Prince Balkonsky. She almost succeeds in eloping with a suitor who happens to be next to her in the here and now of everyday life. Konstantin Levin does not entrust a piece of paper with his marriage proposal; he scribbles the initial letters on the frozen window and his fiancée understands every word without needing to see them written out in full.

In the pages of Dostoyevsky's works, someone is always writing, noting, recording. Dostoyevsky's many writers — the petty functionary Devushkin in *The Poor Folk*, the Underground man in the *Notes from the Underground*, the diarists in the *Notes from the House of the Dead, Winter Notes on Summer Impressions*, and *The Diary of the Writer* — all resort to the written word as their medium of communicating with the world. Even the titles of Dostoyevsky's works contain the multiple and ineluctable words "diary" and "notes."

Every one of Dostoyevsky's busy writers is real and their writing is palpable; they are the very opposite of Malte, Rilke's aesthete. Devushkin and Golyadkin are copying clerks, the Underground Man is a low bureaucrat, and each of them is a man proud of his "neat and regular handwriting" who lives seeking the approval of the senior clerks. The most holy of Dostoyevsky's characters,

Prince Myshkin, "the Idiot," has only one marketable skill, he is a calligrapher. Myshkin's ability to reproduce exotic scripts impresses his potential employer: "You are not simply a good penman, my dear fellow, you are an artist!"

A few of Dostoyevsky's writers are singled out as narcissists. Stepan Verkhovensky of *The Possessed* is one such obsessive writer whom Dostoyevsky describes with sarcasm:

> True, Mr. Verkhovensky was crazy about writing. He wrote to Mrs. Stavrogin even though they lived in the same house, and during his hysterical periods, he turned out two letters a day. I know for certain that she always read those letters very carefully, even when she received two on the same day. Then she folded them neatly, annotated and classified them, and filed them in a special drawer.[11]

Dostoyevsky rejects writing when it fails to communicate, whenever it turns into an obsession and thus becomes writing for writing's sake. For Rilke, any form of writing is sacred. The primary distinction between Malte and all of Dostoyevsky's narrators/writers is that Malte is born into language and his whole life is only a translation of the outer into the inner and the inner into writing. "Dieser junge, belanglose Ausländer, Brigge, wird sich fünf Treppen hoch hinsitzen mussen und schreiben, Tag und Nacht, ja er wird schreiben müssen, das wird das Ende sein . . ." (*Malte,* 26) (This young, insignificant foreigner, Brigge, will have to sit down in his room five flights up and write, day and night: yes, he will have to write, that is how it will end. [*Notebooks,* 30]). For Rilke, writing in itself is always beyond question. He finds charm and value in various "artistic" obsessions that have no value other than art for art's sake (such as Malte's Petersburg neighbors' violin playing and poetry recitations).

With his lifelong interest in Russia, Rilke could not stay away from engaging in the dialogue between Russia's two great novelists, Dostoyevsky and Tolstoy. If in the end, he comes closer to Dostoyevsky on the questions of the life of the spirit, he gets entangled in the debate with Tolstoy on the difficult questions of human life and death.

The Theme of Death in Rilke, Dostoyevsky, and Tolstoy

Malte's diary opens on the note of death: "So, also hierher kommen die Leute, um zu leben, ich würde eher meinen, es stürbe sich hier"(So then, people do come here in order to live, but I would sooner have thought, one died here). From the vantage point of a young writer lost in a foreign city, the readers are taken through the deadly labyrinth of Paris. Impersonal urban death is contagious: it spreads like brushfire through streets, takes over hospitals, reigns in the maternity wards. The city turns into the pandemonium of disease and decline.

Doctors administer to death; they function as cogs in the ominous death mills of the city.

In sheer numbers, Rilke's naturalistic descriptions of urban death measure up only to war casualties in Tolstoy's *Sevastopol Stories* and in the battle scenes of *War and Peace*. Both writers expose the senselessness of death inflicted on a mass scale. Rilke deplores the anti-aesthetic aspect of death in the city while Tolstoy issues a pacifistic anti-war message. For Tolstoy, death is not just a terrifying cessation of the physical human being, but also the end of consciousness and therefore unacceptable on any terms.

Dostoyevsky's characters, often afflicted with poverty and disease, live at death's doorstep day in and day out, but they still become victims of accidents and murders, because Dostoyevsky is not interested in either the aesthetic or the physical aspect of death; he is concerned with death's ethical implications.

Each death is individual and each one takes away the uniqueness of life. It is at this juncture of ethics, where the Russians, Tolstoy and Dostoyevsky, come together on the question of death. In the ultimate count, death is neither a transcendental concept nor a private experience; it simply binds everyone together in the communal responsibility for life. Although Rilke did not make any direct statements concerning Dostoyevsky's themes of death, his dialogue with the Russian writer is transparent in his texts.

Rilke was also well aware of Tolstoy's portrayals of death. He even wanted to obtain copyrights for the translation of Tolstoy's drama *The Live Corpse* and called Tolstoy's novella "The Death of Ivan Ilyich" one of the most powerful descriptions of death he had ever read. Tolstoy was featured in the drafts of Rilke's novel as a great artist who gave up writing for fear of death ("der grosse Todesfurchtige"). To reach eternity, he worked tirelessly at constructing his own legend

Tolstoy starts the story of Ivan Ilyich's life by announcing his death, which was just like everyone else's, lonely and meaningless; in other words, public. His purpose is to take a private look into the dying person's consciousness. At the end of the story he comes to an unexpected conclusion. Every life and death is unique but none of it is individual and everyone goes through the same feelings on his own: "it is myself alone who must live and myself alone who must die."

Rilke shared two of Tolstoy's ideas about death which were alien to Dostoyevsky. He considered that if one had a choice, the "natural" death was the only "right" death to choose and, like Tolstoy, he indulged in descriptions of "grand deaths" on occasion. The scene of the burial service for Count Bezukhov seen through the eyes of his son, Pierre, in *War and Peace* recalls Rilke's description of Kammerherr Brigge's death, as observed by little Malte. The scene of mourning in *War and Peace* is an exercise in hypocrisy. Pierre observes the following scene upon entering the room:

> A little behind them (the clergy) stood the two younger princesses holding handkerchiefs to their eyes, and just in front of them their eldest sister, Katishe, fixing a vicious and determined look on the icons, as though declaring to all that she would not answer for herself if she were to look round. Anna Mihalovna, with a meek and mournful all-forgiving expression on her face, stood by the door with the unknown lady. Prince Vasili, on the other side of the door, near the invalid chair, was leaning his left arm on the carved back of a velvet chair which he had turned round for the purpose. He held a wax taper in his left hand and was crossing himself with his right, raising his eyes each time his fingers touched his forehead. His face wore a calm look of piety and resignation to the will of God. "If you cannot comprehend such sentiments, so much the worse for you," he seemed to be saying.[12]

Tolstoy makes it clear in this description that he does not believe in spectacles, just as he does not believe in sharing death. In Rilke's rendition, the "ideal" death envelopes everyone in its grandiose feeling. Death takes control over peoples' emotions; it dictates their words and controls their movements.

Christoph Detlev's death is powerful because it is governed from within, in full harmony with the dying man's being; nothing from without can influence its natural flow.

> Christoph Detlevs Tod lebte nun schon seit vielen, vielen Tagen auf Ulsgaard und redete mit allen und verlangte. Verlangte die Hunde, verlangte daß man lache, spreche, spiele und still sei und alles zugleich. Verlangte Freunde zu sehen, Frauen und Verstorbene, und verlangte selber zu sterben: verlangte. Verlangte und schrie. (*Malte*, 16).

> [Christoph Detlev's death had been living at Ulsgaard for many, many days now and had spoken to everyone and demanded: . . . Demanded the dogs, demanded that people should laugh, talk, play and be quiet and all at the same time. Demanded to see friends, women and people who were dead, and demanded to die itself: demanded. Demanded and shouted. (*Notebooks*, 21)]

The gap between the dying person and all those around him can not be bridged. In Tolstoy the language of death is understandable only to the naïve and sincere outsiders like Pierre Bezukhov and to the uneducated Russian peasants:

> When Pierre approached, the count was looking straight at him but with the gaze the intent and significance of which no mortal man could fathom. Either this look had simply nothing to say and merely fastened upon him because those eyes must needs look at something, or it had too much to say.
>
> (*War and Peace*, 83)

Rilke stands apart from the Russian "giants" upholding his views on the philosophical meaning of death. To him, who was called, "the last German Romantic," death could be beautiful, self-created, and even lived for. The main difference between Tolstoy's and Rilke's portrayals of death was never finite. He says it best in his First Duino Elegy:

> . . . Und das Totsein ist mühsam . . .
> . . . .
> Aber wir, die so grosse
> Geheimnisse brauchen, denen aus Trauer so oft
> seliger Fortschritt entspringt — : k ö n n t e n wir sein ohne sie?[13]
>
> [. . . it's hard, being dead . . .
> . . . .
> But we, that have need of
> such mighty secrets, we, for whom sorrow's so often
> source of blessedest progress, could we exist without them?]

To say that *The Notebooks of Malte Laurids Brigge* is the most Russian of Rilke's works in its themes and style may seem an exaggeration at first. However, Rilke deals in this novel with the experience that comes closest in spirit to the vocabulary of Russian themes. To accomplish an aesthetic return to Russia, Rilke needed to have lived in Paris and to critically reexamine the icons of Russian life that he had earlier so blindly worshipped. He was guided upon his return by the writings of Tolstoy and Dostoyevsky, whom he read and reread before he could make Russia his own.

Fairfield University

Notes

[1] André Gide, *Dostoyevsky*. trans. L. Varese (New York: New Directions, 1961).

[2] Rainer Maria Rilke, *Die Aufzeichnungen des Malte Laurids Brigge* (Frankfurt am Main: Suhrkamp, 1979), 233. *The Notebooks of Malte Laurids Brigge*, trans. M. D. Herter Norton (New York and London: Norton, 1964), 215.

[3] "[Dostoyevsky] ist mir später sehr wichtig geworden, als ich, durch sein Land und seine Sprache zum äussersten auf ihn vorbereitet, die 'Armen Leute' las und wiederlas und schliesslich einen Teil dieses ahnungslos genialen Buches übersetzte . . ." ([Dostoyevsky] later became very important to me, when through his country and his language I was prepared for him to the utmost, I read and reread "Poor Folk" and finally translated a part of this unsuspecting, brilliant book) (Ingeborg Schnack, *Rainer Maria Rilke: Chronik seines Lebens und seines Werkes*, 2 vols. [Frankfurt am Main: Insel, 1975], 1:292).

[4] "Der Slawe allein kann noch einmal Jesus oder Buddha geboren" (Moller van den Bruck, "Einleitung," *Die Dämonen* [Leipzig and Munich: Reinhard Piper, 1906]: VIII).

[5] In the words of the Russian critic Volynski, "One cannot understand the Russian peasant without using metaphysics because everything in and around him — is full of mystery and secrets, full of organic processes, from which life emerges" (A. L. Volynski, *Die Russische Litteratur der Gegenwart*, trans. Josef Welnik, [Berlin: Gose and Tetzlaff, 1902]).

[6] Quoted and translated in F. W. J. Hemmings, *The Russian Novel in France* (Oxford: Oxford UP, 1950), 5.

[7] Frederic Lefevre called Rilke in an interview the "last German Romantic," "Novalis de notre temps. Une homme pour qui le monde interieur existe" (The Novalis of our time. A man for whom the interior world exists). Quoted in Hartmann Goertz, *Frankreich und das Erlebnis der Form im Werke Rainer Maria Rilke* (Stuttgart: J. B. Metzler, 1932), 115.

[8] Maurice Betz, *Rilke in Frankreich* (Vienna: Herbert Riechner, 1938), 65. Translations of Betz are my own.

[9] Rilke to Andreas-Salomé, 28 December 1911 (from Duino) *Briefweschel* (Frankfurt am Main: Insel, 1979), 238. Translations are my own.

[10] Fyodor Dostoyevsky, *The Double*, trans. Jessie Coulson (New York: Penguin, 1979), 215.

[11] Fyodor Dostoyevsky, *The Possessed*, trans. Andrew R. MacAndrew (New York: New American Library, 1962), 16.

[12] Leo Tolstoy, *War and Peace*, trans. Rosemary Edmonds (New York: Penguin), 91.

[13] Rainer Maria Rilke, *The Duino Elegies*, trans. J. B. Leishman and Stephen Spender (New York: Norton, 1939). Facing-page translation. The English is on 27 and the German on 26.

KATHERINE CALLEN KING

Antigone's Lyric Heart: Marguerite Yourcenar's Revision of Sophocles' *Antigone*

Chaque fille de Londres ou de Rotterdam cherchant son frère mort sous les débris de maisons bombardées nous rassure sur l'authenticité d'Antigone; Antigone à son tour nous atteste que cet héroism est plus qu'une prouesse individuelle, l'accomplissement, sans cesse renouvelé, d'un devoir aussi ancien que le premier frère et la première soeur.[1]

[Every young woman searching for her dead brother in the ruins of bombed houses in London or Rotterdam assures us of Antigone's authenticity; Antigone in her turn assures us that this heroism is, more than an individual feat, the accomplishment, renewed incessantly, of a duty as old as the first brother and the first sister.]

This passage from an essay written by Marguerite Yourcenar in 1943 describes a fairly straightforward relationship to Greek mythology in which cultural memory provides models for exemplary behavior in situations of crisis. Yourcenar's relationship to the stories shaped by Greek poets was, however, much more complex than this; as Joan Howard has proven in splendid analyses of *Qui n'a pas son Minotaure?* (Who doesn't have his own Minotaur?, 1963), and *Le mystère d'Alceste* (The Mystery of Alcestis, 1963), Yourcenar often appropriated exemplary myths "in the service not of revalorization but rather of demythification," that is, to divest them of their power.[2] In other cases, and this is what I want to examine here, she revalorized the story's mythic power but only while significantly changing the values embodied in the original In this essay I will examine two short prose poems from 1934–35, the height of Yourcenar's Greek period. During these years, Yourcenar rewrote several ancient Greek legends, nine of which she published first separately and later together in *Feux* (*Fires*, 1935), claiming they functioned to both "illuminate" and "mask" a personal crisis.[3] It is interesting that she includes a reworking of Sophocles' *Antigone* in *Feux*,[4] for this particular myth recurs most often on modern stages to illuminate and mask *political* rather than personal crises.[5] Indeed, Yourcenar would write in the preface to the 1974 edition that "Antigone ou le choix" ("Antigone or the Choice") is more laden with current events and the shadows of political danger than any other of *Feux*'s stories.[6] Any sense of anomaly disappears, however, if we consider Yourcenar's lyric response to Sophocles as a perfect example of the 1960s feminist creed: the personal is political. Although I will refer occasionally to the personal events that "Antigone" may mask, what is ultimately more interesting to me is the world view illuminated by its gendered play between "nature" and "culture."

Although Yourcenar claimed always not to be a feminist, issues of gender — especially the unfortunate antagonism between male and female perspectives — play an important role in much of her work.[7] It is certainly not surprising that they should play an important role in her response to Sophocles' drama, a tragedy overtly concerned with female will versus male authority. What may be more surprising to readers more familiar with Yourcenar's later work is how feminist her response is.

Before I examine Yourcenar's lyric revision of Sophocles' tragedy, it is necessary to sketch out my understanding of Sophocles' use of gender in the *Antigone*, an analysis indebted to scholars Page duBois, Marilyn Katz, Bernard Knox, Sheila Murnaghan, Charles Segal, and Froma Zeitlin.[8] Antigone, the protagonist, represents an aristocratic clan-centered social structure, responsibility to the clan's gods, personal duty directed especially towards the ancestors, empowerment through love, and simple human feeling. Creon, the male protagonist, represents an anti-aristocratic city-centered social structure, a mediated civic relationship to the gods, civic duty, power based on wealth or exchange, and legal and logical thinking. *She* looks to the past, *he* to the present. Neither achieves a future, which, the play suggests, would require an (Athenian) democratic social structure to create a harmonizing hierarchy (male on top, of course) between the gendered opposing modi operandi.[9]

The male Chorus of Theban Elders sympathizes with Antigone, but, despite having some forebodings about the gods' wishes, they support Creon politically. They accept his definitions of friend and enemy, and they equate disobedience to power with foolishness and being "in love with death."[10] Although they believe Haimon is talking sense[11] and urge his father to listen to him, they give stronger approval[12] to Creon's speech, which argues that order is more important than justice (666–7) and concludes "I must never be weaker than a woman, . . . would rather be displaced, if necessary, by a man, and would not be called weaker than a woman."[13] The Elders' final response to Haimon's refusal to accept Creon's arguments and authority is to say that he has been made irrational by love.

In their "Ode to Unconquerable Eros" (Third *Stasimon*), the Elders opine that Love is a troublemaker, driving lovers mad and drawing just minds to injustice.[14] Love has stirred up this family quarrel (793), Love that is as powerful as the great *thesmoí*, which are, we must infer, the laws of human society that dictate obedience to fathers and rulers (796–99). Aphrodite, they say, plays with us as she will. No matter how correct Haimon's arguments may be, therefore, the Elders condemn his insubordination, and they portray heterosexual love, the foundation of the family, as dangerous, inimical to the city.[15]

Immediately after singing this ode, the Elders see Antigone being led to death and discover an emotion, pity or sympathy, that carries *them*, like Haimon, beyond the *thesmoí*. Their rebellion, however, extends no further than tears, and their subsequent lyric interchange with Antigone shows that they are not going to let their sympathy for her overwhelm their reason.

When they see Antigone approach, they weep, but when she laments her untimely death, they put the blame squarely on her: "You go to the grave without glory, without praise, by your own freely chosen action" (817–21).[16] When Antigone compares herself to the rock-enclosed Niobe, they are quick to point out the *difference* between her and Niobe and to make the psychologically astute but comfortless observation that mortals like to hear themselves compared to gods especially when they are about to die (834–38). When she asks them to stop mocking her and laments her alienated, isolated, intermediate state between living and dead, they respond again that it is her own fault — her rashness made her crash against the throne of Justice (853–55). The only extenuation they offer is to suggest that she is redeeming an ancestral debt (856), and the only effect this suggestion has is to increase her anguish as she recollects anew her mother's, father's, and brother's disastrous marriages (857–71). The Elders' response to this anguish is a small concession — "Reverent action is a kind of piety" — and a large admonition: "authority cannot brook disobedience; this is your own fault" (872–75).[17] No wonder Antigone replies that she goes to her grave unmourned (876–82).

My point is this: the *emotions* of the male Chorus sympathize with Antigone, but their *rational* selves critique her and support the body politic. Despite their obvious belief that Creon's punishment of Antigone is misguided,[18] there is absolutely no doubt in their minds that *family piety* must be subordinate to *civic order*. Would Athenians have judged them wrong? Probably not. As Simon Goldhill has pointed out, despite "all the political strife and violence that dominates the histories of the Greek cities, there is surprisingly little evidence of the modern contention that an 'unjust law' should be disobeyed" (95).

Nonetheless, Antigone is as clearly heroic as Creon is hubristic. It is this "nonetheless" that brings me back to the question of gender. What is the effect of Sophocles' emphasis on the gender of his heroic and hubristic protagonists? Are their failings as well as their strengths related to their gender? The fact that the male Chorus retains its sober median position supporting order shows that in Creon's case the answer is no: his virtues — concern for the patriarchal public sphere and hierarchy — are male, but his failing — hubris — is merely human.[19]

Ismene's final yielding to her sister's "passionate" position, on the other hand, reinforces a feeling that Antigone's strength and weakness are essentially one and the same and female. Devotion to family and to the burial rites that are the special concern of women is beneficial to the community,[20] but in the context of a clash between familial and civic values (i.e. Athenian aristocracy and democracy), it may be harmful. In other words, Antigone's gender is problematic, Creon's is not. Her "weakness," however, is not *sui generis* but created by Creon, who, as leader of a tyranny not a democracy, forces her into the public realm and into rejecting the necessary patriarchal political hierarchy by refusing her her proper role.

Following duBois ("Antigone" 382), I would suggest that gender in *Antigone* is used to represent a clash of social systems rather than a battle of the sexes. The play is not about female heroism or male hubris but about the disaster that will ensue if the aristocracy is not successfully integrated into a polis-centered social system. Creon's failure sends a direct message to the male citizens in the audience: like women — and like Love — the aristocracy remains dangerous to civic order. Like the female to the male, it naturally needs to be firmly subordinate to the democratic polis, but it cannot be totally repressed.

If Sophocles' play ultimately focuses on Creon, Yourcenar's short story, despite also incorporating synopses of Sophocles' two Oedipus plays, has no focus other than Antigone. There is no dialogue, and Yourcenar does not confront issues explicitly as Sophocles does in his confrontations between Creon and Antigone, Creon and Haimon. Male and female oppose each other not directly but through imagery, as Yourcenar's prose responds lyrically to the odes of Sophocles' Chorus, particularly those of the parodos and the third stasimon on love.

Yourcenar's gendered opposition concerns systems of thought rather than concrete political systems of order. Nonetheless, the political climate of the mid-1930s — the increasing danger posed by Hitler and Mussolini and the culture of fascism — pulses behind Yourcenar's lyrical prose. A devastating personal experience blends with a terrifying political situation in this most political of the love stories in *Feux*, with what we may call a feminist result: Yourcenar's "Antigone" allies the masculine with culture and masculine culture with destruction.

One of Yourcenar's key images — the sun — appears to be a response to the victory ode that accompanies the Chorus's entrance into the theatrical space of Sophocles' play. The Chorus's first words celebrate a "radiant sun, most beautiful ever to shine on seven-gated Thebes, eye of golden day."[21] Yourcenar's first sentence is: "Que dit midi profond?" (75) (What does high noon signify?). For two pages she proceeds to answer this question, transforming the Theban sun into a metaphorical "affreux soleil" (fearsome sun) that images hate instead of victory (75).

Yourcenar's noonday sun is set in opposition to the female Sphinx, whose death has left all the city's secrets exposed to the light of day: "Depuis la mort de la Sphinge, la ville ignoble est sans secrets: tout y vient au jour" (75). Opposing images of refreshing shadow and water chased away by this sun make it clear that its truth-revealing sway is a thoroughly negative thing.[22] Yourcenar next creates a new motive for Jocasta's earlier suicide: she strangled herself "pour ne plus voir le soleil" (75–76) (in order not to see the sun). This sun dries up hearts, which therefore call for blood; its radiation eats away at consciences without healing them; it turns lovers into coupling dogs (76). To sum up: the sun is portrayed as the source of war, suicide, maiming, loss of humanity.

But there is more. When Yourcenar writes that Oedipus "est devenu aveugle à force de manipuler ces rais sombres" (76) (became blind through manipulating its gloomy rays), she seems to be evoking that same "sun" deployed by Sophocles at a critical moment of the *Oedipus Tyrannos*. There, when the Chorus asks Oedipus how he could have dared to put out his eyes, what god drove him do it, Oedipus replies:

> It was Apollo, Apollo, friends, / who brought this terrible terrible suffering of mine to pass. / But it was my own wretched hand that struck, none other. / For why should I have sight / when there is nothing pleasurable I could see?[23]
> (*O. T.* 1329–35)

It seems clear, therefore, that Yourcenar's sun represents Oedipus's old enemy Apollo, i.e. the *knowledge* that made his incestuous marriage possible and the devastating *awareness of crime* that caused him to blind himself in Sophocles' tragedy. Throughout Sophocles' work, however, Apollo is admirable, while in this and another of Yourcenar's early revisions of Greek myth he is not. We can amplify our understanding of his function in "Antigone" by examining in some detail a roughly contemporary prose poem in which he appears in an equally negative role.

In 1934 Yourcenar wrote what may have been the precursor to the revised myths collected in *Feux*,[24] a short "travel" piece about a visit to Mycenae entitled "Apollon tragique."[25] The choice of title is significant because, since its imaginative focus is Aeschylos's *Agamemnon* and its major mythic figure is Cassandra, the piece could well have supported a different eponym. In addition to intensifying the reader's attention to Apollo, the title also encourages readers to ponder the adjective "tragique": coupled with the name of a god it can hardly bear its usual simple meaning: the condition of being violently forced to acknowledge human limitations, especially the mortal limitation of death. Readers must consider instead two alternative meanings — "Apollo of the tragic stage" and "Apollo cause of [a] human tragedy." Both turn out to be relevant.

The summer sun in Argos is no doubt murderous — Sartre too evokes it in *Les Mouches*, his own anti-fascist version of the *Oresteia* — but Yourcenar directs its rays to most specific metaphysical effect as she glides smoothly back and forth between metaphor and physical fact, mythic past and contemporary experience. Our guided tour of modern Mycenae begins, as will the story of ancient Thebes, at foreboding noon: "Midi: l'heure du crime à Mycènes" (427) (Noon: the hour of crime in Mycenae). Yourcenar's readers are expected to know what the crime at Mycenae is — Clytemnestra's murder of Agamemnon — but their expectations are immediately twisted when they meet a quotation from the *Agamemnon*, Cassandra's first words before she begins prophesying the past and imminent calamities of the House of Atreus: "'Apollon, ô Apollon, mon meurtrier . . .'/ Qui hurle ainsi? Cassandre" (427) ("Apollo, O Apollo, my killer . . ."/ Who cries thus? Cassandra; compare *Agamemnon*, ll. 1080–81). The fatal value-laden conflict between Apollo and Cassandra will frame and dominate that between the king and queen of Mycenae in Yourcenar's retelling of the story.

Apollo is a murderer. Is he thus the criminal? By no means. This term is reserved for the human women who lend their mythic spirits to Mycenae. He is, however, intimately related to "crime." Immediately after establishing Apollo and Cassandra as her primary antagonists, Yourcenar writes:

> Troie est prise, des feux de joie flambent sur les sommets de l'Argolide, et les poètes vont faire durer ces feux pendent près de trente siècles. Les pentes de Mycènes sont fleuries de pavots rouges, et comme pavoisées par ordre de Clytemnestre. Mais leur couleur n'est pas celle du crime; rien que celle de l'été.
> (427)

> [Troy is taken, fires of joy flame on the summits of the Argolid, and poets will make these flames endure for nearly thirty centuries. The slopes of Mycenae blossom with red poppies, and seem to rejoice by Clytemnestra's order. But their color is not that of crime, merely that of summer.]

Here we have heat and light from another related source: poets, whose art comes from Apollo, keep the flames of martial victory and marital murder burning to the present day. The power of poets is shown by Yourcenar's choice not to use the red color of the poppies to represent Clytemnestra's crime, a choice that stands out because it is the only time in this lyric essay that she does *not* translate physical fact into metaphor. With this choice she expands her contrast between fire and flowers to include one between the cultural imputation of meaning — such as "crime" — and the simple expression of nature. The way she opposes the beauty of poetry to the beauty of nature evokes also, of course, the contamination of nature by culture.

After three sentences that sketch in the events of the first two-thirds of the *Agamemnon*, Yourcenar turns her attention back to Cassandra to view Apollonian "crime" from the perspective of a female "poet":

> Aimée d'Apollon, Cassandre s'est jadis refusée au dieu. En connaissance de cause, cette femme qui sait l'avenir a préféré les servitudes humaines aux étreintes du dieu. Sa punition pour avoir refusé le soleil semble découler de son crime: ses prédictions demeureront obscures; Apollon ne lui a pas accordé qu'on comprenne ses oracles. Tout se passe comme si on ne l'entendait pas crier. Les calamités n'ont pas cessé de s'abattre sur son peuple en dépit de cette folle qui prophétise dans l'ombre. (427–428)

> [Beloved by Apollo, Cassandra in time gone by refused the god. Understanding what she was doing, this woman who knows the future preferred human servitude to the embraces of the god. Her punishment for having refused the sun seems to flow directly from her crime: her predictions will remain dark, for Apollo did not grant that anyone would understand her oracles. Everything happens as if no one has heard her cry out. Despite this madwoman who prophesies in shadow calamities have not ceased to fall upon her people.]

Cassandra's crime, we may note immediately, is different from the broken promise depicted in Aeschylos' *Agamemnon*, where Cassandra admits to the Chorus that she lied to Apollo in order to be given the gift of prophecy.[26] In "Apollon tragique," she merely rejects divine embraces in favor of "*servitudes humaines*," an action that could be interpreted either as choosing to serve humanity over divinity or as preferring even human slavery to divine play. Apollo's revenge also differs. In Aeschylos's classical world Apollo fittingly punishes Cassandra's false speech with universal disbelief (*Agamemnon*, l. 1213). In Yourcenar's surrealist world, Cassandra's refusing the sun generates a punishment equally fitting: she must prophesy in shadow, her words dark and incomprehensible.

There is a world of difference between Aeschylos's "believe" (πείθω) and Yourcenar's "understand" (comprendre), just as there is between broken promises and a choice to serve one group rather than join another. It is impossible not to interpret Yourcenar's changes in the myth as creating a feminist allegory for the troubled times she is living through, both personally and politically. The female speaker (writer), whose different experience gives her much of value to tell her people,[27] cannot, no matter how skilled, be understood unless she allows herself to be embraced by the dominant masculinist culture. As Yourcenar would indicate many years later (after partially yielding to necessity herself) a woman cannot write from a subject position as a woman; a female character cannot interpret her own experience to the world without being accused of no longer being a woman.[28]

Yourcenar makes her Cassandra feel none of the horror towards Clytemnestra that is expressed by Aeschylos (see esp. *Agamemnon*, ll. 1231–37). Instead of accusing Clytemnestra, who is depicted as "offended" rather than evil, instead of blaming *any* individual human being, Cassandra blames Apollo:

> Cassandre n'accuse ni le roi qui l'entraîne dans la mort, ni l'épouse offensée qui déjà lève sa hache, ni la fatale beauté d'Hélène.... Elle accuse Dieu. Elle remonte au Soleil comme à la cause de tout. Elle sait qu'Apollon se réserve la vengeance: Égisthe et Clytemnestre serviront tout au plus de manche et de tranchant au couteau céleste. (428)

> [Cassandra blames neither the king who drags her into death, nor the offended wife who already raises her axe, nor the fatal beauty of Helen.... She accuses God. She goes back to the Sun as the cause of everything. She knows that Apollo reserves vengeance for himself: Aegisthos and Clytemnestra at most serve as handle and edge of the celestial knife.]

Yourcenar's depicting her humans as instruments of the divine is similar to Aeschylos' world view in the *Oresteia*, where Clytemnestra is the agent of Artemis, Agamemnon of Zeus, and Orestes of Apollo. A major difference between their depictions lies in the absence of female divinity to counter Apollo's divinity. In the *Agamemnon*, goddesses conflict with gods to the great detriment of humans, and then in the other two plays of the trilogy harmony is established by the subordination of the female, both divine and mortal, to the male. Androgynous Athena mediates between Apollo, who disdains female earth-centered culture, and the Furies, who disdain the new patriarchal Olympian culture. Yourcenar will create no mediator, choosing not even to hint at future reconciliation. She will keep her vision within the world of total conflict portrayed in the first play of the trilogy but with the gendered power relations at the end reversed.

The *Agamemnon* ends with the complete (if troubled and temporary) triumph of Clytemnestra, while "Apollon tragique" ends with that of Apollo. The last paragraph in "Apollon tragique" circles back to modern Mycenae, where contemporary humans are driven indoors by the murderous sun to which Cassandra has yielded at last:

> Cassandre s'élance pour rejoindre ce mourant dont elle partagea le lit, tombe au milieu de la cour, frappée d'un coup de soleil. Sur la pente fatale, plus personne. Le gardien des ruines dort dans la loge de concierge du palais qui est maintenant celui d'Égisthe. Au bas de la montée, le propriétaire de l'*Hôtel de la Belle-Hélène* ferme les volets pour échapper au feu du ciel. Apollon, dieu jaloux, règne seul sur la butte de Mycènes, poignard splendide dans un sein d'or. (428)

> [Cassandra rushes to rejoin this dying man whose bed she shared, falls in the middle of the court, struck by a blow from the sun. On this fatal slope, there is

no one. The custodian of the ruins sleeps in the porter's lodge of the palace that now belongs to Aegisthos. At the foot of the hill, the owner of the Hotel of the Beautiful Helen closes the shutters to escape the sky's fire. Apollo, jealous god, reigns alone over the butte of Mycenae, brilliant dagger in a golden breast.]

A blow from the sun fells Cassandra as sunstroke would the modern traveler.[29] Then she appears imagistically in the last line fused with the earth, finally pierced by Apollo, who makes her golden as he makes her his own. The woman is both silenced and gilded by Apollo's deadly beauty.

Yourcenar's physical presence in Mycenae sets free a lyric riot of metaphor and allegory that fuses ancient and modern experience, human action and natural processes. Biographical information about her personal experience is in this case probably important for a full understanding of her imagery here and in *Feux*. This experience includes more than just touring Greece; it also includes (1) a thorough introduction to psychoanalytic theory by her companion André Embirikos, who was both surrealist poet and psychoanalyst, and (2) an early response to the disastrous unrequited passion for her misogynist editor André Fraigneau that she would later try to "exorcise" by writing *Feux*.[30]

In addition to his misogyny, Fraigneau also embraced the masculinist antisemitic fascist philosophy propounded by Hitler and Mussolini.[31] Despite her not finding this philosophy congenial, Yourcenar deified him in her heart, as is reflected in the *pensées* that thread through *Feux*, and in her dreams, as is reflected in another surrealistic work of this same period, *Les Songes et les sorts* (Dreams and Destinies, 1938). One of the "rêves lyriques" (lyrical dreams) dreamed in the years 1931–36 associates the man "plus aimé que Dieu" (218) (more loved than God) with Apollo (216), the man who, indifferent to the woman who trembles for him, sheds along with his coverings "toute trace d'humanité" (every trace of humanity) to restore "sa forme et sa nudité de dieu" (218) (his form and his godlike nudity).[32] In her dream as in her waking poetry, Yourcenar uses the aloof aristocratic classical Apollo to mask the arrogant superiority of Fraigneau, ultimate judge of her intellectual and sexual desirability.

On the basis of internal and external evidence, then, I would like to argue that Apollo, both in "Apollon tragique" and "Antigone," represents either the masculinist power of a rationalist fascism or, more generally, a hierarchic culture predicated on Apolline reason. The female protagonists Cassandra and Antigone represent basic connective emotions that cannot be understood or are not valued by this masculine culture.

Apollo loses, however, some of the fatally effective splendor he displayed against Cassandra when Yourcenar manipulates solar imagery around her later protagonist Antigone. Only one person is impervious to "the arrows of light launched by Apollo's bow" in Mycenae: Antigone's *douleur* (pain), first for her *frère aîné* (elder brother)/father and later for her *frère putréfié* (rotting brother), Polynices, protects her like sunglasses ("Antigone seule supporte les flèches décochées par la lampe à arc d'Apollon, comme si la douleur lui servait de lunettes noires" [76]). *Douleur* has an unusual valence in "Antigone." When coupled with *douleur* even death becomes something positive: Oedipus's Furies immediately change to "déesses protectrices, puisque toute douleur á qui l'on s'abandonne se change en sérénité" (77) (protective goddesses, because all pain to which one abandons oneself changes into serenity). *Douleur* invests Polynices, who "même mort . . . existe comme la douleur" (even dead . . . exists like pain) with new life, while victorious Etéocles "même vivant . . . est momifié déjà dans le mensonge de la gloire" (79) (even alive . . . is already mummified in the lie of glory). The action provoked by this *douleur* is what Yourcenar celebrates in Antigone: sisterly sacrifice called forth by feelings of selfless devotion and loss. It is Antigone's choice to act according to this feeling that Yourcenar later will term "justice."[33]

This "justice" is linked to the natural rather than to the cultural realm. After laying her father-brother to rest in the bed of the Furies at Athens, Antigone returns to Thebes, which Yourcenar characterizes as "la ville qui fait un crime de ce qui n'est qu'un désastre, un exil de ce qui n'est qu'un départ, un châtiment de ce qui n'est qu'une fatalité" (77) (the city that has made a crime out of what was merely a disaster, an exile out of a mere departure, a punishment out of the merely inevitable). Sun-dried Thebes, in other words, takes natural events and makes them worse by applying cultural judgments, much as Creon does in Sophocles' *Antigone* and Apolline poets seem to in "Apollon tragique." Yourcenar counterpoises Antigone's "justice" to such cultural judgments by means of natural — cosmic, earthly, and corporeal — imagery.

True to Sophocles (and to ancient Greek thinking about women), Yourcenar's Antigone is linked to chthonic rather than Olympian forces. Like Cassandra, Antigone is associated with earth, but her opposition to Apollo is expanded from that earlier more basic one. She is like shadow and water during the day, ("En pleine soleil, elle était l'eau pure sur les mains souillées, l'ombre au creux du casque" [82]), a natural source of illumination at night.

Night falls on Thebes as soon as Creon condemns Antigone. It is complete night, just as before it was total day, for "the city without pity ignores twilights" ("La ville sans pitié ignore les crépuscules: le jour noircit d'un seul coup, comme une ampoule brûlée qui ne verse plus de lumière . . ." [81]). In other words, Apolline discriminations must be absolute, with no shades of gray or other muted colors. Thebes is not without light, but its streetlights and searchlights — anachronisms that bring Yourcenar's story into the technical and political reality of the mid-1930s — are not portrayed as illuminating anything. They serve only to hide the stars. The stars gone, time stops ("Le temps n'existe plus dans ce Thebes privé d'astres" [83]). Humans have no destiny, no conscience ("Les hommes sont sans destins, puisque le monde est sans astres" [82]; "Les dormeurs allongés dans le noir absolu ne voient plus leur conscience" [83]).

Just as Antigone's *douleur* protected her from Apollo at high noon ("midi profond"), so now her *agonie* provides the only natural illumination in this darkest midnight ("minuit profond"):

> En pleine nuit, elle devient une lampe. Sa dévotion aux yeux crevés d'Oedipe resplendit sur des millions d'aveugles; sa passion pour son frère putréfié réchauffe hors du temps des myriades de morts. (82)

> [She becomes a lamp. Her devotion to the blind eyes of Oedipus shines over millions of blind people; her passion for her rotting brother warms uncountable dead.]

It is because "you cannot kill light" that Creon puts her underground rather than executing her (" On ne tue pas la lumière; on ne peut que la suffoquer: on met sous le boisseau l'agonie d'Antigone" [82]). Even when she is dead, she emits a phosphorescent glow, one that enables Creon to see his son Haimon hanging dead from her neck ("Une vague phosphorescence émanent d'Antigone lui fait reconnaître Hémon suspendu au cou de l'immense suicidée" [84]).

Yourcenar uses Haimon, "le troisième aspect" (the third aspect) of Antigone's "tragique amour" (tragic love) (83) to conclude her celebration of love and critique of the male culture that was threatening Europe with fascism. But before I examine how she manipulates this young man, I would like briefly to return to Sophocles, who subjects Haimon to uncontrollable Eros solely, it would seem, in order to punish the hubris of his controlling father. Haimon's suicide is presented not as a means to join Antigone in death but as a reaction to his passionate attack on his father's life, a reaction that is described as "anger at self" (αὐτῷ χολωθείς) rather than as love for another. The erotic image of his clasping her in death merely confirms the Chorus's earlier view of the deleterious effects of love. Charles Segal is surely correct when he interprets this scene as reflecting "the failure of the political tie of the male band to pull the youth away from the mother to the city," and sees Haemon as rejecting "not only his father but also his adult male role of political responsibility in the city, succeeding his father to the throne of Thebes" (185).

Yourcenar presents quite an opposing valuation of the relationships between Haimon and Antigone, Haimon and Creon. Haimon attempts no violence toward his father, and the attachment to Antigone that pulls him away from his father is put in terms of his being "converted to the cause of misfortune" ("converti au malheur" 83). Since this phrase comes shortly after a description of Antigone's rejecting in Haimon "l'*affreuse* chance d'enfanter des vainqueurs" (83) (the *fearsome* chance of giving birth to conquerors), Yourcenar's point seems to be that love allows him to cross over from male to female culture. I choose the word "allows" rather than "forces" (as Sophocles' Chorus would have had it) because the adjective *affreuse*, which links "conquerors" to the fearsome sun ("affreux soleil") of the opening sentences, indicates that Yourcenar views this crossing over as a good thing.

Yourcenar's imagery of mother earth in this last section of her meditation on Sophocles is a structuralist's treasure trove. Antigone "retourne au pays des sources, des trésors, des germes" (83) (returns to the region of sources, treasures, germinations), heading for the "antipodes of human reason" ("Elle part à la recherche de son étoile située aux antipodes de la raison humaine . . ." [83]). Just as the "weight of her heart" earlier dragged Antigone to Polynices' corpse (79), so now she and Haimon, "tied one to the other as if to weigh more heavily," are thrust ever more deeply into the tomb with the swaying of their linked bodies ("Liés l'un à l'autre comme pour peser plus lourd, leur lent va-et-vient les enfoncer chaque fois plus avant dans la tombe" [84]). Their palpitating weight restarts the mechanism of the stars (84–5), and, closer to the earth's surface, it fills the dry air with the pulsation of arteries (85). Pulsating arteries create an image of living blood that is quite the opposite of the blood that the "*affreux soleil*" calls forth at the beginning of the story. The "affreuse virginité" (80) that was imposed on Antigone by Apolline Thebes' conception of crime gives way to a new kind of fertility as time begins anew. In this Cartesian universe, Antigone and Haimon embody "l'horloge de Dieu" (85) (God's clock), and within that clock Antigone's heart is termed "le pendule du monde" (the pendulum of the world).

The opposition between love and masculine culture is, therefore, resolved in favor of love. This love is grief, it is agony, it is renunciation, it is tragedy. Love in a man's world, it seems, must be *douleur*. It is, however, the only possible life-affirming response to a culture of conquerors that turns life into death, that "mumifies" people in "le mensonge de la gloire" (79) (the lie of glory), that stops the natural processes of time.[34] Yourcenar's anti-fascist "Antigone" thus contradicts Sophocles' message that love, especially heterosexual love, is dangerous to life and community. After allying love with the feminine (as does Sophocles), "Antigone" situates that feminine at the dead center of a liveable world.

Despite Yourcenar's use of a dubious essentialist feminism, the effective message of her "Antigone" remains relevant today. It is not dissimilar from the message of an African American hero who, like Antigone, died for acting out of love and justice, and whose words will make a fitting epilogue to this essay:

Power at its best is love implementing the demands of justice, and justice at its best is power correcting everything that stands against love.

Martin Luther King, Jr.

University of California, Los Angeles

Notes

[1] Marguerite Yourcenar, "Mythologie grecque et mythologie de la Grèce," in *Essais et mémoires* (Paris: Gallimard, 1989), 440–441. All translations are my own unless otherwise indicated.

[2] Joan E. Howard, *From Violence to Vision: Sacrifice in the Works of Marguerite Yourcenar*, (Carbondale: South Illinois UP, 1992), 5. The analyses are contained in chapters 2 and 3, 9–75.

[3] In her preface to the 1936 edition of *Feux*, Yourcenar wrote: "On ne trouvera ici ni un recueil de poèmes, ni une collection de légendes. L'auteur a entremêlé des pensées, qui furent pour lui des théorèmes de la passion, de récits qui les illustrent, les expliquent, les démontrent, et souvent les masquent" (*Feux* [Paris: Grasset, 1936], 10) (You will find here neither a collection of poems nor a group of myths. The author has intermingled *pensées*, which were for her theorems of passion, with short stories that illuminate, explain, demonstrate and often mask them). In her preface to the 1957 edition she describes *Feux* as a "compte-rendu d'une crise intérieure" (report of an inner crisis). Both are quoted in Josyane Savigneau's biography, *Marguerite Yourcenar: L'Invention d'une vie* (Paris: Gallimard, 1990), 114 and in Joan E. Howard's translation, *Marguerite Yourcenar: Inventing a Life* (Chicago: U of Chicago P, 1993), 104. The English translation here is my own.

[4] Originally published as "Antigone" in *Revue blue: politique et littéraire* 74:13 (4 July 1936), 442–44. I find no significant differences between the original journal publication and the version included in *Feux*.

[5] Walter Hasenclever described his reasons for creating a version of *Antigone* in 1916 (performed in 1917 and 1919 in Leipzig and Frankfurt) as follows: "Written in 1916 in a time when every word was stricken by the censor, the play's task was to protest war and violence by clothing them in ancient garments" (quoted and translated in William R. Elwood, "Hasenclever and Brecht: A Critical Comparison of Two Antigones," *Educational Theatre* 24 [March 1972]: 48–71; see 52). Jean Anouilh's *Antigone*, performed with the unsuspecting approval of Vichy in 1944, is perhaps the best known example in the United States; more recently Argentina, Poland, and Ireland have witnessed highly charged adaptations. Most recently, I attended a moving production that expressed its director's anguish over the civil war in the former Yugoslavia. The program of this production describes the time as "Then and Now" and the place as "Where modern America meets the former Yugoslavia, and political, social, and cultural war zones everywhere" (*Antigone*, adapted by Deanne Stillman, directed by Goran Gajic, The Hudson Guild, Los Angeles, 1996).

[6] *Feux* (Paris: Gallimard, 1974), 11–12, 17. All references to *Feux* will be to this edition unless otherwise specified. An English translation, *Fires*, by Dori Katz in collaboration with Yourcenar was published in New York by Farrar, Straus, Giroux in 1981.

[7] See Joan Howard, *Violence*, 9–75; Judith L. Johnston, "Marguerite Yourcenar's Sexual Politics in Fiction, 1939," in *Faith of a (Woman) Writer*, ed. Alice Kessler-

Harris and William McBrien (New York: Greenwood, 1988), 221–28.; my "Achilles on the Field of Sexual Politics," *LIT* 2 (1991): 201–220; Mary Lydon, "Calling Yourself a Woman: Marguerite Yourcenar and Colette," *differences* 3.3 (1991): 26–44, esp. 31–37; and Linda K. Stillman, "Marguerite Yourcenar and the Phallacy of Indifference," *Studies in Twentieth-Century Literature* 9.2 (1985): 261–277.

[8] Page duBois, "Antigone and the Feminist Critic," *Genre* 19,2 (1986): 371–83; Marilyn A. Katz, "The Character of Tragedy: Women and the Greek Imagination," *Arethusa* 27 (1994): 81–103; Bernard Knox, *The Heroic Temper* (Berkeley: U California P, 1966), 91–116; Sheila Murnaghan "*Antigone* 904–920 and the Institution of Marriage," *American Journal of Philology* 107 (1986): 192–207; Charles Segal, "*Antigone*: Death and Love, Hades and Dionysus," in *Tragedy and Civilization: An Interpretation of Sophocles* (Cambridge: Harvard UP, 1981), 152–206, 441–53; Froma Zeitlin, "Thebes: Theatre of Self and Society in Athenian Drama," in Peter Euben, ed. *Greek Tragedy and Political Theory* (Berkeley and Los Angeles: U California P, 1986), 101–41.

[9] Compare duBois, 378,381; Zeitlin, 133.

[10] μῶρος (220), ἀφροσύνη (383), λόγου τ'ἄνοια (601–2). The text cited and quoted throughout is Sophocles, *Antigone*, ed. Richard C. Jebb, (Cambridge: Cambridge UP 1902, rprt. 1963).

[11] εὖ γὰρ εἴρεται διπλέᾳ (725).

[12] λέγειν φρονούντως . . . δοκεῖς (682).

[13] τούτοι γυναικὸς οὐδαμῶς ἡσσητέα.
κρεῖσσον γάρ, εἴπερ δεῖ, πρὸς ἀνδρὸς ἐκπεσεῖν,
κοὐκ ἂν γυναικῶν ἥσσονες καλοίμεθ' ἄν. (678–79).

[14] ὁ δ' ἔχων μέμηνεν (790); δικαίων ἀδίκους φρένας παρασπᾷς (791).

[15] As Simon Goldhill puts it: "Eros marks [the husband-wife] relationship as one of a possible irrational and overwhelming force, a principle that threatens the principles of law and order" (*Reading Greek Tragedy* [Cambridge: Cambridge UP, 1986], 102).

[16] οὐκοῦν κλεινὴ καὶ ἔπαινον ἔχουσ' / ἐς τόδε ἀπέρχει κεῦθος νεκύων, / . . . αὐτόνομος (817–18, 821).

[17] σέβειν μὲν εὐσέβειά τις, / κράτος δ' ὅτῳ κράτος μέλει, / παραβατὸν οὐδαμᾷ πέλει· σὲ δ' αὐτόγνωτος ὤλες' ὀργά (872–75).

[18] Gail Holst-Warhaft argues that the stanza about Lykurgos in the subsequent ode (Fourth *Stasimon*) shows that to a degree Antigone's appeal to the Chorus has won their "support . . . and set revenge in motion" (*Dangerous Voices: Women's laments and Greek literature* [London and New York: Routledge, 1992], 164). The Chorus's feeling that Creon may have been wrong to forbid burial, however, has been apparent from as early as verse 279, and their song here in no way celebrates the possibility of female heroism. Danae and Kleopatra are victims pure and simple; the mythic Danae, who was saved by Zeus in the end, was perfectly submissive to the law of her unjust father.

[19] This idea, of course, is made easier by the fact that ancient Greeks viewed the male as the basic human being and the female as a variant. See Page duBois, *Centaurs and Amazons* (Ann Arbor: U of Michigan P, 1982), and Nicole Loraux, *Les enfants d'Athéna: Idées athéniennes sur la citoyenneté et la division des sexes* (Paris: Découverte, 1984), for particularly good discussions of this issue.

[20] Donna C. Kurtz's and John Boardman's *Greek Burial Customs* (London: Thames and Hudson, 1971), 142–161, provides the earliest and still authoritative account of women's key role in funerary ritual. Marilyn Katz cites this account in support of her argument that Antigone is fulfilling a proper female role in burial ("Character," 93). For analysis of the sixth- and fifth-century reforms that restricted this role in the interest of household or οἶκος-based patriarchal democracy (as opposed to clan or γένος-based aristocracy) see Margaret Alexiou, *The ritual lament in Greek tradition* (London: Cambridge UP, 1976), 14–21. For analysis that links these reforms to the imperial state's need for a standing army, see Holst-Warhaft (*Dangerous*, 116, 119–21), who bases her argument on Nicole Loraux's persuasive analysis in *L'invention d'Athènes: histoire de l'oraison funebre dans la cité classique* (Paris & New York: Mouton, 1981) of the Athenian funeral oration as "politico/military" in character. S. C. Humphreys gives a convenient description of funerary custom on 86–87 of *The Family, Women, and Death* (Ann Arbor: U of Michigan P, 1993).

[21] ἀκτὶς ἀελίου, τὸ κάλλιστον ἑπταπύλῳ φανὲν /Θήβᾳ τῶν προτέρων φάος, / ἐφάνθης ποτ', ὦ χρυσέας / ἀμέρας βλέφαρον, ...

(*Antigone*, 100–104).

[22] "L'ombre baisse au ras des maisons, au pied des arbres, comme l'eau fade au fond des citernes: les chambres ne sont plus des puits d'obscurité, des magasins de fraîcheur" (75).

[23] Ἀπόλλων τάδ' ἦν, Ἀπόλλων, φίλοι, / ὁ κακὰ κακὰ τελῶν ἐμὰ παθέα. / ἔπαισε δ'αὐτόχειρ νιν οὔτις, ἀλλ' ἐγὼ τλάμων. / τί γὰρ ἔδει μ' ὁρᾶν, / ὅτῳ γ' ὁρῶντι μηδὲν ἦν ἰδεῖν γλυκύ; *Oedipus Tyrannus*, ll. 1329–35.

[24] Yourcenar says that the myths collected in *Feux* were written in 1935 (*Feux*, 9).

[25] Published in *Le Voyage en Grèce*, summer 1935, and later included in *En Pèlerin et en étranger* (As a Pilgrim and as a Stranger) (Paris: Gallimard, 1989). I will quote from the reprint in *Essais et mémoires*.

[26] Χο: ἦ καὶ τέκνων εἰς ἔργον ἦλθετον νόμῳ;
Κα: ξυναινέσασα Λοξίαν ἐψευσάμην. (1207–08)

(Cho: And did you come as usual to begetting children?
Ka: [No.] When I promised [to have sex with] Apollo I lied.)

[27] Much later, in 1980, Yourcenar would declare "Every gain that women achieve in the areas of civil rights, urbanism, environmentalism, and in protecting the right of animals, children, and minorities, every victory over war and over the monstrous exploitation of science by the forces of greed and violence, is a triumph for women if not for feminism . . . . I even believe that women may be better equipped to play this role than men, because women are in day-to-day contact with the realities of life, of which

many men remain comparatively ignorant" (*With Open Eyes: Conversations with Matthieu Galey*, trans. Arthur Goldhammer, [Boston: Beacon Press, 1984], 222. For the original French, see: *Les Yeux ouverts. Entretiens avec Matthieu Galey*. [Paris: Centurion, 1980]).

[28] Explaining why she had made Hadrien and not Plotina the narrator of *Mémoires*, Yourcenar wrote: "La vie des femmes est trop limitée, ou trop secrète, qu'une femme se raconte, et le premier reproche qu'on lui fera est de n'être plus femme" (Carnet de notes de *Mémoires d'Hadrien*, quoted by Nicole Chaillot, "Marguerite Yourcenar" in *Femmes et littérature: George Sand, Colette, Marguerite Yourcenar* [Paris: Martinsart, 1980], 147).

[29] *Coup de soleil* = sunstroke, an untranslatable surrealist pun.

[30] Preface to *Feux*, 26. For a discussion of this exorcist function of *Feux*, see Daniel Leuwers "*Feux* et contre-feux" in Leuwers and Jean-Pierre Castellani, eds., *Marguerite Yourcenar: Une écriture de la mémoire* (Marseilles:*SUD* Hors serie, 1990), 247–254. Leuwers analysis is hampered by not yet knowing either the name or the sex of the object of Yourcenar's passion, but its explication of how "fire" moves from amorous passion into a book of passion is nevertheless useful.

[31] According to Josyane Savigneau, we find a good portrait of Fraigneau in the narrator of Yourcenar's *Coup de grace* (1938), the novel that completed the exorcism attempted in *Feux* (*L'invention*, 132–38). Savigneau also quotes at length from Fraigneau's own ungenerous account of the relationship that led to *Feux* (112–13).

[32] "L'Amour et les bandelettes de lin" ([Love and the Linen Bands] *Les Songes et les sorts* [Paris: Grasset, 1938], 215–218) is presented as the last dream in the book. In good surrealist fashion Yourcenar considered the twenty-two lyric, or hallucinatory, dreams she selected to publish to be comparable to poetry (13–14), and she felt that this type of dream "emporterons chez Dieu" (31).

[33] In the "Preface" to the 1974 edition (*Feux*, 26).

[34] Since *douleur* seemingly must coexist with love, I would not apply to "Antigone" Madeleine Boussuges' choice of words when she says that "victoire sur la douleur," victory over pain, is what *Feux* is about (*Marguerite Yourcenar: sagesse et mystique* [Grenoble: Cahiers de l'Alpe, 1987], 244). "Antigone" is not concerned with victory except as something to avoid; and pain is not only inherent to life but is the very pulse of life. It is interesting to consider in this context Yourcenar's words about her relationship to *douleur* some forty years after writing *Feux*. "Let's say that I had an interest, a capacity to participate, in mystery, an interest that was fundamentally religious (in the true sense of the word, from *religare*, to bind together). It may be that I was born not for anxiety but for pain, for the infinite pain of loss, of separation from loved ones, for the pain and outrage that I feel for the suffering of others, animals as well as people, and for the pain of knowing that so many human beings live in such abject poverty and alienation from the light" (*With Open Eyes*, 18).

ELLEN WALDINGER

"That come before the swallow dares" (Thinking about Leonardo's *St Anne Cartoon*)

But how can I tell you about this presence, of love?

And tell about it simply, to someone who expects to hear of something else.

So it's easiest to begin, as if this were the fitting entry-point for a story, by way of one night, four years ago, in Rome. A group of five making our way past the Palazzo Farnese to the Campo dei Fiori: Diane, Danny and I walked together ahead, behind us Jessica and Carlo. Diane asked me did I know classical Rome well? Why couldn't I respond? Diane, who had devoted energy for years as an unofficial and civilized tour guide to the well off or reasonably well-connected, a fount of knowledge really, a professor after all, and the best friend of my horribly snobbish companion (whose snobbism was matched by a mesmerizing lack of culture), was being polite. It was a straightforward question that she'd asked, something to which I could have given a direct enough response and found some pleasant way of conveying the limits and the strengths of what I knew, rather than simply disappearing in the face of Diane's attentive pedantry and stammering, dumbstruck, "A bit."

Was it shame that caught me, whatever bit held down my tongue, these truculent monosyllables, the vacuousness they had tripped me into, and how to reclaim nothing, the dark around us down which the palazzi hung dirty walls, as Diane went on to explain that there was a marvelous Borromini church up the way, and not well known either, in which could be found . . . but I forget.

But memory extended solace, silent pride. I told myself then that had I spoken, I would have talked about a morning in Rome when I was nine. My parents and brother and I were walking up a hill, for some reason in the middle of the street. My mother went up to a man, dressed in grey, sinewy, mustachioed, not elderly yet, and asked him in Italian if there were a pharmacy near. (A blister on my heel. My new patent leather shoes.) But I didn't know she spoke Italian.

I see her perfectly. The street veers up, it seems to lift, grey, off of the pavement, transporting itself into haze. We are still there. The particles of air breathe out our features, the surrounding contains us still, on the street, a young woman and her daughter (my face turned towards her, listening, did she know how proud I was of her?), my father to the side, my brother out of view.

And now, all these years later, thoroughly at home in what wasn't said, I'd found a way to make the silence full of something unspeakable. So that evening, I knew Diane would tell her best friend — the one who'd been berating me for several months and telling me what a nobody I was — that I had nothing to say, was plain old dumb. Still, in her friend, I'd got a brute of my own to make my silence a real torture.

And there was a refuge to be found in what I'd remembered. After all, I told myself, there's no way to show the scene I'd just recalled, and even how the scene happened to me in the moment when it had occurred had not been known by anyone there; so remembering twenty-six years later sounded out that long-past moment's pull into what I could draw back within myself, my mother alive with her question, my father dropped behind, myself knowing how nothing would be said to show my feelings, although I cannot tell you why I got embarrassed and rather than joy I kept a visual scrim that would never go away, an unacknowledged haze between us all.

So, that evening as I listened to Diane pontificate, I told myself again that one cannot say what one knows, since the knowledge I would offer, vision, disclosed only the defeated spaces inside of me:

> Jouet de cet oeil d'eau morne, je n'y puis prendre,
> ô canot immobile! oh! bras trop courts! ni l'une
> ni l'autre fleur: ni la jaune qui m'importune
> là; ni la bleue, amie à l'eau couleur de cendre.
> (Arthur Rimbaud, "Mémoire" [Memory])

> [Plaything of this mournful eye of water, I can't take there, oh immobile rowboat, oh! too short arms! either one or the other flower: not the yellow one that bothers me, there; nor the blue one, friend to the ash-colored water.]
> (all translations are my own)

And since I was in Italy, this experience soon had me thinking about the notion of perspective in painting. For the next three weeks, while my companion blistered with the inappropriateness of our being together, given, as I was told, my lack of connection, or any qualities of interest, or anything you'd want to show your friends, I theorized, to myself, about the unique relation to perspective in the work of Leonardo and of Cézanne.

Perspective in painting assumes, after all, the importance of a point of view. And what being can ever emerge, full with all her past and swarms of feeling, into another's point of view?

Whereas Leonardo's sfumato, the chiaroscuro particling its way through light, through air, rises as if out of the depths of the painted scene, opening what's on view from within its own self.

Most of all it was the London *St. Anne Cartoon* I kept thinking of: the Virgin Mary seated on her mother's lap, although full-grown, and holding the infant Christ who seems almost to come from her belly, like a dream, extending himself into space, whirling from the enclosure of both women, each ushering one into the other, protective still, to extend a blessing to the infant John, who plays at their feet and waits.

And the smile of each mother at her offspring. And the entire story, the destiny of this child, of these children, which both mothers know.

I knew that the Cartoon held a secret for me, something it had to teach me that I couldn't know yet and would have to look for, patiently, with time.

That summer, I could only think that Leonardo's style and technical achievement, this transcendence of perspective whereby the scene, engendering its own light and space, grew within the painting's boundaries — and how the brown air astounds one, building flight and freedom that comes from somewhere deep within, a motion and a spirit, and St. Anne's right knee solidly receives the burgeoning that's all over and that from her lap unfolds, and there Mary sits, the two women's knees mirroring each other's (with light growing everywhere) — realized the painting's subject matter: the story which brought Grace.

If I had any spiritual understanding of what Grace meant, it certainly wasn't tied to a religious belief. I understood only that here in this Cartoon were a mother and her mother, holding one another and the daughter's young son who inexorably stretches his whole being outward, reaching over and past his mother's lap. And he blesses his young cousin. And his young cousin looks at him, willing but abashed, and points upward where over him Anne's left hand is pointing upward too, a gesture that extends her smile. All of them know how the story will play out; how the children will die, and through that death life be affirmed. For that is what is here, even as the hands point to heaven, the fecundity that is here and now, borne through the Virgin Mary, the surge and tug of life embedded in the focused view of death and still promising life to come, Grace.

It was this story that made all the difference, so I told myself, thinking about Cézanne. Wasn't part of the meaning of Cézanne's ever-evolving technique, of painting from the shadows outward, and of allowing the object to be built up through color planes, through the refraction of itself, in which shadow and light are joined, an effort to let the object transcend its otherwise inevitable fixture in the artist's point of view, so that from within itself, in Cézanne's work, the object manifests its being, spreading outward, caught in the painted instance wherein the Mountain (St. Victoire) takes its own contours in the light and captures the space which it has filled? So the act of painting fulfills itself in the object which the painter has, to use one of Cézanne's favorite terms, "réalisé" (realized).

Then the trees, near the Chateau Noir, hover in the darkness they have grappled from the sky, and emerge, through green, through an orange patch of ground where the hill slopes up in the midst of it all, through the slate inference of occasional rocks, into their own febrile density, a mass that is its own reflection finding form.

But there are no people in the landscapes, no human life.

I understood. There was no where, no way to show people accumulating within themselves the resonance of how they've come to be. Not for a living soul, the burgeoning of the Annenberg late Mont St.Victoire, where the mountain seems to slip from itself into where Becoming can happen forever, a stained-glass blue, and still be always steady, reservoirs of such solid stuff.

The historical context of this inability to surface the depths of active human life in a depicted scene accompanied my thoughts as I traveled. And here I thought not of painting but of poetry: the major poetry of the nineteenth century attests that only in memory can human beings truly reveal themselves. And that revelation, the self its own memorial, occurs only in isolate splendor, in the self, alone:

> Rien n'égale en longueur les boiteuses journées,
> Quand sous les lourds flocons des neigeuses années
> L'ennui, fruit de la morne incuriosité,
> Prend les proportions de l'immortalité.
> — Désormais tu ne's plus, ô matière vivante!
> Qu'un granit entouré d'une vague épouvante,
> Assoupi dans le fond d'un Sahara brumeux;
> Un vieux sphinx ignoré du monde insoucieux,
> Oublié sur la carte, et dont l'humeur farouche
> Ne chante qu'aux rayons du soleil qui se couche.
> (Charles Baudelaire, "Spleen")

[Nothing is as long as the limping days, when, under the heavy flakes of snow-drenched years, boredom, the fruit of a mournful lack of curiosity, takes on the proportions of immortality. — All at once you aren't anything, oh living matter! but a block of granite surrounded by a vague terror, half-asleep in the middle of a dim Sahara; an old sphinx ignored by the careless world, forgotten on the map, and whose savage humor sings only to the rays of the setting sun.]

This memorializing is not about the past but the present, about the fact that life as it is desired will not happen now, that what is occurring leaves us out, that an enormous effort must be made to assert this sunken inner life and it is doomed; and the only heroism is to capture that failure in a poem, in the words that keep what no one knew went on.

Of course, traveling that summer, I knew how tired I was of being stuck in my own superannuated precocity, this childhood claim that I didn't have anywhere to be; after all, my companion's great dislike of what, I was now told, was not an inner life but rather a failed one was my goad to force from the present something more than a cause to remember all that was being lost.

And yet how to proceed, and still to bring the shadows into life? Cézanne had found a way to paint so that the shadows of objects engendered the forms out of which those objects grew. I knew, from my own experience, how memory, like a vast repository of shadow from which the remembered images and the unspoken feelings emerge and linger, could issue that seeming wholeness (perfected out of life) where the seen discloses the hidden. And I had, from childhood, turned to poetry as that which charges the very physicality of objects with the life inside, as that imaginary zone where the inner life and the outer life are one:

> he stood and called
> His Legions, Angel Forms, who lay intrans't
> Thick as Autumnal Leaves . . .
> so thick bestrown
> Abject and lost lay these, covering the Flood,
> Under amaz'ment of thir hideous change.
> (John Milton, *Paradise Lost*)

I was stuck, on that first go that summer, looking for what it was the Leonardo Cartoon had to tell me, on applying thoughts about poetry to painting, and finding in the way the Leonardo had brought to mind Cézanne, a possible hypothesis for painting similar to a hypothesis one can make for poetry. That is, perhaps one might find in painting, as in poetry, that when, by the eighteenth century, Actuality (the present, the here-and-now itself) became the subject matter, then painting fell prey to a familiar paradox: that the religious iconography and fantastical (though naturalistically accurate) setting of the Leonardo renders an image that is full of living, whereas the mundane iconography and actual setting of the Cézanne renders only an image that is its own recollection (and from which active human life is therefore gone).

I knew that behind this hypothesis my real question was whether there could be painting, or poetry, today that realized the present being filled by inner life, and did so with the fullness of the Leonardo cartoon, where

> the sense sublime
> Of something far more deeply interfused,
> Whose dwelling is the light of setting suns,
> And the round ocean, and the living air,
> And the blue sky
> (William Wordsworth, "Tintern Abbey")

rendered its presence in the painted scene and through the active human life depicted there. I knew that in the case of Leonardo the point was not to conflate a nineteenth-century understanding of the spiritual destiny of humankind with a Renaissance one. Rather, it was Leonardo's very moment in time that allowed him to fulfill this discovery of the infinite in the natural world. The Renaissance allowed in painting for natural space to be valued as the locus for the painted scene, and thus replaced a hieratic view of the world with a naturalistic one (one based on the natural sciences). Of course this replacement took till the eighteenth century to disclose its intent (to empty the world of the Judeo-Christian God). It is precisely the concurrence of the valuation of nature (so intensely felt by Leonardo) and Christian belief which allows for the Cartoon. So, this amazing opening up of natural space anchors and finds its anchor in the Christian story through which nature is redeemed by human life.

Morning walks, alone, freed to the appeasing endlessness of thought, I could entertain myself again with the elegiac mode to which I was accustomed, where the closest one gets to life is:

> Outside
> > outside myself
> > > there is a world,
> > he rumbled, subject to my incursions
> > — a world
> > > (to me) at rest,
> > > > which I approach
> > concretely —
> > > > (William Carlos Williams, *Paterson*)

But if there were a coupling of my mind's disburdening itself with the countryside I now walked through, noticing the olive groves, the heat, the bend in the road that had not escaped the sun, that engendered sensation, moving through my blood, was creative of nothing but memory still, all my ambitions tripping over the quiet.

But I was beginning to take my failures personally, and to stop pretending their causes were objective truths. It was a deep freeze I'd been in, I knew that. The disdain, the disdainful passion, of my companion shocked me — how could this be, I asked myself, grateful. But to endow this gratitude with intellectual stature, I'd let my mind turn to Cézanne, to wondering about his Bathers — were they not his try to realize active, living, human beings, and not just scenes of nature, or still lifes, or portraits? How awkward the Bathers are, the more they move. How like, in figuration, the violent figures of Cézanne's very early work. For it is always startling, that the Cézanne of the composed portraits, the human form not quite animate, should be the same Cézanne whose chosen subjects early in his career were scenes of violence: murder, rape. It shouldn't be startling at all. A convulsive, destructive force stampedes its way through emptiness:

> Je te frapperai sans colère
> Et sans haine, comme un boucher,
> Comme Moïse le rocher!
> Et je ferai de ta paupière,
>
> Pour abreuver mon Saharah,
> Jaillir les eaux de la souffrance.
> Mon désir gonflé d'espérance
> Sur tes pleurs salés nagera
>
> Comme un vaisseau qui prend le large,
> Et dans mon coeur qu'il soûleront
> Tes chers sanglots retentiront
> Comme un tambour qui bat la charge!
> (Charles Baudelaire, "L'Héautontimorouménos" [The Self-Tormentor])

[I will hit you without anger, and without hate, like a butcher, like Moses hitting the rock! And, to quench my Sahara, I will make the waters of suffering spring from under your eyelid. My desire, swollen with hope, will swim in your salty tears like a ship taking the open water, and in my heart, drunk with your tears, your dear sobs will resonate like a drum beating the charge!]

Cézanne replaced the rapes and murders of his early work with scenes haunted by their own huge energy. That tablecloth, those fruits, that *Boy in a Red Vest*: the colors refracting planes that might find more containment, and through it all a pre-ordained sense of falling, a force in the process of vacating its own expansiveness. And though one might say that through the energy in his technique — that accumulates absence and presence at once, shadow and light, all inhering now in color — Cézanne transcended a rageful emptiness, the awkward Bathers suggest that he knew better, that the violent subject matter of the early work was not resolved in his mature compositions, that something about living would be beyond him still. But while such thoughts would reassure me, strengthen my belief that I was looking for the goal of my own experience, I still needed my shaming, and shameful, companion.

The things I did over the next two years, back in New York, are straightforward enough: starting to build a business, getting a puppy, furnishing my home. After a year and a half, I got free of the companion of that summer. By then, I had started to change.

And this past summer, I finally began to understand what I'd been looking for in the Leonardo. A year earlier, I'd met the person whom I would marry this past May. We were spending the summer in the country, and somehow in

August we realized that we wanted to have a child. And so that same month, when I was asked to contribute to this volume and knew that I would write about the Leonardo, what I'd been looking for in the Cartoon dawned on me.

Writing of the Cartoon, Sidney Freedberg comments on "the emanation that is here of love, in the spirit of the persons and in their loveliness of form" (*Painting of the High Renaissance in Rome and Florence*); it was that resonance everywhere of feeling, awakened by "the loveliness of form," and in the gestures, in the manner in which the children both reach out from and repose in their mothers, in the light clearing shadows: feeling and love, emanating from within and everywhere; connection and possibility of greater connection yet; presence which had now begun to resonate in me.

I now realized that for all those years I had been looking in a dead-ended way: for a vision of how living could reveal experience. That search had led me to poetry, as the place where the inner life finds its own outward form:

> Before I got my eye put out
> I liked as well to see —
> As other Creatures, that have Eyes
> And know no other way —
>
> But were it told to me — Today —
> That I might have the sky
> For mine — I tell you that my Heart
> Would split, for size of me —
> (Emily Dickinson, "Before I got my eye put out")

But it had been a way to envision that I had been looking for, not a way to feel.

Revelation, I'd reasoned, must reveal:

> And Los beheld his Sons, and he beheld his Daughters:
> Every one a translucent Wonder: a Universe within,
> Increasing inwards, into length and breadth, and heighth:
> Starry & glorious . . .
> (William Blake, *Jerusalem*)

But to experience the Visionary is to be traumatized by it; and even had I the power to do so, I would not engage trauma. And so, through that void that seems to be infinite retreat, emptiness reigned in me.

To have my awareness imploded by an incomprehensible world was the stuff of tragedy; as if to play Cassandra. And yet to refuse . . . The poetry I cared for found that moment wherein

> I asked the Orient
> Had it for me a Morn —

> And it should lift its purple Dikes,
> And shatter me with Dawn!
>   (Emily Dickinson, "As if I asked a common alms")

wherein that ecstasy can suddenly reverse:

> Weh mir, wo nehm'ich, wenn
> Es Winter ist, die Blumen, und wo
> Den Sonnenschein
> Und Schatten der Erde?
> Die Mauern stehn
> Sprachlos und kalt, im Winde
> Klirren die Fahnen.
>   (Friedriech Hölderlin, "Hälfte des Lebens" [Half of Life])

[Alas, where can I find, when it is winter, the flowers, and where the sunshine, and the shadows of earth? The walls stand speechless and cold, in the wind, the weathervanes strain.]

Totality was called for, of fullness or of emptiness; where was my everyday life?

Not that I thought this was a new question. I was perfectly aware that for the last two hundred years poets had set about trying to celebrate the everyday. I knew Wordsworth's disclosure that people are themselves only within, that we cannot reveal ourselves in the world of action, that only if we "look with feelings of fraternal love / Upon those unassuming things that hold / A silent station in this beauteous world" can we discover "men as they are men within themselves" (William Wordsworth, *The Prelude*). Hamlet, who has "that within which passes show," has become everyone, unable to act, the self all undisclosed. I knew that sometimes in poetry the everyday did appear, within its own mundanity aloof and heartbreaking, its simple imperiousness overcoming all objections that we cannot just slip away like the rest, as blunt as nature:

> Where are the songs of Spring? Ay, where are they?
> Think not of them . . .
>
> A robin whistles on the garden croft
> And gathering swallows twitter in the skies.
>   (John Keats, "To Autumn")

And I understood something of the darkening confrontation between the self and what cannot express our destiny it is so denatured: "Fourmillante cité, cité pleine de rêves, Où le spectre en plein jour raccroche le passant!" (Swarming city, city full of dreams, where a spectre, in plain day, grabs the passer-by!) (Charles Baudelaire, "Les Sept Vieillards" [The Seven Old Men]). (Of course, in an inevitable poetics, Baudelaire found our nature itself to be monstrous and the life of the city, where we stumble constantly on incomprehensible horrors, to be the flowering of our true selves.)

And that same struggle, between experience and its revelation, between the internal sense of possibility and a reality that stifles, between internal noticings or remembrances of even the slightest moment and the outward look of it from which one's inner life has disappeared, had re-occurred in much of the poetry of the past two hundred years with varying degrees of power and only slightly changing contexts. To voice that struggle had often been the poetry's goal. I did not believe that struggle could itself be transcended.

It could metamorphose itself into a contemporary mode. To let painting illustrate the point: one might say that the *Watchman* and *Periscope (Hart Crane)* and *Out the Window* and *Land's End* paintings of Jasper Johns with their flattened tries at reaching (an arm plummeting from and into nowhere and emptied thus of volume) while color that is caked into its own adherence, or bits of cutlery, or rulers, or chairs, cluster the moment of being whose fragmentation the painted canvas holds, is a painter's response to the contemporary self that can't arrive at its own being and dangles its way through an Ashbery poem:

> Hasn't the sky? Returned from moving the other
> Authority recently dropped, wrested as much of
> That severe sunshine as you need now on the way
> You go . . .
>
>   Each moment
> Of utterance is the true one; likewise none are true,
> Only is the bounding from air to air, a serpentine
> Gesture which hides the truth behind a congruent
> Message, the way air hides the sky, is, in fact,
> Tearing it limb from limb this very moment.
>
>   (John Ashbery, "Clepsydra")

Of course there had been relatively recent moments where a poet thought the struggle overcome and the thing itself revealed with no catching after our human need to turn an object into our experience of it in time:

> the back wings
> of the
>
> hospital where
> nothing
>
> will grow lie
> cinders

> in which shine
> the broken
>
> pieces of a green
> bottle
> > (William Carlos Williams, "Between Walls")

    But the thing itself, even laid out thus for us to marvel, did not satisfy my need to let desolation sound out my own imaginative reach; I preferred

> some Elsie —
> voluptuous water
> expressing with broken
>
> brain the truth about us —
> her great
> ungainly hips and flopping breasts
>
> addressed to cheap
> jewelry
> and rich young men with fine eyes
>
> as if the earth under our feet
> were
> an excrement of some sky
>
> and we degraded prisoners
> destined
> to hunger until we eat filth
>
> while the imagination strains
> after deer
> going by fields of goldenrod in
>
> the stifling heat of September
> Somehow
> it seems to destroy us
>
> It is only in isolate flecks that
> something
> is given off

> No one
> to witness
> and adjust, no one to drive the car
> > (William Carlos Williams, "To Elsie")

And of course it was false that there was nothing in life but desolation. How could poetry realize life's abundance? And how could it uncover not only a moment of truth, but the pace of life?

The modern pull to write narrative poetry taps the desire to represent living in all its detail, to value the ongoing, to voice what occurs. And yet what if the nature of the ongoing is that most of our inner life is lost from it, stays mute inside our selves? Over the past two hundred years the locus for narrative has become prose; since it is the nature of poetry to realize inner life in outer form and the nature of prose to keep the inside and the outside separate, through the particular novelist's method of combining (or keeping apart) his or her focus on what is unspoken, buried in a character's thoughts or dreams or half-aware perceptions, and his or her separate focus on the things that do happen, how people speak and act. How, then, can modern narrative poetry extend the momentary utterance that lyric poetry can voice — in which inner feeling and knowing discover their outward form — into the ups and downs, the maneuverings, the changes through time, of life? (Indeed, to think of writing narrative poetry may be to dream of drama: the lyrical moment of the self extended into event.)

Poetry, I understand, is also possession: as if for that moment of the poem, one's own voice filled the object of one's attention. And so it was to keep me from the quiet in which we all do inhere that poetry held out its promise: to keep the paradox going, that that which comes from me inheres in what we are and cannot tell each other.

But now I recalled that Sidney Freedberg also writes of the Cartoon that in it

> there is a communication of sensuous pleasure to the eye and spirit of the beholder by the qualities of form . . . . (Leonardo) now embraces, within the vital unity of the work of art, the element of pleasurable sensuous response, which becomes peer to and part of an inseparable texture with the properties of intellect and moral good.
> > (Freedberg, *Painting of the High Renaissance in Rome and Florence*)

Doesn't that pleasure in the creation of form match the Cartoon's "embodiment of love?"

I realized that the creation of this pleasure results from the act of giving praise. And that both pleasure and praise are attributes of love.

Thus, if it is possible to make praise the other side of elegy, and not elegy the only mode of life, elegy that the self can never be, that in any moment we are already half-gone, then poetry need not seek to replace living (where remembrance and imagination create a shadow life) but rather to accompany it.

Is it possible then that as my own life opens for me, and for the first time my own feelings do not withdraw, numb with quiet, but grow strong and stronger with love and enter fully with all my attention of mind and heart into the lives of those who are my own by virtue of tenderness and responsibility and care, is it possible that our lives will maintain for me a steadfast need to find themselves again in poetry? Milton's fallen angels speak to us because their anxious hope is ours: to be "not lost in loss itself." But Leonardo's painting shows that Grace which overwhelms death, even of the children. To know such Grace is surely to praise.

But for me to attain a pitch of feeling which suffuses my life with Grace — . The subject of Leonardo's Cartoon immortalizes our hopes for Grace, placing its realization elsewhere, in the divine. And yet my feelings, my altogether human love, my knowing what things can occur in our lives, my hope —

New York City
December 1994

DAVID LENSON

Ptyx: The Metaphysics of the Symbol[1]

An extraterrestrial observer might have trouble understanding the human propensity for saying, writing or depicting one thing while meaning another. Along with other forms of indirection, such as circumlocution and euphemism, the practice of alternative representation is as central to politics and religion as it is to art. It is the antithesis of the mimetic. Throughout the Middle Ages and the Renaissance, the Church, reading into the phenomenal world a greater significance than meets the eye, required the arts to produce allegories — literally, representations which "say something else." The production and reception of the arts (including even music) constituted an interpretive laboratory whose methods paralleled those which Christian doctrine applied to the macrocosm. This process moved invariably from the particular to the general, granting no lasting importance to idiosyncrasies or accidents of style. Universal interpretability gave evidence of God's ubiquity; it rescued the apparent randomness and triviality of the phenomena by infusing them with spirit. Allegory is plainly an exercise in order, but the price of its certainty is that there can be only one correct reading of any representation. If two contrary interpretations are produced, one of them must be wrong (though it is assumed that each commentator proceeds with the *intention* of being correct).

Unlocking and exposing the "real meaning" of a representation presumes that significance is already present in the work, rather than being imposed by the commentator. Success in such commentary therefore depends least of all on originality. What is required is the alignment of a particular text with a body of incontrovertible authority, such as the New Testament or the Patrilogia. If there is only one correct interpretation, then there must be an external and canonical document to establish rectitude. A good interpreter may be distinguished from an inferior one by two criteria: 1) degree of knowledge of the canonical source and skill in citing that document to elucidate the artwork; and 2) thoroughness in accounting for detail, giving an impression of *complete* correctness. This second criterion is important. If one is interpreting in the context of a universal order, it is essential that every last element of the interpreted work be hypotacted under that order. The exposition must be as ubiquitous within the text or image as God is in the world.

Generating a reading was not an activity reserved solely for scholars and monastics. Every recipient of an artwork could offer an interpretation. This is, certainly, a good way to assure and enhance the involvement of the audience. Such customs survive today primarily in relation to cinema, where an exegetical conversation in a bar or coffee shop after a screening is still considered to be an important part of the experience of the genre. Although we lack the canonical grounds to assert beyond doubt the accuracy of our reading — which is often referred by default to the director's intent instead of God's — we still argue as if correctness were possible.

This is so despite the fact that the ecclesiastical and social hierarchies that provided the exegetical basis for allegory gradually diminished in authority during the eighteenth century. Apparently the desire to say one thing and mean another, the instinct for alternative representation, outlived the wherewithal of interpretation, which then took on an increasingly ad hoc character, becoming less universal — and more the function of an individual commentator — than the traditional mediation of iconography. Sometimes the new encoding had political motivations, when direct statement might bring retribution upon the artist (*Gulliver's Travels* or *Candide*), or else it generated idiosyncratic religious allegories, as in the cases of Swedenborg and Blake. It is still more or less possible, however, to advance a "correct" reading in these instances, although it is probably easier to verify that correctness with the benefit of historical retrospect than it was at the time.

It may be surprising to find the following most perceptive glossing of Coleridge's paragraphs on Fancy and the two Imaginations in an essay by Edgar Allan Poe:

> But, as often analogously happens in physical chemistry, so not infrequently does it occur in this chemistry of the intellect, that the admixture of two elements will result in a something that shall have nothing of the qualities of one of them — or even nothing of the qualities of either.[2]

Poe is comparing the difference between Fancy and secondary Imagination with the distinction between mixtures and compounds in chemistry. Fancy puts substances together without changing either one. It unites discrete elements only by their co-occupancy of an interwoven space. These substances, then, are merely untransformed "fixities and definites." Secondary Imagination, on the other hand, makes genuinely new syntheses out of the elements it brings together. With reference to alternative representation, Fancy is clearly the intellectual faculty that produces allegory, linking surface to *sententia* by conscious choice. This is true whether the encoding is originally the author's or the product of a predetermined and exterior ideology.

If the *hortus closus* is to stand for the Virgin Mary, that connection may be made without altering the nature of either garden or Virgin. Coleridge's association of Fancy with memory suggests that allegorical representation may be partly a mnemonic device, a way of reminding the audience of an invisible ideology even though what is actually represented has its origin in the phenomenal plane. Lurking behind the dismissive tone that Coleridge assumes as he writes about Fancy may be a disdain for anything so contrived as allegory, anything so manipulable for ulterior reasons. For although allegory is most readily associated with formal theology, there is nothing mysterious or transcendental in its operation. If it is religious, it pertains to a religion without miracles or *numina*, that is willing to accept spiritual abridgment in order to maintain interpretive certainty.

Fancy may not be experiential at all, since it is "emancipated from the order of time and space," which in Kantian terms removes it from the realm of possible experience. But secondary Imagination has cognition (primary Imagination) as its point of origin. It cannot therefore restrict itself to the production of allegorical equations as does Fancy, since it always continues to partake of the spontaneous and accidental qualities of the phenomenal world. The elements to be fused into an imaginative or chemical compound may be deliberately selected, but it is not possible to know a priori what the qualities of the product will be. With secondary Imagination, Coleridge proposes to liberate the process of alternative representation by discarding Fancy's insistence upon conscious control, "that empirical phenomenon of the will, which we express by the word CHOICE." This is why he refers to secondary Imagination as "co-existing with the conscious will." It need not, indeed must not, replace or even curtail that conscious will, but at the same time it doesn't "receive all its material ready made from the law of association."

We may, as an example of that law of association, employ Fancy to combine a woman and a fish. In that case we know in advance that we shall have something more or less like a mermaid. But we can neither predict nor control what would issue from an imaginative synthesis of the two, any more than we can predict with a priori sureness what we will be smelling or seeing at this time tomorrow afternoon. Even Kant's universalizing forms and categories cannot decree specific intuitions beforehand. Along the spectrum of possibilities for alternative representation, secondary Imagination is a higher kind of metaphor, a rejection of mechanisms of Fancy like simile and equation, or any other rigid linguistic structures that serve to ensure the qualitative preservation of the original elements.

I. A. Richards, in *Coleridge on Imagination*, says about the most celebrated passage from the *Biographia Literaria*:

> Neither Coleridge's grounds for the distinction nor his applications of it have as yet entered our general intellectual tradition. When they do, the order of our universes will have been changed.[3]

The remainder of this discussion is intended as a difference with Richards on the first part of that statement, and an agreement with the second. It is possible to wonder whether Richards's Anglocentrism didn't blind him to the possibility that it was not in England but France that the idea of a radically transforming secondary Imagination entered the mainstream of literary art.

By the nineteenth century, direct roads from the surface of the artwork to *sententia* begin to grow over and disappear. There are two steps in this process, and it is arguable that they are historical stages, one emerging with German and English Romanticism and the other coming decades later in France. They hinge upon the gradual rejection of Fancy and allegory, resulting first in the development of *emblematic* representation, and later in the evolution of Symbolism. Generally speaking, this progression is one of dissociation of tenor and vehicle, or of signifier and signified, in such a way that meaning is diminished and interpretation concomitantly devalued. It is a growth in autonomy of the object recreated by secondary Imagination, at the expense of both the originating material world and the primary Imagination that perceives it.

Between allegory and symbolism lies the vast and uncertain territory of emblematic representation. "Emblem" is etymologically related to "symbol," both deriving from the Greek verb *ballein* meaning "to throw" and eventually "to put." *Emballein* translates as "throw in," "put in," or "inlay." Unlike allegorical representation, where one simply says one thing and means another in a fixed relationship, emblematic representation uses a single sign to account for a wide range of significations. The emblem is "thrown in" or "inlaid" upon the surface of phenomenal reality like one anomalous tile in a mosaic. It does not belong to the realm of Fancy alone, as allegory does, for in allegory both representation and significance are internally consistent. Just as the surface of a work like *Pilgrim's Progress* is coherent in itself, and may be read satisfactorily on a superficial level, so too the system of meaning to which it alludes is integral and complete in itself. This is not the case in emblematic representations, where the emblem seems foreign to the surface in which it is set.

Emblems may yield several layers of interpretation, with no one any more demonstrably correct than the others, leading from the specific to the abstract. If I see, in an otherwise phenomenally consistent American city, some red, white and blue bunting on a building, I am aware that I am seeing something that contains meaning which the city that surrounds it does not inherently possess. Given even an allegory-trained interpretive capacity, I would recognize the bunting as a general emblem of the United States. Spatially, I might surmise that its presence on that particular building signifies something about what transpires inside; perhaps it is a government building, or the headquarters of a patriotic organization. Temporally, I might see the significance of the bunting as restricted to that particular day; perhaps it is a national holiday, or the grand opening of a business. I might assume that the institution or enterprise inside the building is, for whatever reason, reaffirming its allegiance to America, so that the deployment of the emblem is a gesture of advocacy.

Now, national colors in and of themselves are an abbreviation, signifying a complex, interdependent series of beliefs. If the building houses a business, it may be proclaiming adherence to the American economic system, although, of course, it is possible that it is merely decorating the facade in a conventional way, one designed to generate an instinctively favorable but contentless response. If it is a national holiday, on the other hand, the display might have a historical meaning. There could be a political interpretation as well: perhaps America is being affirmed in opposition to an enemy, or to some domestic insurgency that the building's inhabitant feels is imperiling the nation. But in all likelihood, the bunting alludes to more than one of the above "signifieds."

Even in this simplistic example, there is a spectrum of signification issuing from a concise representation "inlaid" upon the phenomenal surface. This is clearly more sophisticated than the mere "fixities and definites" of Fancy. And yet nothing has been dissolved, diffused, dissipated or re-created. Building, bunting and Empire are all unaltered. Emblematic representation belongs to that "second best" component of secondary Imagination, the less radical of its functions and therefore the first to be assimilated easily into the arts. This is the part that "struggles to idealize and to unify." In our example, the bunting is meant to *unify* a complicated system of beliefs into a single sign which attempts to *idealize* a nation, its inhabitants, its history, its economy, and even its social and moral conventions.

This idealization is accomplished in part by the isolation and distinctness of emblems against their backgrounds — the "inlaying." This gives us another clue about their nature. An emblem is an imprint of consciousness upon the phenomenal world. I nearly wrote "footprint," for emblems show that something conscious has passed and left its mark. In literary contexts, authors offset them in similar ways. In a purportedly mimetic work, that is, an untransformed representation of primary Imagination in turn representing phenomenal reality, an emblem may be offset as distinctly as bunting against the stone wall.

This technique is developed to great sophistication in, for example, American romances of the nineteenth century. In *The Scarlet Letter*, the "A" placed around Hester Prynne's neck stands out luridly from the surface of the narrative and is plainly intended to have significance. But, like our bunting, it has several "correct" interpretations. It is Adultery, on the allegorical level, but it is also the Alpha of creation, and eventually leads to more general meanings about Hester's character: that she is set apart from the ordinary by some inexpressible grade-A superiority, and that she retains much of the innocence of an Edenic beginning. In *Moby-Dick*, emblems of even more ambiguous significance are scattered throughout the text. The gold doubloon nailed to the mast by Ahab as a reward for the first sighting of the white whale means something completely different to each crew member who perceives and interprets it. So too the whale itself, set apart from the representational surface by its unusual color, becomes the most ambiguous emblem of all, until it comes eventually to signify something like significance itself.

All emblems, then, whether inlaid upon the phenomena or upon the surface of a textual representation, call beyond themselves to richer layers of meaning which cannot be subdued by any single "correct" interpretation. The emblem is infused with a consciousness that transcends its context. The interpreter becomes a seer. Like a *vates* of antiquity he peruses the phenomenal world for omens, intuitions endowed with idealizing and unifying powers, and with the intimation of extraordinary significance, all the while knowing that any of a multiplicity of readings may be correct even though none can hold a final or exclusive claim. This may lead, as in Hawthorne and Melville, to connotations of a religious or metaphysical nature, suggestions of both the numinous and the noumena. In either case, the consistency of the artwork's surface is disrupted.

In Gérard de Nerval's "Vers Dorés" (Golden Verses), the emblematic technique of alternative representation is pressed to its utmost complexity. Here the phenomenal world becomes a series of glyphs. Emblems occur in greater density than before, and threaten altogether to usurp the "setting" or nonsignifying realm.

> Eh quoi! tout est sensible
> — Pythagore

> Homme, libre penseur! te crois-tu seul pensant
> Dans ce monde où la vie éclat en toute chose?
> Des forces que tu tiens ta liberté dispose,
> Mais de tous tes conseils l'univers est absent.
>
> Respecte dans la bête un esprit agissant:
> Chaque fleur est une âme à la Nature éclose;
> Un mystère d'amour dans le métal repose;
> "Tout est sensible!" Et tout sur ton être est puissant.
>
> Crains, dans le mur aveugle, un regard qui t'épie:
> À la matière même un verbe est attaché . . .
> Ne la fais pas servir à quelque usage impie!
>
> Souvent dans l'être obscur habite un Dieu caché;
> Et comme un oeil naissant couvert par ses paupières,
> Un pur esprit s'accroit sous l'écorce des pierres![4]

> [Eh, what! everything is sentient!
> — Pythagoras
>
> Man, free thinker! you think you're the only thinking thing
> In this world where everything explodes with life?
> What powers you have your liberty can dispose,
> But the universe is gone from all your councils.
>
> Respect in animals an active mind:
> Every flower is a soul opened to nature;
> A mystery of love sleeps in metal;
> "Everything is sentient!" And everything has power over you.
>
> Dread in the blind wall an eye that is watching you:
> To matter itself a verb is attached . . .
> Don't make it serve some impious purpose!
>
> Often in the dark being lives a hidden God;
> And like an eye being born, covered by its lids,
> A pure mind grows under the rind of stones!]

    Nerval accuses humanity of operating solely on the level of Fancy and failing to attain the richness and complexity of secondary Imagination. This helps to explain the use of "liberty" in the first stanza, recalling Coleridge's restriction of Fancy to conscious choice. Human councils (a word with stuffy, "official" overtones) deny life to all possible objects, and do not perceive even to the fullest potential of *primary* Imagination. For if they did, they would recognize that perception, as "a repetition in the infinite mind of the eternal act of creation in the infinite I AM," can confer a universality unavailable through choice or liberty. Because they play only with "fixities and definites" they sacrifice any claim to universality. Nerval insists that if we were alert to the emblematic quality of nature, we would find consciousness in apparently material objects. "To matter itself a verb is attached" avers that what seems to be an object may be a subject as well, and may have the potential for intuition and action. More than that, these transformed subjects may have power over us, and may not be content with passive coexistence. Animals, flowers and even metals, endowed with a kind of latent or inapparent consciousness, must not be made to serve impious, materialistic ends. They are inhabited by hidden gods. The numinous and the noumenal are equated.

    Nerval's transcendental signifying does not allow any single "correct" interpretation. Emblems may be isolated, but cannot be limited to unitary meanings. In the proliferation of emblems in "Vers Dorés" it is possible to detect a movement toward true symbolism. For Nerval, alternative representations are not a series of narrow passages from one level of consciousness to another. Instead, the existence of a complete heterocosm lying beyond the perceptual veil is intimated. It is as if the Kantian thing-in-itself had become sentient, no longer a vague material substratum of nature. Or this may echo the Swedenborgian quest for spiritual correspondences to the phenomena. In either case, the idealizing and unifying capacities of secondary Imagination are well illustrated in this poem. Beyond the apparently random surface of perception lies a spiritual realm which idealizes in two ways: it asserts both the overall ascendancy of mind over matter and the perfection of that transcendental consciousness. (In other words, it is idealist in both the philosophical and popular usages of the term). Still, the poem operates as revelation rather than transformation, so that it does not yet illustrate the highest function of secondary Imagination, the activity which results in the production of true symbols.

"Symbol" comes from *sumballein*, meaning "put together." The cognate noun, *sumbolon*, means "token" or "mark," referring to a procedure used in commerce whereby two merchants agreeing to a contract would divide a coin or other object in half, with the two halves to be rejoined upon the contract's fulfillment. Separating friends would use a similar procedure to pledge their intent to meet again. A symbol, then, is etymologically a reunion of something once sundered. This brings to mind Coleridge's remarks in chapter 12 of the *Biographia* about the union of subject and object, and the mutual dependency of those terms. "During the act of knowledge itself, the objective and subjective are so instantly united, that we cannot determine to which of the two the priority belongs. There is here no first, and no second; both are coinstantaneous and one" (255). Subject and object are thus like opposite sides of the same coin, or the two halves of a *sumbolon* reunited. This is Coleridge's "infinite I AM," what Hegel calls the *An-Sich-Für-Sich*. The higher component of secondary Imagination, which "dissolves, diffuses, dissipates, in order to re-create," should have as its result a heterocosm in which, as Coleridge says, "the act of contemplation makes the thing contemplated" (251–52). Thesis VII asserts that "the spirit in all the objects which it views, views only itself" (278). Here is the passage in which that phrase occurs:

> If then I know myself only through myself, it is contradictory to require any other predicate of self, but that of self-consciousness. Only in the self-consciousness of a spirit is there the required identity of object and of representation; for herein consists the essence of a spirit, that it is self-representative. If therefore this be the one only immediate truth, in the certainty of which the reality of our collective knowledge is grounded, it must follow that the spirit in all the objects which it views, views only itself. If this could be proved, the immediate reality of all intuitive knowledge would be assured. It has been shown, that a spirit is that, which is its own object, yet not originally an object, but an absolute subject for which all, itself included, may become an object. It must

therefore be an ACT; for every object is, as an *object*, dead, fixed, incapable in itself of any action, and necessarily finite. Again the spirit (originally the identity of subject and object) must in some sense dissolve this identity, in order to be conscious of it: fit alter et idem . . . . (276–79)

Symbols are representations which promise a new, higher objectivity of the spirit. Secondary Imagination must first perform its destructive function, dissolving the non-signifying phenomenal world and re-creating it on another plane where its material nature is identical with its spiritual content.

Nerval's poem is still in the emblematic mode, however, because the poet is exhorting us to take cognizance of a world of spirit which still remains alien and outside us. There is something sinister, even paranoid, in the line cautioning the reader to "dread in the blind wall the eye that is watching you." All we can do with this transcendental reality is to respect it. As we move toward symbolic representation, however, the possibility of genuine integration with transcendental consciousness is raised. Baudelaire's sonnet "Correspondances" is an important step in this direction:

> La Nature est un temple où de vivants piliers
> Laissent parfois sortir de confuses paroles;
> L'homme y passe à travers des forêts de symboles
> Qui l'observent avec des regards familiers.
>
> Comme de longs échos qui de loin se confondent
> Dans une ténébreuse et profonde unité,
> Vaste comme la nuit and comme la clarté,
> Les parfums, les couleurs et les sons se répondent.
>
> Il est des parfums frais comme les chairs d'enfants,
> Doux comme les hautbois, verts comme les prairies,
> — Et d'autres, corrompus, riches et triomphants,
>
> Ayant l'expansion des choses infinies,
> Comme l'ambre, le musc, le benjoin et l'encens,
> Qui chantent les transports de l'esprit et des sens.[5]
>
> [Nature is a temple where living pillars
> Sometimes blurt out confused words;
> There man passes across forests of symbols
> That watch him with familiar eyes.
>
> Like long echoes from far away which melt
> Into a shadowy and profound unity,
> Vast as night and light,
> Odors, colors and sounds correspond.

> There are odors fresh as children's skin,
> Sweet as oboes, green as plains,
> — And others, corrupt, rich and victorious,
>
> Having the expansion of infinite things,
> Like amber, musk, benzoin and incense,
> That sing the ecstasies of senses and the mind.]

If Nerval's poem is dense with emblems of spirit which can be interpreted (although not in any one "correct" way), in Baudelaire's we find "forests of symbols" for which the possibility of interpretation is never even raised. For no true symbol is ever a symbol *of* anything. It is always a token of the reunion of subject and object; hence the potential harmony between humanity and the forest of symbols. The "regard" no longer comes from a blind wall, and need no longer be dreaded. We now have a familiar relationship with it.

Because of the dubious transition from the first quatrain to the rest of the sonnet, the reader is forced to supply a connection between the annunciation of symbolic reciprocity and the ensuing statements about synaesthesia. It seems that we are meant to understand the harmony of the senses, which leads to "ecstasies of senses *and* the mind," as something which will be available in the world re-created by secondary Imagination. Since, as Coleridge says, that faculty has among its various powers that of unification, it is not surprising that the "senses" in this transcendental realm are not restricted to their compartmentalized perceptual functions. Because they may now yield some direct apprehension of the noumenal realm, they will all possess "the expansion of infinite things." Since there can be but one infinity, they necessarily unify. So mathematicians tell us that parallel lines intersect at numerical infinity. It is also instructive to see in "Correspondances" the confluence, once again, of metaphysics, aesthetics, religion and ethics. Nature is a temple in which one can experience "transports" or religious ecstasies. This is reminiscent of Nerval's hidden god. Various forms of sensual beauty are united, and the innocent ("chairs d'enfants") exists side by side with the corrupt and rich.

The doctrine of correspondences is of course Swedenborgian (and not Kantian or Coleridgian) in origin, and the way in which Baudelaire modifies it is instructive. Swedenborg, in *Heaven and Hell*, presents it as follows:

> The whole natural world corresponds to the spiritual world — not just the natural world in general, but actually in details. So anything in the natural world that occurs from the spiritual world is called a correspondent. It is vital to understand that the natural world emerges and endures from the spiritual world, just like an effect from the cause that produces it.[6]

Swedenborg goes on to delineate these correspondences with an almost preposterous specificity:

> In general, a garden corresponds to heaven viewed as to its discernment and wisdom.... Trees, species by species, correspond to perception and insights of what is good and true, the raw material of discernment and wisdom....
> (93)
>
> And what about caterpillars, the most unattractive members of the animal kingdom? They know how to get nourishment from the juice of appropriate leaves, and how after a precise time to form a cocoon around themselves — to put themselves in a womb, so to speak — and to hatch offspring of their own kind in this way. Some of them change into nymphs and chrysalids first, and make new threads. Then, after exhausting labor, they are fitted out with a new body adorned with wings. They fly through the air as though it were their heaven, they consummate their marriages, lay their eggs, and provide a posterity for themselves. (90)

For Swedenborg, nature is altogether an alternative representation, but it is completely interpretable, and therefore remains a simple allegory. Baudelaire modifies "correspondence" to signify a transcendental representation that will not succumb to interpretation at all. But although the poem provides a schematic for the mechanism of transformation, it does not contain any symbols per se.

The roughly contemporary sonnet "Tristesses de la Lune" (Sorrows of the Moon) gives a detailed account of the generation of a true symbol:

> Ce soir, la lune rêve avec plus de paresse;
> Ainsi qu'un beauté, sur de nombreux coussins,
> Qui d'une main discrète et légère caresse
> Avant de s'endormir le contour de ses seins,
>
> Sur le dos satiné des molles avalanches,
> Mourante, elle se livre de longs pamoisons,
> Et promène ses yeux sur les visions blanches
> Qui montent dans l'azur comme des floraisons.
>
> Quand parfois sur ce globe, en sa langueur oisive,
> Elle laisse filer une larme furtive,
> Un poète pieux, ennemi du sommeil,
>
> Dans le creux de sa main prend cette larme pale,
> Aux reflets irisés comme un fragment d'opale,
> Et la met dans son coeur loin des yeux du soleil (63)
>
> [Tonight the moon dreams more lazily;
> Like a beautiful woman on her many cushions

Who caresses with a light discreet hand
The contour of her breast as she falls asleep,

On the satin back of soft avalanches,
Dying, she gives in to long faints,
And sweeps her eyes over the white visions
That rise like flowers into the azure.

When in her idle languor she sometimes lets
A furtive tear fall onto this globe,
A pious poet, enemy of sleep,

Takes in the palm of his hand this pale tear
With veined reflections like a fragment of opal,
And puts it in his heart, far from the eyes of the sun.]

The poem begins with an image of the moon among clouds. But the moon is never allowed even an instant of phenomenal existence. Dissolved, diffused, and dissipated from the start, it is personified as a woman reclining on her couch and engaged in lazy autoeroticism. The poem's vocabulary of death and sleep suggests that this personification is not fully conscious, either dreaming, dying or swooning — versions of consciousness in extremis. She, herself a vision, has in turn a metavision of flowers rising into the infinite azure. Moved, she lets a tear fall to earth. A pious poet, enemy of sleep (and hence friend of consciousness), takes the tear, which solidifies into something like an opal, and "internalizes" it. This tear/opal is a kind of proto-symbol, returned to an apparently material existence on another, re-created plane of existence. It is characteristic of symbols that there is no mimetic explanation for their generation. Where emblems are inlaid upon phenomena or upon mimetic representations of phenomena, symbols are joined together by imaginative recreation. The two halves of the *sumbolon*, subject and object, are reunited.

While "Correspondances" is a theoretical statement, "Tristesses de la Lune" is a practical symbolist *ars poetica*. It illustrates the process of which symbols are the products. From the personified moon's waning consciousness something is re-created and given a lithic solidity. Since this process is irreversible, symbols resist interpretation however strongly they may seem to demand it. The tear/opal bulges with significance, being at once subject and object, yet it is impossible to say what its significance is. Moonlight certainly cannot be deduced from it. Where emblems are still informally interpretable, symbols radiate an intrinsic "feeling of meaning." They call beyond themselves, as if signifying, but any attempt to specify that significance leads only to reflexive statements, like "The symbol signifies significance," or worse, "The symbol symbolizes significance itself," or simply "The symbol symbolizes itself." Although phenomena are the raw materials of symbols, any one-for-one correlation is dissolved by the action of secondary Imagination. As the only non-referential alternative representations, symbols resemble dreams in that their character is fundamentally atmospheric. Exegesis is therefore not only pointless but destructive: recounting a dream always distorts its nature and misses its essence.

Baudelaire is not rigorous in his use of symbols. They are part of a poetic arsenal that includes emblems, allegory and even a certain amount of mimesis. He would agree with Schopenhauer's dictum that "life and dreams are pages of one and the same book."[7] For Stéphane Mallarmé, the goal is to operate exclusively in the heterocosm of objects re-created by secondary Imagination. Not only is this strategy non-referential, it is not even concerned with the process of transformation. The symbol, the product, is its sole preoccupation. What Mallarmé tries to represent is, in brief, the dream without the dreamer, the vision abandoned by any generative or sustaining consciousness. Art becomes an unconditional ontology accessible only through the artwork that embodies it.

> Ses purs ongles très haut dédiant leur onyx,
> L'Angoisse, ce minuit, soutient, lampadophore,
> Maint rêve vespéral brulé par le Phénix
> Que ne recueille pas de cinéraire amphore
>
> Sur les crédences, au salon vide : nul ptyx,
> Aboli bibelot d'inanité sonore,
> (Car le Maître est allé puiser des pleurs au Styx
> Avec ce seul objet dont le Néant s'honore.)
>
> Mais proche la croisée au nord vacante, un or
> Agonise selon peut-être le décor
> Des licornes ruant du feu contre une nixe,
>
> Elle, défunte nue en le miroir, encor
> Que, dans l'oubli fermé par le cadre, se fixe
> De scintillations sitôt le septuor.[8]

[Her pure nails up high offering their onyx,
Anguish, this midnight, sustains, lampbearer,
Many a vesperal dream burnt by the Phoenix
That no cinerary urn gathers

On the sideboards, in the empty room: no ptyx,
Abolished trinket of sonorous inanity,
(Since the Master has gone to draw tears from the Styx
With that lone object by which Nothing is honored).

But near the window vacant to the north a gold
Is dying perhaps according to the decor
Of unicorns kicking fire against a nixie,

She, defunct and naked in the mirror, while
In the forgetfulness closed by the frame, the dipper
Of scintillations at once is fixed.]

Access to this poem takes place through the apparently allegorical figure of Anguish. Despite the capitalization, however, this is not precisely a personification, since Anguish is transformed not into a person but a figure sculpted into the base of a lamp. It is thus a representation at two removes from mimesis; it metamorphoses from disembodied consciousness (its name designating a free-floating emotion) to unconscious statuary without the intermediating stage of incorporation. It is impossible to know whose anguish it is that informs the scene. Throughout the poem anything human is similarly absent, especially the poet. This sets the stage for a great many images of negation, illustrative of Mallarmé's tenet that absence is superior to presence because of its greater suggestiveness.

> Je dis: une fleur! et, hors de l'oubli où ma voix relègue aucun contour, en tant que quelque chose d'autre que les calices sus, musicalement se lève, idée meme et suave, l'absente de tous bouquets. (368)

> [I say: a flower! and, out of the oblivion where my voice relegates any contour, as something other than the known calyces, musically there rises, suave, the very idea, the absence of all bouquets.]

Accordingly no cinerary amphora on the sideboards will gather the ashes of dreams. The lamp in Anguish's hands, with their onyx fingernails, gives off not light but vesperal dreams. This lamp does not burn, and so its sole function is denied. Instead its dreams are burnt by the Phoenix; normally we think of the Phoenix as being burnt itself, and not as burning anything else. The room, which we have seen to contain an ornate lamp and more than one credenza, we are quickly told is empty. So the transformed world both exists and does not exist at the same time. Or it exists, but is not "real."

Another oxymoron, "nul ptyx," negates a word which already does not exist, so the phrase might as well be translated as "no nothing." "Ptyx" does, however, have connotations if not denotations. It seems to be in apposition to the amphora, and accordingly most readings assume that it is some sort of vessel, probably the one the Master uses to draw tears from the Styx. The word sounds Greek, an atmospheric device reinforced by the poem's classical overtones and by its extensive use of the letter "y," whose French name is "i grec." "Ptyx" may be cognate with the Greek *ptux*, which denotes a writing tablet, or, in the plural, "folds." Pindar uses this word in the First Olympian Ode in the phrase *humnon ptuchais*, "folds of song."⁹ In the "Ouverture" to *Hérodiade*, Mallarmé has a similar construction in "les plis jaunes de la pensée" (42) or "yellow folds of thought." The ptyx is then a vessel with distant reverberations of a writing tablet (vessel for poetry) or a single "wrinkle of thought" (vessel for song or consciousness).

With the dazzling phrase "aboli bibelot d'inanité sonore," this object is doubly negated. If a trinket of emptiness is abolished, doesn't that imply "something?" This latest infinite regress of oxymorons is, however, "explained" in the seventh and eighth lines. The vessel exists, but is absent, "For the Master has gone to draw tears from the Styx / With this sole object by which Nothing is honored." "Le Maître" is not only an epithet of Mallarmé, bestowed by his contemporaries and gladly assumed and retained by the poet; it is also the authorial consciousness of the poem. The dreamer whose dream we are experiencing has departed from it, taking this symbolic object with him. This double absence is the most salient feature of the octave. The autonomous room of the imagination, with its mental furniture, contains one symbol, the lamp, notable for its presence, and another, the vessel, notable for its absence. An urn honors Nothing because it is a form shaped around its own emptiness. Or, it is form containing emptiness. As a "bibelot" it is ornamental, in keeping with the decor of the room from which it has been taken. Its nature therefore reflects that of the poem as a whole, or possibly of poems in general: ornate forms surrounding emptiness. But the amphora is missing, along with the poet, while the poem still exists and is present, although it is a dream of Nothingness dreamt by no one.

Just as an amphora by definition must have an opening in its otherwise closed form, so too the dreamt room of the poem has a "window vacant to the north" through which some light enters, first from a dying sun and finally from the seven stars of Ursa Major. It is by this light, and not by the light of the lamp, that we see the decor — unicorns kicking fire against a nixie, a struggle among non-existent creatures. Mallarmé no doubt relishes the word "nixe" for its negative sound. The nixie is presumably depicted in a mural, tapestry or wallpaper of some sort, thus taking it yet one step farther from existence. Even the depiction of such a non-existent creature cannot be seen directly, but only in a mirror, "the forgetfulness closed by the frame." She is thus several layers deep in absence and art — a myth represented on a wall, and seen through a mirror in a poem. At this long remove, we are able to perceive only that she is "defunct and naked," two more terms of negation. Mallarmé, in *Hérodiade* and in "L'Après-midi d'un Faune," associates nakedness with whiteness, emptiness, negativity. This poem, opening with the burning lamp of Anguish, ends with the cold and indifferent light of distant stars. If there is "motion" of any kind, then, it is away from an implicit allegory of Anguish toward some sort of resignation, of surrendering to the Void. When the Master departs, it is for the floor of Hades, where, in the Greek myth, the shades have no chance of salvation, but only the hope of reaching that other river, Lethe, which will accomplish the final negation: the obliteration of consciousness itself.

Whatever the analogy between the symbol (ptyx) and its poem, one cannot say that the symbol is a symbol of the poem, any more than one may rightly say that the poem is *about* anything. In fact, what makes this poem so perfect an illustration of Mallarmé's symbolic technique is that it is precisely and deliberately about Nothing. Just as the content of the amphora is emptiness, to be filled only with tears of oblivion, so the poem has only negative significance. Any interpretative activity would be blasphemous. If secondary Imagination sacrifices the phenomenality of an object in order to "re-create" it on another plane, then this is a later stage of the process, where the Imagination withdraws from its own creation. The role of the reader simply could not be more extraneous. We come upon the poem like archaeologists opening a chamber sealed long ago by some disaster. Our presence seems to defile the silence.

To recapitulate, pure symbolism concentrates as closely as possible on the products of the secondary Imagination, without dwelling upon its processes or, still less, upon the original phenomena that have been transformed. Subject and object are reunited, and the two halves of the *sumbolon* are joined into an ideality more vivid because it cannot and does not exist. Its concerted uselessness illustrates Kant's definition of beauty as "the form of purposiveness in an object so far as this form is perceived in it without the concept of a purpose."[10] In its drift into silence, negation and Nothingness, "Ses purs ongles . . ." presents a sort of Schopenauerian fable of the futility of will and the fragility of representation. The slogan "Art for Art's Sake" is inadequate as a synopsis of this method. "Art without a sake" would be better. Mallarmé's art is not so much an end in itself as a highly imperfect, all-too-human instrument for salvaging consciousness from the categories of time and space, for separating it from experience. "Of" must be permanently removed from "symbol."

University of Massachusetts, Amherst

Notes

[1] The following essay assumes that this familiar text from Coleridge's *Biographia Literaria* is indeed familiar:

> The IMAGINATION then, I consider either as primary, or secondary. The primary IMAGINATION I hold to be the living Power and prime Agent of all human Perception, and as a repetition in the finite mind of the eternal act of creation in the infinite I AM. The secondary Imagination I consider as an echo of the former, co-existing with the conscious will, yet still as identical with the primary in the *kind* of its agency, and differing only in *degree*, and in the *mode* of its operation. It dissolves, diffuses, dissipates, in order to recreate; or where this process is rendered impossible, yet still at all events it struggles to idealize and to unify. It is essentially vital, even as all objects (*as* objects) are essentially fixed and dead.
>
> FANCY, on the contrary, has no other counters to play with, but fixities and definites. The Fancy is indeed no other than a mode of Memory emancipated from the order of time and space; while it is blended with, and modified by that empirical phenomenon of the will, which we express by the word CHOICE. But equally with the ordinary memory the Fancy must receive all its material ready made from the law of association.

Samuel Taylor Coleridge, *Biographia Literaria*, ed. James Engell and W. Jackson Bate, 2 vols. (Princeton: Princeton UP, 1983) 1:305–6. All page references are to this volume and edition.

[2] Robert L. Hough, ed., *Literary Criticism of Edgar Allan Poe* (Lincoln, Nebraska: U of Nebraska P, 1965), 15.

[3] I. A. Richards, *Coleridge on Imagination* (Bloomington: U of Indiana P, 1960), 72.

[4] Gérard de Nerval, *Oeuvres*, ed. Albert Beguin and Jean Richer (Paris: Gallimard, 1960), 8–9. All translations are my own.

[5] Charles Baudelaire, *Oeuvres complètes*, ed. Y.-G. Le Dantec, rev. Claude Pichois (Paris: Gallimard, 1961), 11. All citations are from this edition. All translations are my own.

[6] Emanuel Swedenborg, *Heaven and Hell*, trans. George F. Dole (New York: Swedenborg Foundation, 1984), 81. All citations are from this edition.

[7] Arthur Schopenhauer, *The World as Will and Representation*, trans. E.F.J. Payne (Indian Hills, Colorado: Falcon's Wing, 1958), 18.

[8] Stéphane Mallarmé, *Oeuvres complètes*, ed. Henri Mondor and G. Jean-Aubry (Paris: Gallimard, 1945), 68–69. All citations are from this edition. All translations are my own.

[9] Pindar, *The Olympian and Pythian Odes*, ed. Basil L. Gildersleeve (New York: American, 1899), 5.

[10] Immanuel Kant, *Analytic of the Beautiful*, trans. Walter Cerf (Indianapolis: Bobbs-Merrill, 1963), 45.

Part II:

Narrative Transformations

ANCA VLASOPOLOS

Free-Floating Marginals and Contagious Degeneracy in the London and Paris of the Mid- and Late Nineteenth Century

No scientific "discoveries" in the nineteenth century filtered so rapidly to the popular imagination and held such sway over formulations of public policy as those made in the area of life sciences. Nor is this chapter of the life sciences and its impact on public discourse closed, subject to antiquarian interest or recoveries of a distant *mentalité*. We hunt for analogies between the animal kingdom and human society, and we still engage in the quantification of our heredity. Sociobiology, or biological determinism, is with us every time we fill out our medical history. We are spending vast resources on the Human Genome Project. We continue to suspect marginals and outsiders of carrying contagion and degeneration, and, more irrationally, of transmitting contagious degeneracy. Our public policies are often guided by the latest "scientific" investment in sustainable hierarchies.

Without nostalgia, we can look at past discourses of power and recognize that they were less absolute than the discourse of science. Whereas a theological world view, inherently built on hierarchy, nevertheless allowed, in Stephen Jay Gould's words, "conversion and assimilation," and at least the illusion of an equality of redemption, the scientific narrative of hereditary difference that arose in the early decades of the nineteenth century and continues to the present, with one major and brief interruption, allows no escape. Again, to quote Gould, "The death knell of the old eugenics in America was sounded more by Hitler's particular use of once-favored arguments for sterilization and racial purification than by advances in genetic knowledge."[1]

Although what follows is a series of readings of nineteenth-century literary texts that participate in the dissemination of the "contagious degeneracy" discourse, I want to make two disclaimers: one, the scientific master narrative underlying literary production is itself far from seamless; the scientific investment in upholding hierarchy needed constant adjustment in the face of flawed evidence, with literature lagging some decades behind the successive discreditation and reconstitution of inherited differences. Two, the literary texts themselves are far more subtle, complicated, contradictory, and disordered than might be suggested by the occasional bald statement in lockstep with the scientific climate made by an author in or outside a specific text.

Debate continues among historians, political scientists, and scientific writers about the continuity or discontinuity of biological hierarchy. Any analysis of the discourse itself is complicated by the fact that areas of knowledge we now regard as distinct — medicine, psychology, biology, paleontology, philology, anthropology — were part of the same grand enterprise of establishing the origins of species and the descent of man. For instance, in his study of fascism, Sternhell declares that while "fascism was an integral part . . . of European culture," we should not identify it with Nazism precisely because of Nazism's complete dependence on biological determinism and fascism's only partial dependence on the same.[2] Pick, however, insists on "the historical specificity of the model of degeneration which . . . inflected so much writing of the period."[3] Kraut focuses on a single aspect of the degeneration model, namely "immigrant menace" in the United States and its contaminating potential.[4] Proctor reminds us that although the Nazis may have corrupted and abused science, "scientists themselves participated in the construction of Nazi racial policy," while Olender analyzes the continuum from the discovery of Indo-European — through comparative philology to history to human sciences and ultimately to "racial science" — for its uses in placing "the monotheistic stagnation of the Semites" and their descendants, the Jews of Europe, within the new mythology of a "science of human origins."[5] In describing the fine tuning necessary to sustain various a priori conclusions about hierarchy, Gould explains: "'Inferior' groups are interchangeable in the general theory of biological determinism. They are continually juxtaposed, and one is made to serve as a surrogate for all — for the general proposition holds that society follows nature, and that social rank reflects inner worth" (103).

While I cannot resolve debates about historical specificity versus a unified scientific discourse of hierarchy, I wish to examine those interchangeable groups that take turns at representing the undesirable within biological determinism. The link between sexuality, especially female sexuality, and pathology has been thoroughly explored by Showalter, Gilman, Laqueur, etc.[6] Yet the emphasis on female sexuality occasionally obscures instead of illuminating the interchangeability of "inferior" groups and the irrationality at the heart of a notion like contagious degeneracy. Gilman, for instance, with his penchant for the psychoanalytic as cultural explanation, "naturalizes" the process by which certain groups become interchangeable: "The black [implicitly the Jew, the 'white Negro'], the proletarian, the child, the woman, the avant-garde are all associated in a web of analogies . . . . The role of sexuality in shaping these fantasies . . . is not merely an artifact of the nineteenth and early twentieth centuries. Human sexuality is a wellspring for much of our fantasy life" (41).

Be that as it may, the medicalization of discourses of power, in which psychoanalysts participate with as much gusto and as few controls as other scientific practitioners, is a historically recent phenomenon that needs to be examined in socioeconomic and political contexts. As Moscucci observes, "At a time of increasing scepticism about the interpretive power of metaphysics, conservatives and reformers alike looked to science as the new foundation for political and social action. The most controversial issues of the day, from the emancipation of blacks to the Irish Question, were to be submitted 'to Agassiz and Huxley, not to Kant or Calvin, church or Pope.'"[7] As studies of biological determinism make clear, those groups that by turns challenged established or aspiring hierarchies became subject to "scientific" analyses that would prove them more distant from the human evolutionary ideal than their dominant counterparts in the culture.

I too am liable to charges of a priori conclusions in my selection of literary texts that reproduce the "web of analogies" linking marginals and outsiders so as to relegate them to contagious, atavistic sub-humanity. However, these texts are so contradictory as to defeat in unexpected ways their own social theses or aesthetic programs while at the same time subscribing to one prominent element in the nineteenth-century discourse of contagion and degeneracy that I deferred discussing until this point, namely, the great city. Again, there is no uniformity of opinion about the role that great cities played in the deployment of the hierarchical discourse of contagious degeneracy. Pick, for instance, attends to this component of the "late nineteenth-century fascination with the ancestry and atavism of the crowd" in French literature by arguing that the focus of the degeneration locus shifts from the individual "and even the family . . . to society itself — crowds, masses, cities, modernity" (4). He traces the rise of a "massive new literature" of crime in the cities that "fetishised, romanticised and reviled the criminal mysteries of a Paris, a Naples, a London. Dangerous classes and dangerous races multiplied in literature" (21). But Pick insists on the cultural specificities of the eugenics movement in terms of public policy, so that France, England, and the U. S. appear less culpable in instituting laws that led to the Final Solution, and "the population of the imperial metropolis" less subjected to the racist language of imperialism, than the countries that came under "Western political control" (37).

In his study of the 1880s culture, Greenslade finds, conversely, that the great city serves as site of a widespread, contagious degeneration that could endanger civilization.[8] He identifies the confusion and irrationality attendant on the "science" of eugenics, which decried the fertility of Londoners on the one hand and, on the other, their tendency to die out, to deplete rural areas of healthy stock, and to incorporate into an already vulnerable public organism the "scavenging beast," the immigrant. In her study on criminality, Zedner emphasizes the threat posed to the emergent middle class by urban chaos more than by eugenic fears: "Middle-class reformers' obsession with the condition of the urban slum arose less out of alarm about its insalubrity or the dangers of disease than from their perception of it as a breeding ground of disorder."[9]

Disorder, however, as the fictional, lyric, and dramatic narratives that I examine suggest, often appears under the authoritative metaphor of genetic disease and contagion. As Zedner herself notes, "Certain locations, particularly inner city slums, were identified as veritable 'crime areas' of dense, frenetic criminal activity. Much effort was devoted to exposing the 'promiscuous herding' and 'scenes of profligacy,' the 'polluting language,' and the 'vicious abandonment' they engendered" (51–52). Yet what contemporary criminologists generally attribute to the conditions of the poor, the majority of scientists in the nineteenth and early twentieth centuries saw as inherent hereditary causes of the moral distress of lower classes or inferior groups. In our present resuscitation of quantifications of intelligence, draconian immigration policies, cuts to welfare, we are witnessing the resurgence of a similar discourse, with antecedents in the "sciences" of the last century and the policies that gave us mass sterilizations, heredity-based immigration laws, and the Final Solution.

The mid-century problem, posed in a variety of texts and haunting literature well into the twentieth century, centers on the modern industrial city as a site of uncertain and shifting spaces in which the *femes covert* within family government, "public" women, children, domestics, and other lower-class inhabitants circulate so freely that the distinctions of class and status, even of race, remain dangerously submerged. "Scientific" texts in the late nineteenth century achieved great vogue precisely because they tried to provide a morphological classification of vice, degeneracy, and criminality that would permit the onlooker to distinguish the prostitute from the "honest" woman, the lower-class depraved child from the middle-class innocent, the ape-like criminal from the loyal citizen.[10] Yet, at the same time that "scientists" avowed for the detecting accuracy of anthropometrics, they insisted upon the insidiousness of degeneration and its disguises under clothes, veils, social conventions.

I shall turn now to a series of texts demonstrating that neither the Right nor the Left was exempt from the seduction of the science of human evolution. Yet literary texts, despite their cultural uses, often bear testimony against the aims of their makers, at least in part. Men of letters (and my analysis here is limited to texts produced by males) found themselves caught in the same paradox as the eugenicists: while the available scientific evidence overwhelmingly supported the notion of female inferiority or at least debility, men nonetheless had to mate with this inferior of the species in order to exert their genetic imperative. Thus, in the texts that follow the "evolutionary" assessment of women moves from arguments against tainted and tainting heredity to detection of contagious degeneracy in women and in other marginals and their hallucinatory doublings; the ruptures occur in moments when the stigma of degeneracy both is and is not detectable. Textual moments of unease suggest the difficulty of reproducing an already contradictory and irrational master discourse within fictional bounds.

The first two texts in question exist in a dialogical relationship, since Augier conceived of *Le mariage d'Olympe* (1855) (*Olympia's Marriage*) as answer to Dumas fils' idealized fallen woman in *La dame aux camélias* (1852) (*Camille*).[11] Whereas Dumas fils, himself the product of an illicit union, argues for the possibility of redemptive love even for a fallen woman, his play (and novel) nevertheless reproduces the inextricable link between disease and prostitution and justifies upper-middle-class horror of misalliances as tainted heredity. *Camille* shows us a heroine already symbolically sick of her métier as kept woman and literally sick of the unnamed disease that will kill her. The hope of redemptive love that unites Marguerite and Armand is also to take them away from the city that has corrupted Marguerite, who declares, "J'ai rêvé campagne, pureté; je me suis souvenue de mon enfance — on a toujours eu une enfance, — quoi que l'on soit devenue" (I dreamed of the countryside, of purity; I remembered my childhood — we all have had a childhood, no matter what becomes of us) (395).

The sojourn in the country restores Marguerite's health but not her reputation. Even before M. Duval's arrival, she acknowledges that her past forbids her from marrying Armand. The arguments made by the patriarch center on Marguerite's corrupting influence on both Armand's genetic future — "Cette liaison . . . n'aura eu ni la chasteté pour base, ni la religion pour appui, *ni la famille pour résultat*" (this connection will rest on neither chastity, nor religion, and *will not lead to a family*) (400; emphasis mine) — and his sister's — "L'avenir d'une jeune fille qui ne vous a fait aucun mal peut donc être brisé par vous" (you will have destroyed the future of a young girl who's done you no wrong) (399). Whereas the sister's marriage is imperiled by the break in social conventions of Armand's misalliance, his own futurity in terms of children is endangered by Marguerite's inability and unwillingness to bear children. She admits to herself her own ineradicable corruption: "Regarde donc la fange de ton passé! Quel homme voudrait t'apppeler sa femme? Quel enfant voudrait t'appeler sa mère?" (Look at the mire of your past. What man would want to call you wife? What child would want to call you mother?) (401). The imagery of slime used here is a recurring index of atavism in evolutionary discourses. Marguerite goes back to Paris, the site of her fall, and to the disease that will devour her. Thus, while making a case for the natural nobility of a woman whose conscience prevents her from ruining her lover's and his family's future, Dumas replicates the dichotomy of country purity and city corruption, as well as emphasizing the inescapable consequences of a woman's stained past.

Safeguarding the genetic future of the well-to-do provides the mainspring of Augier's *Le mariage d'Olympe*. This rebuke to Dumas fils emphasizes the irremediable degeneracy of demi-mondaines and the danger they pose to young men of sound heredity whom they seduce amid the confusion of class boundaries caused by the great city. As the Marquis de Puygiron clarifies from the first, the world has been going to the dogs since la Vendée of 1832. The Baron de Montrichard enlightens the old man as to how badly things stand mainly by reference to the "rise" in the world of kept women: "Elles ont passé des régions occultes de la société dans les régions avouées" (They have moved from obscurity to public acknowledgment). In an allusion to Dumas' play, he adds, "le théâtre a pu les mettre en scène" (They even appear on stage). Unlike Marguerite, however, the kept women in Augier's play are hardly self-sacrificing. They marry their prey, naive youths (485). The question then is whether such a change can be redemptive for these "repentant Magdalens," and the answer is the Marquis' resonant compound of social dominance and biological determinism: "'Mettez un canard sur un lac au milieu des cygnes, vous verrez qu'il regrettera sa mare et finira par y retourner.' *Montrichard:* 'La nostalgie de la boue!'" (Place a duck in a lake among swans, and you'll see that it'll long for its swamp and will end up returning to it. *M*: The longing for mud!) (486). The mire, as the undifferentiated, unevolved origin of the prostitute, becomes a leitmotif. Unlike Marguerite's innocent childhood, Olympe's has been corrupt from the beginning. Montrichard speculates that she lost her innocence from the age of four, and she offers no rebuttal. Like Nana in Zola's novel, Olympe is "vicieuse" from heredity, hence from early childhood. She succeeds in entrapping a young man incapable of detecting the mark of degeneracy by which experienced men can tell the tainted woman. As in *Nana*, where birthmarks function as markers of women's latent or overt sexual depravity, so in *Le mariage* Montrichard recognizes Olympe by the "petit signe rose" (little pink mole) on her nape, whose existence ought to have remained hidden or unremarked upon (489). Whereas Marguerite is seen only in the context of her present life and is allowed to suggest for herself an earlier, pure self, Olympe has a mother who arrives as embodiment of the heroine's irrepressible origin. Both women, irremediably venal, want more money and more vulgar pleasures, in a downward movement toward the slime. In discussing her awakened husband's reluctance to grant her a separation, Olympe declares, "Il a peur que je ne galvaude son nom" (He's afraid I'll drag his name through the mud) (505); when, left with her mother in the aristocratic apartment, she takes a break from the formal manners governing familial intercourse, Olympe displays such crass vulgarity that Montrichard remarks in an aside, "La nostalgie de la boue" (506). In the denouement, when Henri discloses to his uncle the identity of Olympe, he throws himself on his knees before the Marquis and begs forgiveness "d'avoir souillé de sa [Olympe's] présence votre chaste maison" (for having sullied your chaste home with her presence) (515). Throughout the play, Augier gives the imagery of mud, sullied honor, and dirtied name explanatory power for the woman's inability to rise above her origins. The "scientific" certainty of the duck longing for its swamp and of the incompatibility between ducks and swans justifies the violence of the ending, when the Marquis kills Olympe to save the honor of his granddaughter and then proceeds to commit suicide, fully convinced of God's forgiveness.

Yet Augier's play departs from his own thesis, as does *Camille's* from its author's. Just as Dumas fils reintroduces images of bodily corruption and genetic taint/sterility in representing a woman whose actions, not nature, have become depraved, so Augier in creating the extremely vital and entertaining hybrid Olympe/Pauline presents a contrast between Olympe's wit and vitality, and the exaggerated goodness of the Marquis and his family. That she is able to deceive these good people for as long as she does — in excess of a year — suggests a native intelligence and adaptability that contrasts in a dramatically sympathetic way with the mental stagnation of her victims. Despite a conclusion in which order has been restored at the cost of Olympe's and the Marquis's lives, an ending beyond which we are strongly directed to foresee Henri's marriage with his virginal cousin and his securing himself a "clean" progeny, the play belongs to the ruthless Olympe, who proves herself more worthy of natural selection than Augier's plot allows her to be and who is exterminated by the upper class, not defeated by her own weakness.

Like Augier and Dumas fils, Dickens in *Bleak House* undertakes to explore the nature of female heredity and permits himself several transparent statements of thesis, which are subverted in various ways in the novel. However, Dickens creates a panoramic context that directs our attention toward a different generative corruption, that of civil law. Indicted as responsible for the slum Tom-all-Alone's, Chancery stands at the heart of city corruption. From Tom radiate the ills that Dickens represents through characters that move across symbolic, socioeconomic, and topographical boundaries that should have remained impermeable. Dickens's omniscient narrator makes plain the moral lesson of Tom-all-Alone's:

> Tom goes to perdition head foremost in his old determined spirit. But he has his revenge. Even the winds are his messengers, and they serve him in these hours of darkness. There is not a drop of Tom's corrupted blood but propagates infection and contagion somewhere . . . . There is not an atom of Tom's slime, not a cubic inch of any pestilential gas in which he lives, not one obscenity or degradation about him, not an ignorance, not a wickedness, not a brutality of his committing, but shall work its retribution, through every order of society, up to the proudest of the proud, and to the highest of the high.[12]

It is hard to resist Dickens's reformist agenda; for instance, Marshall and Jahn respectively contrast Dickens's ethics favorably with Baudelaire's "aestheticized city" and to Darwin's "progressive evolutionary ethics."[13] By so doing they uncritically replicate the very language of corruption that was used to contain and condemn the sociopolitical turbulence of the great cities, Jahn by talking about "London's emerging swamp" (372), Marshall by accusing critics of buying into Baudelaire's "high modernism" and not looking at cities as "places of terror, anxiety, and deprivation" (29). More to the point is Pritchard's analysis of Dickens's Gothic city, which "in its infinite complexity and mystery, becomes the ultimate indecipherable text."[14] In this respect, Dickens's London bears striking similarities to Baudelaire's Paris.

Yet if we follow the trajectory of infectious degeneracy spreading from Tom-all-Alone's, we can see that *Bleak House* is not immune to replicating the evolutionary determinism and unredemptive fanatic Christianity that its author sets out to repudiate. Dickens's project about the nature of woman is enormously seductive: he makes a case for the possibility of inner goodness triumphing over heredity in his heroine and part-time narrator, Esther Summerson. Yet despite Esther's unimpeachable qualities Dickens must redeem her from the pollution of her birth by requiring that her sexual attractiveness be cleansed by slum-borne infection. Significantly, the illness comes upon Esther via orphans and marginals (Jenny, Charley), doublings of her own self but for Jarndyce's intervention. Of these the most peripatetic and pathetic, as well as pathological, is Jo, the utterly abandoned child, who unwittingly becomes a scourge to the very culture that has bred him — to the Dedlock aristocracy, to the pinnacle of law represented by Tulkinghorn, and even to Esther, whose fault of birth, Dickens insists, is not her fault, but which is punished nonetheless. Through her disfiguration, Esther is wrenched from genetic duplication of her sinful mother, whose face she no longer mirrors and thus whose fate — her empty life, her rapid decline and deterioration into the very mud of the paupers' graveyard — she is no longer in danger of sharing.

Infection in the world of *Bleak House* and in the Victorian imagination functions along symbolic rather than etiologic lines. Jo carries the smallpox, a disease standing for venereal contagion since the Renaissance. He transmits it to the prepubescent Charley, who recovers unscathed, and to Esther, whose sexual desirability has to be marred by it so that her moral nature can be the single inspiration to love. When Jo is rediscovered in Tom-all-Alone's, he is dying of pneumonia or tuberculosis, both highly infectious and generally lethal diseases. Yet neither disfigures; since their contagious potential serves no symbolic purpose, Dickens has Woodcourt declare them non-infectious.

Dickens's replication of contagious degeneracy does not stop with a plot that requires extirpation of potential sin from Esther's features. Several villains of *Bleak House* exhibit anticipations of the theory of recapitulation. This concept holds that "the *adults* of *inferior* groups must be like *children* of *superior* groups, for the child represents a primitive adult ancestor" (Gould, 115). The whole Smallweed family has inscribed on it inferiority of intellect, imagination, and physique. They are described in terms of a perverted childhood that denotes imbecility and primitivism: "There has been only one child in the Smallweed family for several generations. Little old men and women there have been, but no child, until Mr. Smallweed's grandmother, now living, became weak in her intellect, and fell (for the first time) into a childish state" (257). The entire family appears as an evolutionary throwback: "Hence the gratifying fact, that it has no child born to it, and that the complete little men and women whom it has produced, have been observed to bear a likeness to old monkeys with something depressing on their minds" (258). The heavy-handed irony Dickens directs at the Smallweeds, in conjunction with his hatred of men whose living comes from the "God of Compound Interest," foreshadows late-century anti-Semitism, in which the Jews appear as evolutionary throwbacks whose emotional life centered on their worship of the same "God."

The apex of the rogues' gallery is Krook, whose pack-rat habits lead to the undoing of the Dedlocks as well as of Richard's hopes, and who perishes from an internal transmutation from organism to inorganic fuel, Dickens's most dramatic but not unique devolutionary reversal of life into matter. The fallen woman fares no better. In her quest for her mother, Esther comes upon a body amid a slush and thaw that dissolve boundaries between solidity and liquids: "On the step of the gate, drenched in the fearful wet of such a place, which oozed and splashed down everywhere, I saw . . . a woman lying" (713). Just as matter itself hovers between states, so identity founders, and the corpse, mistaken for a poor woman's, turns out to be Lady Dedlock.

The hallucinatory scenes — of orphans (Jo, Phil, Guster), of poor and fallen women, of villains mirroring one another, of Krook's nauseating conflagration — all take place in London. Distance from London signifies removal, though it does not guarantee safety, from contagion; Bleak House stands as counterpoint to Tom-all-Alone's, recuperative benevolence versus malign neglect. Thus, the new Bleak House, its inhabitants, and its familiars are situated "down into Yorkshire," "in the country," away from the irredeemable city.

For Baudelaire, as for his contemporaries, Paris in the throes of urban renewal becomes the site of collapsing boundaries between classes, races, the "public" and "honest" woman. Odd as it may seem given Baudelaire's self-conscious "decadence" and Dickens's reformist stance, both create the imagery of corrupt liquefaction to describe the fallen woman and the marginal poor, and in Baudelaire the colonial as well. In *Les fleurs du mal* (1857) (Flowers of Evil), however, Baudelaire presents a narrator (and a male audience) complicit with woman's sin, so that desire itself becomes an agent of contamination. Woman's unreliability finds its parallel in the upheaval undergone by Paris at the time when Baudelaire was writing the volume.

In the cycle of the Vénus Noire, inspired by the colonial Jeanne Duval, woman is a repository of parts, an uncontrollable city, and a decomposing corpse. As the exoticism of "La chevelure" (The Mane) gives way to XXIV, the next poem in the sequence, the narrator who made use of the woman's hair to be transported to the outposts of empire now addresses the woman as "bête implacable et cruelle" (implacable and cruel beast).[15] The following poem creates the most telling conjunction of the woman's body and the city; it begins with a triple pun on "ruelle," which in this context can mean the bedside — the space between a bed and the wall — a narrow city street, and the vagina: "Tu mettrais l'univers entier dans ta ruelle,/Femme impure!" (You'd take into your alley the whole world, tainted woman) (ll. 1–2). Thus woman erases the chasm between the intimate home and the public street. The multiplicity of her betrayals parallels the indiscriminate nature of city amusement; like the "public" city the woman is an engine that indiscriminately destroys by its indifference, and especially destroys genius. As such, the woman is a "machine aveugle et sourde" (blind and deaf engine) (l. 9), an instrument in Nature's hands, and a "fangeuse grandeur" (slimy greatness), an oxymoron that combines the speaker's thrall to the woman's beauty with his recoil from her inferiority.

The most ferocious attack on woman's sexuality as a source of corruption occurs in "Une Charogne" (Carrion) where the corpse displays itself in the manner of a sexual invitation, "Les jambes dans l'air, comme une femme lubrique" (legs in the air like a woman in heat) (l. 5), the better to show the putrefaction that consumes the body, transforming it from solid to metaphoric liquid — larvae that flow "comme un épais liquide" (like viscous liquid) (l. 19) — to gaseous matter — "le corps, enflé d'un souffle vague" (the body, swollen by undulating gas) (l. 23). The corpse presents a hallucinatory self-multiplication that prophesies the beloved's fate, the perverted reproduction as "horrible infection" instead of progeny.

Two poems of *Tableaux parisiens* (Parisian Scenes) best capture the sense of displacement and uncertainty that makes Paris a counterpart of females and marginals let loose by the breakdown of a city that had kept vestiges of feudal order. In "Le Cygne" (The Swan) the poet himself begins in the traditional role of woman, his imagination fertilized by something which is already a simulacrum, "Ce Simoïs menteur" (This lying Simoïs). The masculine "vieux Paris" [*masc.* old], like the world mourned by the captive Andromache is no longer, in its stead the fickle feminine "ville" [*fem.* city] that changes its shape faster than the span of a man's faithfulness, "que le coeur d'un mortel" (than man's heart) (l. 8). The poem builds on a superimposition of phantasmagoria of the poet's remembrance onto the present order, already itself disrupted by memories of the disorder that wrecked neighborhoods prior to urban renewal. The fake Simoïs implicitly floods its borders, blurring boundaries that are further breached by the swan's escape from its cage, by the poet's hallucinatory bric-à-brac of memories — "palais neufs, échafaudages, blocs,/Vieux faubourgs" (new palaces, scaffolds, buildings,/Old quarters) (ll. 30–31) — upon which he attempts to impose allegorical order, only to seek for it in the same obsessive and vain way as the swan looking for water and the "négresse, amaigrie et phtisique,/Piétinant dans la boue, et cherchant, l'oeil hagard,/Les cocotiers absents de la superbe Afrique/Derrière la muraille immense du brouillard" (the Negress, emaciated, tubercular,/Trotting in the mud, seeking with haggard eyes/The absent palm trees of proud Africa) (ll. 40–44); his search, too, trails into the non-finito of the dispossessed, "Aux captifs, aux vaincus! . . . à bien d'autres encor!" (the prisoners, the defeated . . . many others, too) (l. 52). Both the swan and the "négresse" suffer the ills of urban culture, amid which they degenerate into insanity and disease, as does the narrator in the poem following.[16]

The city as site of degeneration and disorder appears even more obsessively in "Les sept vieillards" (The Seven Oldsters) where the poet falls prey to the nightmare of an uncontrollable, perverse multiplication of the very dregs of urban culture. The "fourmillante cité" (teeming city), disquieting in its multitudes and subsisting on the inexplicable, furnishes the poet with an image of decadence that haunted European culture to the brink of the Final Solution, namely, the threatening, unnatural reproduction of loathsome Jewry. The notes to the Pléiade edition obscure the racialist nature of the hallucination in "Les sept vieillards" by identifying "juif à trois pattes" (three-legged — as in animal vs. human — Jew) as the Wandering Jew of biblical myth. Yet the imagery of the poem belies literary distancing in favor of the terror of contagious degeneration that Baudelaire frequently refigures in his text. Like Dickens's London in the opening of *Bleak House*, Baudelaire's Paris hides its "mystères" behind "un brouillard sale et jaune" (a dirty yellow fog) (l. 9). Out of this obscurity arises the specter of the degenerate old man, who replicates on his own body the stigmata of large-city pollution: "un vieillard dont les guenilles jaunes / Imitaient la couleur de ce ciel pluvieux" (an oldster whose yellowed ankles / Mimicked the color of the rainy sky) (ll. 13–14). His nature reveals itself in his evil, poisonous eye and in his beard, which sticks out like Judas's; with this analogy Baudelaire invokes the epitome of malignant betrayal. The old man's body, broken at unnatural angles, is no less repulsive than his mind, and the narrator fashions a link between the old man's gait and his alliance with maleficent powers, as well as with subhuman manifestations and the liquefaction of urban mire.

As if this specter is not enough, the speaker, like Dickens's narrator giving the genealogy of the Smallweeds, hallucinates a succession of seven clones of the same old man: "je comptai sept fois, de minute en minute, / Ce sinistre vieillard qui se multipliait!" (I counted seven times, minute by minute, / This sinister old man who replicated himself) (ll. 35–36). Only his flight saves him from seeing perhaps eight or more replicas of monstrous birth — "Dégoûtant Phénix, fils et père de lui-même" (disgusting Phoenix, of self both son and father) (l. 43). Yet even behind locked doors the speaker is haunted to madness by the vision of the bestial Jew replicating himself infinitely in the heart of civilization. As the poem concludes, the speaker loses all sense of boundaries and floats "sur une mer monstrueuse et sans bords" (on a monstrous, shoreless sea) (l. 52).

More useful than to accuse Baudelaire of misogyny and anti-Semitism is to note that his literary imagination is fed by and in turn feeds a culture seeking for markers of hereditary inferiority and haunted by the fear of contagion from those forcibly brought into and kept within the great cities — loose women, mendicants, colonials, Jews, the urban poor.[17] Neither genre nor literary allegiances nor political alliances suffice to protect an author from the power of the dominant discourse of his / her time and to prompt a consistent resistance to reproducing chief elements of the same discourse. The naturalist Zola, like the aesthete Baudelaire, gives us in his *Nana* a summation of the discourse of contagious degeneracy as it flourished in the latter decades of the nineteenth century. Whereas the mid-century writers had the luxury of composing within a "scientific" discourse still in flux, by 1878 when Zola begins *Nana*, concepts of tainted heredity and its dangers to civilization have already become hardened in the popular imagination. Ironically, the man instrumental in opening the Dreyfus case — in which "natural" loyalty to nation is the chief issue — to public scrutiny nonetheless places himself at the center of the "science" of heredity. Zola's elaborate genealogies for the Rougons-Macquart series, his firm belief in "facts" whose accuracy has long since been dispelled led him to create texts whose fictionality is more glaring today than the artifices of Gothic or supernatural novels.[18]

In *Nana* contagion and its risk to civilization appear in the person of Nana as the revenge of the lower classes on their oppressors. Like Dickens, Zola writes a highly symbolic passage whose purpose is to disclose the meaning of the text. It appears in the description of a wedding reception at the house of Nana's principal keeper: "La fêlure [de la maison Muffat] augmentait; elle lézardait la maison, elle annonçait l'effondrement prochain" (The crack grew larger, foundering the House of Muffat, proclaiming its imminent ruin).[19] Zola juxtaposes the "familles gâtées" (ruined progeniture) of the poor, which result from hunger, misery, and alcoholism, to the crumbling of the "vieille race" (old line) of the Muffats done in by their own craving for Nana. By invoking the very people who are Nana's antecedents — the drunkards among the poor — at the ball that signals the destruction of the upper class, Zola hammers home the point that Nana, having obtained the status of depraved deity, serves unwittingly as the scourge of the urban underclass to their oppressors.

As with *Bleak House*, however, the text of *Nana* escapes the didactic control of its creator and presents improbabilities, as well as an ambiguous and inconsistent view of Nana and the world she destroys. Zola describes Nana in terms as loaded with opprobrium as Dickens's description of the Smallweeds; she is fat, stupid, lazy, destructive, lustful, incapable of maternal affection or any moral feeling. At the same time, in her calm moments she is a wise counselor to her lovers, loyal to her origins and unashamed of them, disinterested about money, uncannily shrewd about exacerbating desire in the men who court her, and she obsessively keeps returning to her degenerate little boy, from whom she catches the chicken pox that kills her. Through these contradictions, Nana does take on the role of deity — the "blond Venus" containing within her the caprices, power, and opposites of the goddess. Her sexuality becomes an unleashed force that sweeps the city of Paris.[20]

In relation to Nana's victims, Zola's text exhibits similar ambiguities. On the one hand, Nana's lovers are seen as debased by their thrall; on the other, they are treated with a certain ironic compassion as men who sacrifice everything to the "grande passion" inspired by Nana's sexuality. The poor from whom Nana derives are shown as corrupt and indeed degenerate. The upper-class men have the saving grace of a self-consciousness about sinking into depravity that lifts them above the stupefying narcissism of Nana.

In *Nana* Zola allies himself to the nascent "science" of human sexuality and to the incipient psychological discourse that regards woman's physiology and mentality as deviant. Both the eponymous heroine and the Countess Sabine exhibit the sign of perverted sexuality, as did Augier's Olympe, and this birthmark announces to the man intent on seducing the countess that, although "cette femme ne couchait avec personne" (this woman slept with no one) she may succumb to him, as she indeed does (85).[21] The promiscuous woman is fated to produce degenerate offspring or be sterile, and in Nana's illegitimate son we see the marks of degeneration that so frightened and continue to frighten biological determinists: "le petit Louis et ses plaintes tristes d'enfant rongé de mal, quelque pourriture léguée par un père inconnu" (little Louis and his sad ailments of a child eaten by illness, a rot passed on by an unknown father) (436). But despite being promised throughout the text a Nana as a successful weapon of class warfare, who like a weapon remains unchanged by her uses — "Nana . . . restait victorieuse avec sa chair de marbre, son sexe assez fort pour détruire tout ce monde et *n'en être pas entâmé*" (remained triumphant in her marble flesh, in a sexuality strong enough to destroy this world and *not be tainted*) (49; emphasis mine) — what we see vividly is not so much the old order crumbling from Nana's infectious degeneracy as her dissolution into the liquidity of disease.

Ironically, the maternal sentiment, whose absence Zola mocks throughout the text, is the instrument of Nana's death. Punning on "la petite vérole" as both venereal disease and the pox, Zola has Nana catch the infection from her offspring and liquefy before our eyes: "Les pustules avaient envahi la figure entière . . . d'un aspect grisâtre de boue, elles semblaient déjà une moisissure de la terre, sur cette bouillie informe, où l'on ne retrouvait plus les traits" (The pustules had covered her whole face ... gray-looking like mud, they seemed already to be a mildew growing on this mess of porridge whose features could no longer be discerned) (474). Thus Nana, like Baudelaire's Vénus Noire, like the denatured mother of *Bleak House*, succumbs to the dissolution into amorphous slime suggesting a failed evolution.

The very existence of Nana as a genealogical being depends upon the excesses and the blurred boundaries allowed in the great city. In the country episode of *Nana,* Nana's would-be upper-class lovers refrain from saluting the kept women who are being entertained by Nana as the two groups encounter each other on the road. The identity of the women keeps them apart from the rural society of all classes. The city, by contrast, is the site where the women of easy virtue are elevated to spectacle, launched into public circulation, and allowed the scope to contaminate middle- and upper-class families. Nowhere is the breakdown of boundaries more apparent than in the scene at the races, where initially the seating arrangements keep the prostitutes on the margins, away from the court and the women of rank and virtue. Yet at the climax of the scene, taken with the performance of the filly named for Nana, the whole multitude, including kept women and the empress, is united in the cry, "Vive Nana!" (379) and in the confusion between acclaim for the winning filly and the glorious prostitute: "l'on ne savait plus si c'était la bête ou la femme qui emplissait les coeurs" (they no longer knew if the beast or the woman filled their hearts) (381). Zola's language implies the lack of distinction between the two, and he creates an undifferentiating crowd that only Paris and its amusements make possible.

I have focused here on the large city as site of contagious degeneracy, but degeneracy itself became so firmly entrenched even in the face of contrary scientific evidence because it was — and is — so amorphous and convenient a catch-all for sociopolitical and economic anxieties. As we approach another fin de siècle, how far have we traveled from the nexus of hereditary determinism, contagious degeneracy, fear of civilization's degeneration, and hostility to the anonymity and unenforceable boundaries of great cities that allow for disguised races, genders, classes? What of our own anxieties and their intersection with scientific truth?

We live in an era of permeable national borders and new sites of disguised identities, such as cyberspace. Perhaps as a response, our science is invested in convincing us of the uniformity of all bodies as texts to be "read" not only for past and present pathology but genetic fate. Meanwhile, the discourse of difference that began in the humanities and social sciences as a long-due and legitimate interrogation of universality or nationality as constituted by the white, middle-class, heterosexual, Christian Euro-male has now become a reflex, a point of reference in a closed system of academic jargon with rare translation to social practice. We have fragmented individual experience to the point where each utterance is subject to critique as uniquely located and incommensurable with any other. Thus, while "difference" prevents us from creating the solidarities that might best oppose repressive policies, it has yet to be deployed as a critique of the uses of scientific technologies to construct universal models of bodies and to predict human fates but not to ameliorate the conditions of those bodies and fates. As we look back at contagious degeneracy and its insidious uses through two centuries, should we not force ourselves to wonder about the legacy of science and letters we intellectuals in the last decade of *this* century are passing on to the next?

Wayne State University

Notes

[1] Stephen Jay Gould, *The Mismeasure of Man* (New York: Norton, 1981), 22. All further references are to this text.

[2] Zeev Sternhell, *The Birth of Fascist Ideology: From Cultural Rebellion to Political Revolution*, trans. David Maisel (Princeton: Princeton UP, 1994), 3–5, 9.

[3] Daniel Pick, *Faces of Degeneration: A European Disorder, c. 1848-c.1918* (Cambridge, England: Cambridge UP, 1989), 2–3.

[4] Alan M. Kraut, *Silent Travelers: Germs, Genes, and the "Immigrant Menace"* (New York: Basic Books, 1994).

[5] Robert Proctor, *Racial Hygiene: Medicine Under the Nazis* (Cambridge, MA: Harvard UP, 1988), 3; Maurice Olender, *The Languages of Paradise: Race, Religion, and Philology in the Nineteenth Century*, trans. Arthur Goldhammer (Cambridge, MA: Harvard UP, 1992), 7–13.

[6] Elaine Showalter, *The Female Malady: Women, Madness, and English Culture, 1830–1980* (New York and London: Penguin, 1985); Sander Gilman, *Difference and Pathology: Stereotypes of Sexuality, Race, and Madness* (Ithaca: Cornell UP, 1985); further references are to this text; Thomas Laqueur, *Making Sex: Body and Gender from the Greeks to Freud* (Cambridge, MA: Harvard UP, 1990).

[7] Ornella Moscucci, "Hermaphroditism and Sex Difference: The Construction of Gender in Victorian England," *Science and Sensibility: Gender and Scientific Enquiry, 1780–1945*, ed. Marina Benjamin (Oxford: Basil Blackwell, 1991), 174–195; quotation 174.

[8] William Greenslade, *Degeneration, Culture, and the Novel 1880–1940* (New York: Cambridge UP, 1994), 16–17.

[9] Lucia Zedner, *Women, Crime, and Custody in Victorian England* (Oxford: Oxford UP, 1991), 13.

[10] Cesare Lombroso, *L'Homme criminel* (Paris: F. Alcan, 1887); Max Nordau, *Degeneration* (1892), quoted in Pick.

[11] Emile Augier, *Le mariage d'Olympe*, and Dumas (fils), Alexandre, *La Dame aux camélias*, in *Nineteenth Century French Plays*, ed. Joseph L. Borgerhoff (New York: Appleton-Century- Croft, 1959). All French translations are mine; page references follow in parentheses.

[12] Charles Dickens, *Bleak House*, ed. George Ford and Sylvère Monod (New York: Norton, 1977), 553. All further references are to this edition.

[13] Brenda Marshall, "Dickens and Another Modernity: The Eruption of the Real," *Literature and Psychology* 37.4 (1991): 29–46; Karen Jahn, "Fit to Survive: Christian Ethics in *Bleak House*," *Studies in the Novel* 18 (1986): 367–80.

[14] Allan Pritchard, "The Urban Gothic of *Bleak House*," *Nineteenth-Century Literature* 45 (Mar. 1991): 432–52.

[15] Charles Baudelaire, *Oeuvres complètes*, ed. Claude Pichois, 2 vols, (Paris: Gallimard, 1975), vol.1; ll. 7–9. Parenthetical references in text are to line numbers.

[16] In *The Symbolic Method of Coleridge, Baudelaire, and Yeats* (Detroit: Wayne State UP, 1983), I argued for a single, continuous poetic voice in *Les fleurs du mal*.

[17] Constrictions of space do not allow me to examine Baudelaire's attempt in *Spleen de Paris* to represent the terrifying return of the gaze on the part of the poor.

[18] A number of fin-de-siècle writers who put stock in science created texts that now require the audience's willing suspension of knowledge; see Ibsen's *Ghosts*, Strindberg's *Miss Julie*, Shaw's *Man and Superman*, Yeats's notions of proletarian degeneracy and its contagious influence on culture.

[19] Émile Zola, *Nana*, ed. Henri Mitterand (Paris: Gallimard, 1977). All further references are to this edition.

[20] Peter Brooks, "Storied Bodies, Or Nana at Last Unveil'd," *Critical Inquiry* 16 (1989): 1–32.

[21] Naomi Schor, in *Zola's Crowds* (Baltimore: Johns Hopkins UP, 1978), discusses the "interpenetration of home and brothel" in *L'éducation sentimentale* and in Zola's description of Countess Sabine's birthmark.

ROSS SHIDELER

Hardy, Darwin, *Tess* and the Father's Changing Name

At first glance, the novels of Thomas Hardy may seem like the antitheses of what Ralph Freedman called "the lyrical" novel. Yet Freedman himself mentions Hardy's *Jude the Obscure* as connected to the lyrical prose tradition he defines,[1] and readers tend to respond to both the lyricism of Hardy's imagery and the prose of his plots. For Freedman, one criterion of the traditional novel is "objectivity," usually depicted by a distance between the author and/or narrator and the main character, whereas in a lyrical novel the closeness of the narrator and main character often results in a sense of subjectivity that blends time and space and blurs temporal or spatial differentiation (1–2, 16, 31).

Thomas Hardy succeeds at times in approaching a lyricism that one might expect to find in the writing of more poetic authors. This paper connects with a European literary tradition more related to Émile Zola's Naturalism and Henrik Ibsen's portrayals of the bourgeois family in crisis than to Virginia Woolf's lyrical prose. But in looking back at Freedman's classic text, I find that it adds a new depth to my own current reading of Hardy's *Tess of the d'Urbervilles*.[2] This paper, therefore, utilizes a Darwinian and family theory context to discuss Hardy's depiction of the breakdown of the patriarchal family structure in England. Yet even as Hardy seems to be closer to Zola's novels than to Rilke's *The Notebooks of Malte Laurids Brigge* or Virginia Woolf's novels, characteristics of what Freedman identifies in those works appear in some of Hardy's novels including *Tess*.

Freedman argues that "In the lyrical novel, narrator and protagonist combine to create a self in which experience is fashioned as imagery"(31). One has the sense that Hardy and his protagonist, Tess, come together in particular images that define her life. One may also look at Tess in light of Freedman's version of "a hero's allegorical quest" (31) in which a protagonist's "inner condition" appears in a specific object or situation. As we shall see, Tess's journey through life with all of its symbolic encounters takes on a different and perhaps slightly more positive resolution if we read it from Freedman's perspective.

Therefore, though the following pages present a reading that focuses on "the Name-of-the-Father" within a Darwinian, Lacanian and feminist context, part of it relates to Freedman's work. Tess is to a degree a passive protagonist, as Freedman implies about Jude, but more importantly her experiences are shaped as much by the authority instilled in the name and image of the husband and father as by the causal events of the novel. When the novel reaches its most powerful moments, usually in particularly symbolic scenes, one senses a closeness of the narrator with his protagonist.

Darwin and the Degenerating Family

To begin a discussion of Hardy's portrait of the degeneration of what we now call "family values," one should note that Henrik Ibsen had awakened all of Europe to the crises and conflicts of the middle-class family with his social dramas. The Swedish playwright and novelist August Strindberg continued Ibsen's theme, but dramatized an angry resistance to the displacement of the father and the disintegration of the family which Ibsen had portrayed in works like *A Doll House* and *Ghosts*. In both *Tess* and *Jude the Obscure*, Hardy depicts families living in a deterministic Darwinian world and trapped in deadly if silken webs of Christian ideals and patriarchal traditions. My own use of Darwin somewhat relates to Gillian Beer's work[3] and implicitly contains two fundamental elements. The first is the displacement, or at least the subtle dispersion, of the divine father, since Darwin could not put his theory into place without challenging the notion of a divine creator and creation. Second, Darwin's theory of evolution by natural selection resulted in what can be called a biocentric vision of life, a new emphasis upon life in and of itself rather than in the context of some divine or universal scheme.

As a number of critics have established, Hardy was much influenced by Darwinism in various forms,[4] and Hardy's attendance at Darwin's funeral in 1882 substantiates his admiration for that reluctant revolutionary (Rutland, 54). In terms of the general historical context, Herbert Spencer influenced the young Hardy (Rutland, 20), and the Darwinian psychologist Henry Maudsley — discussed by Elaine Showalter[5] and Cynthia Eagle Russett[6] — played a role in shaping Hardy's thought. In *Darwin's Plots* Gillian Beer has suggested some original premises of what one might call a Darwinian textuality in Thomas Hardy's writing, and George Levine has discussed him in this context as well.[7] Hardy's immersion in the social and cultural debate pertaining to the discussion of evolution also appears in his *Literary Notebooks*.[8]

My argument focuses on *Tess* and Hardy's unique meld of Darwinism, women grasping for control of their lives, and a crisis of religious and patriarchal authority in the family — thematic elements previously seen on the European continent in authors like Ibsen and Strindberg but still shocking to nineteenth-century readers.

Many of Hardy's novels bring together protagonists in a world in which religious and moral structures fragment and rip apart the characters themselves. (There are, of course, moralizing figures aplenty, but they often play ambivalent or negative roles — Angel and his family in *Tess*, for instance.) Similarly, Hardy often presents the struggle between a woman trying to be "strong" and one or several profoundly flawed men. These conflicts result in disruptive, broken families, limited by predetermined notions of masculinity and femininity; the competition within these families reveals an evolving vision of a biocentered world — a world in which life itself is seen as the central fact of being — in which, for instance, female characters are given a sexual identity (Morgan, x; Boumelha, 129; Cunningham, 96–104).[9] Hardy pulls together themes and images that appeared throughout European literature, and he blends them into a powerful if profoundly sad picture of a tremulous patriarchy struggling to impose its weakening paradigm onto European and American societies in transition. As Margaret Higonnet puts it, "he complicates our understanding of a narrative authority that rests on unified social discourse."[10] Part of my own argument is that late nineteenth-century European "unified social discourse" rested on loosely defined, but nevertheless somewhat consistent patriarchal structures.

These structures undergo a closer and darker analysis as Hardy's novels progress. Perhaps the bleakness of his last two novels derives to some extent from the seemingly inevitable ruination and destruction of their major characters, characters who try to live up to the Victorian moral standards of home and family, yet who are defeated nonetheless.[11] Tess and Angel reflect, unfortunately, the emotional turmoil and complicated moral dilemma which may arise when a moral standard, supposedly rooted in a Christian patriarchal tradition, makes no sense for the lives of those who find themselves trapped in it. Without denying *Tess*'s ambiguity about women and their roles, one can still read it as a story about the Christian patriarchy's ruin and execution of a healthy, sexually attractive and innocent young woman; the subtitle "A Pure Woman Faithfully Presented by Thomas Hardy" certainly supports the premise of Tess's unjustified downfall.

Similar themes were common during the 1880s and 90s. Ibsen wrote *Hedda Gabler* in 1890, while Hardy published *Tess* in 1891. Strindberg wrote *The Father* and *Miss Julie* in 1887 and 1888. Hardy's skeptical vision with its implicit criticism of Christian morality tends to be closer to Ibsen's. This contrast with contemporary Christianity explains in part why Victorian critics so roundly attacked Hardy, for although Victorian society may have accepted in a limited fashion Darwin's theories, it was not about to give up the Christian morality that characterized the century.[12] *Tess* and *Jude* both reflect Hardy's deep-seated evolutionary and biocentric vision and his critique of Christian dogma.[13] That *Tess* was attacked by critics for its immorality and its unchristian vision is not surprising; that Hardy's dark vision may be related to his own marriage seems even less so.

Tess and *Jude* were both written at a time in Hardy's life when the very premises of the family were troubling to him. Frustrated with his wife Emma and tempted both by the cultural life of London and by some of the intelligent women there, he must have felt severely restricted if not imprisoned by his marriage.[14] Additionally, Hardy must have been ambivalent about the genteel country life, which to many people he seemed to personify, and which in terms of its quiet solitude allowed him to write his novels. Both *Tess* and *Jude* reveal a certain hostility toward provincial life and a longing for some satisfying intellectual and physical relationship. In this context, Tess's unhappy experiences of home and family, and her desire for love, however elusive, seem to parallel Hardy's personal and philosophical position. Since Hardy thought of his own family history in terms of its decline, the tale's emotional connection to Hardy's life seems more than plausible (Millgate, 294).

Tess of the d'Urbervilles contains two stories crucial to this paper: the first is the story of the patriarchal family's continued degeneration, and the second is the search for the originary family: those nearly-forgotten (fore)fathers whose traces fill the countryside only to reinforce the absence of that original father/family. The undermining of the patriarchal family occurs at the lower-class level of Tess's drunken father, Jack Durbeyfield, and the impoverished family he leaves behind, as well as at the merchant-class level of the misnamed d'Urbervilles. Perhaps appropriately, the Stoke-d'Urberville family no longer has the father who appropriated its noble name, but only a blind mother and a lecherous son.

Tess: A Father by any other Name is still an Absent Father

Jack (John) Durbeyfield's initial discovery of his noble heritage gives him a sense of origin which Michel Foucault might describe as "a profound historicity [that] penetrates into the heart of things."[15] The revelation of Jack's unknown history starts the wheels of the Durbeyfield family's fate into motion. The confusing and ultimately misplaced sense of origin, ironically provided by a country parson — yet another representative of the divine father and his name — raises Jack's estimation of himself and precipitates Tess's destruction. Michael Ragussis has shrewdly discussed the significance of "naming" in *Tess* and shown how Tess's "body becomes the crucial tool by which she is subjugated because it is a body in the service of a name, the family name."[16] But Tess's subjugation results in one sense from the family's belief in the bastardization of their original name.

"Durbeyfield" for them becomes the trace of their noble forefathers, the proof of their relation to this absent presence in their lives, and of the nobility which the Durbeyfields could in theory regain. All the members of the family except Tess believe that the d'Urberville name has the potential to reinstate them in an almost Edenic world. Only Tess, who is sent off to find what real social or economic value the father's ancient name might have, is reluctant to accept its significance. Yet, as Ragussis demonstrates, either Durbeyfield or d'Urberville can be used against her (147). The displaced name of the fallen Father in this case becomes a more complex taking and rejecting of the name than even Ibsen's Nora Helmer, as she forged her dead father's name, could have imagined. Tess, born with the supposedly bastardized name of her father, is sent out to reclaim the father's name she never had, and this is the beginning of what one might call her "allegorical quest."

In this sense the family name becomes an image, such as the Christian crusader's silver chalice, and that image permeates the novel and produces some of its most powerful and symbolic scenes. At a Freudian level, however, the father's name has powerful connotations. Although my analysis has a historical bias that tends to reject a traditional Freudian position, Jacques Lacan's phrase "nom-de-père" offers a useful perspective.[17] Lacan has created the notion of the Name-of-the-Father to expand upon Freud's Oedipal complex and to identify the linguistic nature of the complex. For Lacan the Name-of-the-Father is associated with the symbolic father, with law:

> [Freud's] reflexion led him to link the appearance of the signifier of the Father, as the author of the Law, to death, even to the murder of the Father, thus showing that although this murder is the fruitful moment of the debt through which the subject binds himself for life to the Law, *the symbolic Father*, in so far as he signifies this Law, *is certainly the dead Father*. (*Écrits*, 199; my italics)

The connection drawn by Lacan corresponds with my own perception of the father's name as a post-Darwinian sign of the dead (F)ather. Although the Freudian connotations inescapably remain associated with the Name-of-the-Father, I use the phrase to emphasize the relation between God the Father, the Word (of) God, fathers, and words, i.e., language itself. Apart from its Lacanian and Oedipal associations, the phrase may also be connected with the Christian and patriarchal systems that have shaped virtually every aspect of Western culture.

As Ragussis has pointed out, although he gives it no Lacanian framework, the father's name, in various configurations, serves as a structural device in *Tess*. But, as one could anticipate in this post-Darwinian context, the actual father, Jack Durbeyfield, plays only a limited and pathetic role. The father's *name* rather than his person continually connects with authority, with identity, personal and familial. The name of the d'Urbervilles, however, has been located in an imaginary or mythologized history; thus, even as the opening plot historicizes the Durbeyfield family, it places it within a patriarchal tradition that posits an ideal family history.

In other words, while the weak and alcoholic Jack figures the Durbeyfield family, the degenerate Durbeyfield family in turn supposedly represents the now extinct d'Urbervilles, a once noble and wealthy family fallen from grace. In this case, using a limited version of Lacan's "Name-of-the-Father," Jack Durbeyfield symbolizes not only the dead d'Urbervilles (who seem to represent an almost divine governing authority), but the decay of the family and of the religious patriarchy upon which it was based. Perhaps Hardy echoes or parodies here a Darwinian universe with the entombed figures of the d'Urbervilles serving as fossils of an extinct species. The Durbeyfields then become some distant cousin that has evolved in a fashion the original family would have found disgusting.[18]

It is Hardy's genius that the duality of names is used throughout the novel to invoke simultaneously the authority of the past and the death of the originary authority. Tess's enforced search to find and then to escape the destiny of the Durbeyfield-d'Urberville family mirrors humanity's search for an always absent patriarchal authority to rescue it from this blighted world. The family itself, then, or theories of what it is and how it should function, contribute substantially to the naming structure discussed by Ragussis.

Tess plays both an abnormal and a central role in the families which structure the novel; initially, she functions at times as both father and mother in her Durbeyfield family, but as the novel progresses she becomes ensnared in the confusing and conflicting values of the false aristocratic Stoke-d'Urberville family and the seemingly dogmatic Christian patriarchalism of the Clare family. Yet in spite of her struggle to define and create an identity that she and they will accept, Tess is not really a New Woman figure in the sense of the literary movement of the 1890s. Nevertheless, like Ibsen's and Strindberg's women, she embodies many of the characteristics associated with the type. Gail Cunningham draws the parallel between Tess and Zola's and Ibsen's women:

> *Tess of the d'Urbervilles* appeared to its first readers as not only the most strongly argued of Hardy's novels, but also the most outspoken in its treatment of sexuality. It came to a public already jittery about the undermining of morals by French and Norwegian writers, but one not yet familiar with the ways in which this license could be harnessed to the feminist bandwagon. Tess is not a New Woman, but the novel which is built around her embodies essential features of the New Woman fiction which followed it — disrespect for polite reticence about sex, combined with the presentation of a case in favour of some aspect of woman's emancipation. In calling Tess a "pure woman" Hardy was aggressively advertising his polemical intention; . . .[19]

Hardy demonstrates Tess's purity and independence in the novel's earliest family scenes. When Tess comes to get her parents from Rolliver's Inn (17), both parents accept her authority and seem to recognize their own deficiencies;

her mother, Joan Durbeyfield, is described as a child herself (26), and her father is the comically pathetic and alcoholic "Sir John."

Before dawn the next day, Jack Durbeyfield's drunkenness leads to Tess's dark journey and the death of the family horse, Prince (another brilliant name by Hardy, for instead of a Prince coming to save Tess, one dies). Prince's death in turn forces Tess to travel to the The Chase in pursuit of "family" connections. The dual claims of her obligation to support her family and to seek out "kinship" lead to Tess's rape by Alec d'Urberville at The Chase, and, of course, to her return home once she is, to use the appropriate cliché, "in the family way."

The rest of the novel explores the theory and nature of the family: it progresses from Tess's broken-down Durbeyfield family to the exploitative and misleadingly-named Alec Stoke-d'Urberville, and, finally, to the religious Clare family and Angel's — and Tess's — own visions of what a wife is supposed to be. Although Hardy's view of women, like Darwin's, cannot escape a Victorian male perspective, in his last two novels Hardy confronts the theory and the reality of the rural nineteenth-century family.[20] All the families and family structures that Hardy examines suffer from a crisis of authority, from profound flaws in the earthly and the divine patriarchy. The lack of a divine father, the belief that such an originary patriarch and his family once existed, and the inability of any of the earthly husbands and fathers to fill that absence, create the conflicts that define both *Tess* and *Jude*.

In *Tess*, her father's incapacity, caused by his drunkenness the night before, precipitates Tess's journey. When Tess and her brother Abraham ride in the rickety wagon on their predawn trip to deliver the beehives, Abraham raises the issue of God's presence on the other side of the stars. Tess's by now famous statement that they live on a blighted world (21) reinforces the Darwinian nature of their world. But it also admits the lack of an organizing principle, a divine father who might save the family and Tess from their fates.

Thus, the plot of *Tess* hinges on the triangular intersection of the absence or questioning of a divine father, the weakness of a family father, and the rise, and in this case the fall, of a strong woman. Tess's strength of character is emphasized from the beginning of the novel. Gail Cunningham refers to both her uniqueness and her strength when she meets Alec:

> Tess herself is unique among Hardy's heroines in being quite clearly the victim of men's cruelty.... It is most unusual to find one of Hardy's heroines standing out against the generality of feminine behaviour as Tess does when Alec d'Urberville sneeringly retorts to her excuse that she had not understood his meaning till it was too late, ... 'Did it never strike your mind that what every woman says some women may feel?' (97)

As the dominant member of the Durbeyfield family, Tess shoulders most of the family burdens and is, therefore, apart from her gender and beauty, the logical, i.e., "the fittest," person to seek out the family's d'Urberville kin and assure the Durbeyfield family's survival. One must question, as Tess unknowingly does, if anyone can bring back the original family, can restore the bastardized Durbeyfields to their genealogical nobility, for Tess can no more reawaken the original d'Urberville family than she can return to the Garden of Eden. Her unhappy stay at the d'Urberville estate, resulting in her rape by Alec, deprives her of whatever illusions she might have had as a young girl.

Lacan's descriptions of what one actually inherits from the father's name seems apt here:

> The father, the Name-of-the-father, sustains the structure of desire with the structure of the law — but the inheritance of the father is that which Kierkegaard designates for us, namely, his sin.[21]

Thus, Tess finds herself a sinner and an outcast Eve upon her return home. Her condemned status is reinforced when she meets the painter of Christian epigrams — "Thy, Damnation, Slumbereth, Not" — (62) on roadsigns. She huffily declares that she does not "believe God said such things" (63) as she turns away from the painter. But the all-too-symbolic event carries with it the weight of the social condemnation that she feels for the "sin" of her pregnancy. Nevertheless, "even for her name's sake she scarcely wished to marry" d'Urberville (64).

After her return, Tess, in spite of her guilt, begins to waver in her belief in God; nature becomes his replacement.

> The midnight airs and gusts, moaning amongst the tightly-wrapped buds and bark of the winter twigs, were formulae of bitter reproach. A wet day was the expression of irremediable grief at the weakness in the mind of some vague ethical being whom she could not class definitely as the God of her childhood, and could not comprehend as any other. (67)

This passage resonates with crises of faith being described throughout Europe and particularly in Scandinavia.[22] As for Tess, the narrator declares that Tess's sense of guilt is essentially irrelevant to an indifferent nature and argues that she would have enjoyed her maternity had she been alone on an island (71).[23] But she cannot be alone because her family needs her.

The consistent references to the splashes of red on Tess — from the ribbon on her dress at the Cerealia, to the blood from Prince's fatal wound and the prick from Alec's rose — establish her as a sacrificial victim.[24] Hardy often seems to play off the tensions of Tess as a pagan goddess and as a figure who sacrifices herself to save the family, a Christ figure. In this case, however, the savior sacrifices herself, or is sacrificed, in the name of a father (God or d'Urberville) whom she knows does not exist. Indeed, her quest from the beginning is to prove that the name of the father has no meaning for her or her family.

This tension between Tess's natural or pagan strength and her Christian guilt as an unwed mother shapes her relationship with Angel. How appropriate that his name should define him as a Christian messenger, for Angel's apparent break with his family and their Christianity is illusory.[25] Marjorie Garson contrasts him with Alec: "One is dangerous because of his excessive sensuality, the other because of his excessive spirituality; the two together combine to destroy the heroine" (136).

Angel's apparent heterodoxy cannot overcome his patriarchal need for a virgin wife. When he finally learns Tess's story, he views her as impure, no longer the woman he thought she was. He describes quite clearly the relation between her family and "her conduct."

> I think that parson who unearthed your pedigree would have done better if he had held his tongue. I cannot help associating your decline as a family with this other fact — of your want of firmness. Decrepit families imply decrepit wills, decrepit conduct. Heaven, why did you give me a handle for despising you more by informing me of your descent! Here was I thinking you a new-sprung child of nature: there were you, the belated seedling of an effete aristocracy!
> (182)

The passage not only recalls Torvald Helmer's accusation in *The Doll House* that Nora reflects her father's weaknesses, but also scenes from Strindberg's *Miss Julie* and *Getting Married* in which the weakening aristocratic bloodlines lead to the moral and physical decline of the family. For Hardy, the degeneration renders explicit the demise of the illusory family.

Angel sees Tess's moral weakness as a direct result of the Durbeyfield family. His exclamation of "Heaven" is not surprising, for while he claims to have seen her as a "child of nature," he really had seen her as a Madonna of nature, a contradiction in terms, as today's "Madonna" enjoys pointing out to her public. For Angel, Tess has become a perversion of nature, just as her name perverts some original nobility before whom both Angel and his family would kneel. The sense of perversion, of monstrousness in Tess must be canceled out before Angel can see her as the woman he "married."[26]

Angel's romanticized view of nature continues to haunt him, for later he takes up the same issue that Strindberg uses with Tekla in *Creditors*, the possession of a woman by the first man to have sex with her. Angel asks: "How can we live together while that man lives? — he being your husband in Nature and not I. If he were dead it might be different . . ." (190). If literature is a fair guide, few concepts delineate as clearly as Angel's question the grip that patriarchal attitudes held on nineteenth-century rural and urban Victorian society. Alec d'Urberville makes exactly the same assumption when he sees Tess after his conversion and attempts to convince her to marry him: "But has not a sense of what is morally right and proper any weight with you?" (248). His question really means: does she accept his rape and later seduction of her as an act of moral possession? Alec repeats this claim when he tries to convince her to leave the hay field and join him (261). The two men's agreement on this topic must inevitably lead to the death of Alec before Angel can "possess" Tess. Yet the attitude of the two men towards sex differs greatly; Angel seems to lack any strong sexual drive, while Alec has an excess of it.

The novel's narrator almost condemns Angel's ethereal attitude, noting that if Angel had possessed more "animalism he would have been the nobler man" (191). But Angel's paternally-based imagination allows him only one perspective, that of the wounded father-figure. The entire framework of Angel and Tess's later relationship, even after Alec's death, continues in a dark and almost clichéd father-daughter pattern in which the father metes out punishment or reward, and the daughter accepts his decision as part of her familial duty. Tess's one warning, "you know best what my punishment ought to be; only — only — don't make it more than I can bear!" (199), reveals more of her inability to bear the punishment than her rejection of his right to give it. Opposite Angel's almost frigid love is Alec's excessive passion. Somewhat comically, his "animalism" turns into religious fanaticism after his conversion by Pastor Clare (241–2), but then it returns to his normal chauvinist lust when he meets Tess again.

In many ways, throughout the novel only Tess has a healthy sense of her own biocentric physicality.[27] As Rosemarie Morgan's reading of Tess's sexuality argues, Tess represents "a sexually vital consciousness" (84). Tess rejects both Angel's offer of financial support and Alec's propositions, and she endures the torturous farm labor at the expense of her body and its sexual vitality. Ultimately, however, Tess succumbs to the patriarchal determinism (the "President of the Immortals" [314]) which had imposed its rules on her from the beginning.

The dominance of the patriarchal structures permeates all of Tess's experiences, although she is continually described in terms that show her alienation from traditional Christianity. For instance, she says to Alec, "go, in the name of your own Christianity!" (249), but when he later returns he has rejected all religion. Alec's loss of faith apparently gives him the freedom to restate his claim on Tess: "I was your master once! I will be your master again. If you are any man's wife you are mine!" (261). In the first two sentences, Alec seems to invoke a Darwinian male dominance, but in the next sentence he implies a patriarchal morality. While Tess succeeds in resisting Alec this time, when she finally takes her father's place and becomes the family provider she falls victim to Alec.

Once again the law of the absent/present father controls the lives of Tess and her family. When Jack Durbeyfield dies, the family loses its lease and becomes homeless (276). Alive as a father, Jack Durbeyfield was virtually useless, yet his name and male identity allowed the family to live in their house. That their home is lost through the father's death reinforces the power of the patriarchal tradition, even as his dying and leaving his family destitute establishes the father's inadequacy and forces Tess back to Alec. This inability to find or create her own identity apart from a divinely and/or socially valorized (i.e., patriarchal) name destroys Tess. In the absence of all support from her father or her husband, the absent harp-playing Angel, Tess begins to accept Alec's claim on her person, "in a physical sense this man alone was her husband" (282).

The acceptance of Alec as her "physical" husband leads to Tess's final loss of identity through the ironically redemptive return of Angel. Her return to Angel comes only after she takes the falsely-appropriated name-of-the-(fore)father, d'Urberville, for when Angel finds her in Sandborne at The Herons lodging house she is living under the name of Mrs. d'Urberville. As Michael Ragussis has noted, Tess had originally hoped that Angel would help her to escape the d'Urberville name. "From start to finish, Tess experiences her life as a gulf between herself and a name (whether "d'Urberville" or "Clare")" (150). Ragussis discusses Angel as a godlike being for the four milkmaids, "the 'He' whose name they dared not pronounce" (151). In commenting on Tess's memory of Angel's words, Ragussis concludes that "in her worship of Angel, Tess serves another form of patriarchy, another form of the letter of the law" (150). Within the Lacanian framework that I have suggested, Ragussis's words verify how completely oppressive patriarchal structures, originally embodied for Tess in the degenerate Jack Durbeyfield, dominate Hardy's novel. The narrative returns the reader again and again to the inadequacies of this name-of-the-father world.

When Angel finally finds Tess, she is "like a corpse upon the current" (299). Having failed to create a personal identity separate from the patriarchal name that has plagued her, Tess already appears near death. She, on the other hand, views Angel almost as a Christ figure, one who has been resurrected for her and who has come to resurrect her. She blames Alec: "I hate him now, because he told me a lie — that you would not come again; and you *have* come!" (299). When Tess stabs Alec d'Urberville, she eliminates his proprietary claim upon her, but she also kills her father's longed-for name, the letter of a law she rejects. Tess attempts to kill the trace of her inadequate dead father; that is, she murders the Durbeyfield-d'Urberville claim upon her. As we have seen, the tradition of the dead fathers has always made claims upon her, and it is those claims, from her father and his ancestors, to Alec, to Angel, that drive the narrative forward, not her demands of them. Unfortunately, after Tess kills her father's Durbeyfield/d'Urberville name, she gives herself over to another, Clare. The salvation offered by the return of the saving patriarchal Angel presents one of the novel's final contradictions: by murdering Alec, Tess commits herself to Stonehenge and the pagan law for which it stands, but a Christian "Angel" by definition cannot live in a pagan world.

We can return to Ralph Freedman's notion of the "allegorical quest" for a different and perhaps more positive reading of Hardy's conclusion. In the final pages of the novel, although we are gradually distanced from her consciousness, Tess becomes a symbolic presence who has reached the end of her journey. In this sense, the symbolism of Stonehenge becomes even more powerful for it represents a moment of completion, if not of triumph for Tess. For Freedman:

> A hero's allegorical quest depicted by means of symbolic encounters is replaced by an enactment of his inner condition caught in a specific object or situation through which the higher truth is portrayed. (31)

This may be twisting Freedman to suit my own purposes, but to see Tess's story as an allegorical quest in which she seeks to find and to escape the name of the father adds to the richness of our experience and memory of the text. Those memories linger on various images: Tess in the Cerealia — the beginning of her journey; or working at the harvest or in the beet fields; or finally, having freed herself of her deadly inheritance, resting on the slab at Stonehenge.

Within the framework of that almost positive if symbolic conclusion to her quest (in Freedman's terms, her inner life now parallels her exterior situation), one would like to think of d'Urberville's murder and Tess's flight as a statement for a stronger, biocentric Tess, a woman who rejects the patriarchal tradition for a human one. Then, if not Tess herself, perhaps her sister could be allowed to develop fully and freely, limited less by the laws of society than by simple mortality. However, Tess's love for Angel still leaves her committed to the patriarchy that has imprisoned her. In spite of her rejection of Christianity, she accepts its definition of her as bad and as someone who should be executed (311).

Her rejection of the Christian patriarchy, of the religious tradition with which the d'Urberville name has been associated, becomes clear at Stonehenge. ("And you used to say at Talbothays that I was a heathen. So now I am at home" [311].)[28] But Tess's symbolic transformation from Christian to pagan, and her final message, leaves an only moderately reformed patriarchy intact, for when Tess asks Angel to care for Liza-Lu she turns over to him "a spiritualized image" of herself, another "pure woman," like herself, only this time, one fears, one with less independence. Although saddened and wiser, Angel at last has the virtuous and dependent wife he always wanted.[29] From all indications, Liza-Lu will not be a New Woman, but rather, one fears, she will fit the mold of women outlined by Darwin: pure, moral, tender, selfless, and sexually passive.[30]

In a novel which so powerfully suggests that the forces of nature have more importance than the rules of Victorian society, is the final message then the impossibility of escape from the patriarchy? Since Hardy has written a novel in many ways so sympathetic to women, and so hostile to the Victorian and Christian patriarchal traditions that oppressed them, one must admire it, and love Tess. Yet its dark and patriarchally reinforcing closing scene saddens us unless we read it emphasizing its lyrical quality, the allegorical journey suggested by Freedman. In such a reading, although the narrator and the protagonist seem quite separate and not therefore characteristic of a lyrical novel, the final paragraph becomes a kind of dark apotheosis for Tess, a transformation from persecuted woman to a symbolic, almost mythical figure. Nevertheless, though much of the book supports principles of modern feminism, its conclusion leaves us skeptical of Angel and Liza-Lu's future relationship.

> 'Justice' was done, and the President of the Immortals, in Aeschylean phrase, had ended his sport with Tess. And the d'Urberville knights and dames slept on in their tombs unknowing. The two speechless gazers bent themselves down to earth, as if in prayer, and remained thus a long time, absolutely motionless: the flag continued to wave silently. As soon as they had strength they arose, joined hands again, and went on. (314)

The dominance of the patriarchy in this passage is almost overwhelming, from the whimsical sport of the "President of the Immortals" to the indifference of the "d'Urberville knights and dames." That the two speechless gazers are praying is hardly a positive gesture, since Tess so clearly rejected, and was rejected by, the Christian tradition which underlies those prayers. Similarly, even as the waving flag on the tower cornice might connote the end of Tess's journey to a happier, freer paganism (suggested from the beginning by the Cerealia), the pennant also announces a militaristic system of patriotism and justice. The two bent figures remind one of Adam and Eve being driven out of Eden, and by their joining hands, we know they go out to begin a new family; unfortunately, one fears the new family, with Angel Clare as its patriarch, will look very much like the old one that drove Tess in pursuit of her father's name to the Chase and hence to her death.

University of California, Los Angeles

Notes

[1] Ralph Freedman, *The Lyrical Novel: Studies in Hermann Hesse, André Gide, and Virginia Woolf* (Princeton: Princeton UP, 1963), 39.

[2] Thomas Hardy, *Tess of the d'Urbervilles*, ed. Scott Elledge (New York: Norton, 1991); hereafter referred to as *Tess* with page numbers from this edition.

[3] In an influential and persuasive volume, Beer relates Darwin's theories to narrative techniques in English literature (*Darwin's Plots: Evolutionary Narrative in Darwin, George Eliot and Nineteenth-Century Fiction* [London: Routledge and Kegan Paul, 1983], 238–58).

[4] As D. F. Bratchell (*The Impact of Darwinism: Texts and commentary illustrating nineteenth century religious, scientific and literary attitudes* [Amersham, Buckinghamshire: Avebury, 1981]) and Leo J. Henkin, (*Darwinism in the English Novel 1860–1910: The Impact of Evolution on Victorian Fiction* [New York: Russell and Russell, 1963]), among others, have demonstrated, Darwin's influence cut a wide swath in the British novel. Roger Ebbatson discusses Hardy as "The Complete Darwinian" (*The Evolutionary Self: Hardy, Forster, Lawrence* [Totowa, N. J.: Barnes and Noble; Brighton, Sussex: Harvester, 1982], 1–40), and argues for Hardy's "creative misreading of Darwin" (41). Penny Boumelha has argued for the Darwinian context of Hardy's novels, specifically as it relates to "Sexual Ideology and the 'Nature' of Women" in *Thomas Hardy and Women: Sexual Ideology and Narrative Form* (Totowa, N. J.: Barnes and Noble; Brighton, Sussex: Harvester, 1982), 15–19. William Rutland referred as far back as 1938 to the influence on Hardy of Darwin's *The Origin of Species* in *Thomas Hardy: A Study of his Writings and their Background* (Oxford: Basil Blackwell, 1938), 54. Elliot Gose, Jr. has written about Darwinism and Initiation in *Tess* ("Psychic Evolution: Darwinism and Initiation in *Tess of the d'Urbervilles*," *Nineteenth-Century Fiction* 18.3 [1963]: 261–72; reprinted in the 1991 Norton edition of *Tess of the d'Urbervilles*), and, more recently, Peter R. Morton in *The Vital Science: Biology and the Literary Imagination, 1860–1900* (London: George Allen and Unwin, 1984, 194–211) has discussed Hardy's "neo-Darwinism."

[5] Elaine Showalter, *The Female Malady: Women, Madness, and English Culture, 1830–1980* (1985. New York: Penguin, 1987), 112–16.

[6] In *Sexual Science: The Victorian Construction of Womanhood* (Cambridge: Harvard UP, 1989), Cynthia Eagle Russett provides a wide-ranging view of post-Darwinian science and its ugly consequences for women. Her comments on Henry Maudsley, interspersed throughout her book, as well as her discussion of Cesare Lombroso, provide an informative, if horrifying, context for my own work.

[7] *Darwin and the Novelists: Patterns of Science in Victorian Fiction* (Cambridge: Harvard UP, 1988), 230–33.

[8] *The Literary Notebooks of Thomas Hardy*, ed. Lennart A. Björk, 2 vols. (New York: New York UP, 1985).

⁹ Penny Boumelha provides an informative literary context for Hardy in her chapter "Women and the New Fiction 1880–1900."

¹⁰ Margaret Higonnet, ed., *The Sense of Sex: Feminist Perspectives on Hardy* (Urbana: U of Illinois P, 1993), 4.

¹¹ In *Marriage and Morals Among the Victorians* (New York: Knopf, 1986), Gertrude Himmelfarb suggests how crucial those moral standards were to Victorian society. (See particularly 21–22.)

¹² Gertrude Himmelfarb discusses this topic extensively. The following quotation suggests the complexity of the problem:

> Feeling guilty about the loss of their religious faith, suspecting that that loss might expose them to the temptations of immorality and the perils of nihilism, anticipating the Nietzschean dictum that if God does not exist everything is permitted, they were determined to make of morality a substitute for religion — to make of it, indeed, a form of religion. (21)

¹³ In the Introduction to Hardy's *Literary Notebooks*, Lennart Björk comments that

> In *Tess*, for instance, there are unmistakable impressions of Hardy's reading of Comte and other positivists in the 1870s. Indeed, no less a positivist than Frederick Harrison greeted *Tess* as a 'Positivist allegory or sermon.' (Vol. 2, xxvi)

Peter R. Morton comments on the neo-Darwinism in *Tess*:

> The neo-Darwinism in *Tess* is by no means simply a question of a few citations from the *Origin* forced into the story. Instead, Hardy's use of the very freshest data on degeneration, sexual selection, and, above all, on heredity is in the strictest sense aesthetic, for these themes actually commingle with and order the narrative flow. (*The Vital Science*, 196)

¹⁴ Michael Millgate, *Thomas Hardy: A Biography* (Oxford: Oxford UP, 1982), 313.

¹⁵ Michel Foucault, *The Order of Things: An Archaeology of the Human Sciences* (New York: Pantheon, 1970), xxiii.

¹⁶ Michael Ragussis, *Acts of Naming: The Family Plot in Fiction* (New York: Oxford UP, 1986), 136.

¹⁷ Lacan's example of this concept comes from Ernest Jones, who apparently refused to accept that men in some Australian tribes did not recognize that coitus produces pregnancy. For Lacan, however, this makes no difference:

> For, if the symbolic context requires it, paternity will nonetheless be attributed to the fact that the woman met a spirit....
>
> It is certainly this that demonstrates that the attribution of procreation to the father can only be the effect of a pure signifier, of a recognition, not of a real father, but of what religion has taught us to refer to as the Name-of-the-Father. (*Écrits: A Selection*, trans. Alan Sheridan [New York: Norton, 1977], 199)

¹⁸ In her unpublished dissertation, "Family Lineage and Narrative Lines: Genealogy and Fiction in Hardy" (Harvard University, 1992), Tess O'Toole studies the relation

between genealogy and fiction in Hardy's family histories. She comments, "The fallen state of the d'Urbervilles, for example, recalls the trajectory of degeneration that structures Zola's Rougon-Macquart series" (12). Peter Morton argues persuasively for Hardy's use of the neo-Darwinian August Weismann (1834–1914) as the scientific source for Hardy's depiction of the degenerating Durbeyfield family (204–6).

[19] Gail Cunningham, *The New Woman and the Victorian Novel* (London: MacMillan, 1978), 103.

[20] The comparison with Darwin seems necessary since various Hardy critics, such as Penny Boumelha, Gail Cunningham and Margaret Higonnet often point out how Hardy limits women to traditional or "natural" roles, even as he argues for their freedom from unfair laws or social restrictions.

[21] Jacques Lacan, *The Four Fundamental Concepts of Psycho-Analysis*, ed. Jacques-Alain Miller, trans. Alan Sheridan (1978; New York: Norton, 1981), 34.

[22] Jens Peter Jacobsen portrays similar crises in *Mogens* and *Niels Lyhne*, and August Strindberg describes one in *The Son of a Servant*.

[23] Hardy's use of determinism and nature has been even more extensively discussed than Tess's victimage. Marjorie Garson has a fine analysis in *Hardy's Fables of Integrity* (Oxford: Clarendon, 1991), 130–51, and Leon Waldoff's "Psychological Determinism in *Tess of the d'Urbervilles*" offers another interesting perspective (Dale Kramer, ed., *Critical Approaches to the Fiction of Thomas Hardy* [London: Macmillan, 1979], 135–54). The quotation also raises the highly controversial question of Hardy's "sexism," the attitude implicit here in the value and effects of motherhood.

[24] Elliot Gose relates these scenes to a "symbolic initiation among primitive tribes" (*Nineteenth-Century Fiction* 18.3 [1963], 264) as well as to Tess's gradual rejection of her victim status.

[25] Ragussis's discussion of the double meaning of Tess's and Angel's names offers additional insight into this discussion (140).

[26] In reference to Angel's vision of Tess as perfect or Madonna-like, Rosemarie Morgan argues that "Hardy abhorred what he called the 'perfect woman' in fiction," and, she continues, "his heroines' best faculties are presented in the context of their less-than-perfect natures in a less-than-perfect world not yet ready to take them at their face value" *(Women and Sexuality in the Novels of Thomas Hardy* [London: Routledge, 1988], xiv). With a slightly different perspective, Gail Cunningham notes that when "Angel Clare sees Tess as a 'fresh and virginal daughter of Nature' he is, though ironically mistaken in his own terms, very close to the truth in Hardy's" (100).

[27] As O'Toole points out, many critics have commented on the importance of Hardy's physical embodiment of his characters. (2–3).

[28] It need hardly be noted that Tess accepts both her Christian and Pagan definitions from Angel, thus restricting herself even at her death to his standards.

[29] Boumelha and O'Toole comment on this scene in terms of its rejection of a "guilty sexuality" (Boumelha, 125; O'Toole, 140).

[30] Chapter 29 of Charles Darwin's *The Descent of Man and Selection in Relation to Sex* (1871; 2nd ed. New York: D. Appleton, 1898). See particularly 575–77.

JONATHAN FREEDMAN

Mania and the Middlebrow: The Case of *Trilby*

A critic writing at the present moment may I hope be forgiven for greeting recent eruptions of public outrage at avant-garde art and at the literary academy with a certain degree of fascination. For the anger that right-wing politicians and pressure groups have manufactured first at government support of the arts and at what they call academic "political correctness" has had the ironic but indisputable merit of reaffirming the power of these arenas to rouse any public response at all. Thanks to the combined efforts of Robert Mapplethorpe and Stanley Fish — or of Patrick Buchanan and the N. A. S. — high culture and its academic criticism in bourgeois America again *matter* — matter as much as did Stravinsky's *Rite of Spring* in 1913, to cite a classic precedent, or Salman Rushdie's *Satanic Verses* in 1989, to cite a more recent one. And to such a critic, this development is not only engrossing; it is thoroughly unexpected. After all, a crucial tenet of eighties post-modernism was the claim that the avant-garde had lost its ability to challenge the bourgeois audience — that this capacity was undone from within by the tendency of Benjaminian shock to lose its power under repetition and from without by the bourgeois audience's zest for those works that aimed most pointedly to affront it.[1] And academics of the same period held that the concerns of literary critics had come — problematically for some, triumphantly for others — fully to exceed the capacities of the common reader.[2] These recent controversies would appear to have successfully reestablished the status quo in both venues: to have recast the artistic avant-garde in its familiar, fantasmatic drama of transgression, repression, and artistic heroism; to have restored academics to the cultural centrality they possess in their most grandiose dreams — or most terrifying nightmares.

One can only hope that the politicians, preachers, and columnists who have fomented these hysterias will soon trot along to their next — I, for one, doubt it. But even if they should do so, this spasm of outrage will remain noteworthy — if only, paradoxically, for its very ordinariness. For such complex cultural contortions, such paradoxical warpings of the sociocultural field, turn out to be the rule rather than the exception — at least as far as the relation of that mythical entity, the American middlebrow, to that equally mythical entity, its "high" or "legitimate" culture, is concerned. Such contortions, I shall be arguing, are built into the very terms by which the American middlebrow audience was first constructed and thereafter maintained — an enterprise that involved as much cultural trepidation, terror, and *ressentiment* as it did what Pierre Bourdieu has so incisively called "cultural good-will." When viewed in this light, current controversies take on added piquancy. Cultural hostility, hostility *to* "culture," is nothing new for the American middlebrow, and nothing inexplicable. It follows inevitably from the bargain that middlebrow Americans made years ago — one which gave them increasing access to the world of "high" culture, but at a price: that increasing dependency on institutions that augmented their hostility even as they allayed their insecurity.

In what follows, I want to flesh out this argument by focusing on one of the extraordinary waves of enthusiasm for the epigones of Anglo-European high culture that washed over the American public in the late nineteenth century which included "manias" for such diverse figures as Oscar Wilde, Jenny Lind, Robert Browning. The "craze" or "mania" I wish to analyze here was aroused by a book: George Du Maurier's novel *Trilby*. For both *Trilby* and *Trilby*-mania (as this enthusiasm was rapidly dubbed) are uniquely suited to exploring the questions I am trying to pose here. The novel was one of the first, and certainly one of the most successful, of the great middlebrow bestsellers — works that provided a patina of cultural authority to an increasingly status-conscious segment of the mass audience anxiously seeking social legitimacy through knowledge of "high culture." But it was unique in possessing a distinctively self-referential dimension — as, more importantly, did its reception. The novel thematized its own audience's responses to high culture; these responses were avidly mimicked by a fin-de-siècle American public which made *Trilby* not just a success, as it had been in England, but a sensation.

It is this last phenomenon I find the most intriguing of all. For in its mimetic response to *Trilby*, we see the American middlebrow public learning how to be a middlebrow public — learning what kinds of art they ought to respond to, how they ought to respond to that art, how to place themselves vis-à-vis other classes and subcultures by means of that response. We shall see that public thereby constructing themselves in the odd and somewhat paradoxical position of high-culture *maniacs* — as devotees of high culture whose devotion was extreme, even out of control. It is both the unleashing and the organization, the venting and the ordering, of these energies, I shall argue, that we witness in *Trilby*-mania — and both result from a negotiation undertaken between middlebrow readers and the organs of middlebrow culture, who built together the cultural alliances we still confront at the present time.

I make these claims with some confidence because critics have recently given us a precise language for articulating them: Lawrence Levine, Joan

Shelley Rubin, and Janice Radway have written brilliantly on the rise of the middlebrow taste-fragment, and its various cultural ramifications, and I have learned much from each of them.[3] But I have learned most, and wrestled longest, with the brilliant and problematic work of Pierre Bourdieu. For in *Distinction: A Social Critique of the Judgment of Taste*, Bourdieu offers a powerful if problematic vocabulary for describing the relation between aesthetic response and social power — an elaborate if frequently over-elaborated lexicon of the patterns of domination that define and are in turn defined by judgments of "taste." More specifically, Bourdieu offers the most satisfying account I know of the nature and fate of that much-maligned figure, the middlebrow. Unlike high-culture critics like Virginia Woolf[4] who first defined that figure with a satiric shock born of class condescension, or those fifties American critics like Dwight MacDonald who vociferated against middlebrow culture with a resentment born, one suspects, of their dependency upon that culture, Bourdieu reads the middlebrow immanently, sympathetically, as a figure of perpetual, but perpetually frustrated, cultural aspiration expressed "inter alia, by a particularly frequent choice of the most unconditioned testimonies of cultural docility (a choice of 'well-bred' friends, a taste for 'educational' or 'instructive' entertainments), often combined with a sense of unworthiness ('paintings are nice but difficult')."[5] Bourdieu's middlebrow seeks status through the attainment of high-cultural competence, but denied by birth, education, and social circumstance to cultural data or to any assurance in making aesthetic judgments, the middlebrow is perpetually conscious that legitimate culture is not made for him, and is often made against him.

Bourdieu's middlebrow is, then, more than just a docile numskull; that figure, rather, is — as Michael Denning has recently emphasized — something of a comic hero impaled on the horns of a cultural dilemma. (Tellingly, Bourdieu compares the middlebrow to Leopold Bloom, that perpetual outsider who brandishes his shards of cultural knowledge as a ticket to the social acceptance his birth denies him.) For the very cultural *reverence* of the middlebrow places that figure in the midst of a self-defeating paradox. Although the middlebrow always gets it *wrong*, he also gets what no other social player possesses — a genuine involvement in the cultural which is as emotionally intense as it is perpetually frustrated. In "his symbolic class struggle with the certified holders of cultural competence" (330) "avidity combines with anxiety," (328) and the middlebrow grasps as hard as he can at cultural artifacts as if they were objects of sacred value. Neither the dominant classes, who treat taste as their birthright, nor the working ones, who make a virtue of their exclusion from the culturally canonical, need or are able to establish so vibrant, complex, *cathected* relation to high culture. Yet it is precisely this cathexis that frustrates the social ambitions of the middlebrow. For what the middlebrow yearns to achieve is the very antithesis of his own response: the ease, effortlessness, self-confidence that mark the "sense" — and the reality — of *true* high-cultural "distinction":

> The petit bourgeois do not know how to play the game of culture as a game. They take culture too seriously to go in for bluff or imposture or even for the distance and casualness which show true familiarity; too seriously even to escape permanent fear of ignorance or blunders, or to sidestep tests by responding with the indifference of those who are not competing. (330)

There are two possible outcomes to the ensuing dilemma. The first, which Bourdieu fails to consider, is to reject high culture altogether: to demonize it or subject it to the symbolic violence of parody or satire. Rage *at* high culture, in other words, is as likely an outcome of the middlebrow's social drama as rage *for* high culture. A second, less extreme solution is for middlebrows to generate a cultural system of their own, or, more accurately, to turn to a cultural system created for that purpose. The middlebrow turns for aid and comfort — for the legitimation that legitimate culture withholds — to those authorities that mediate between high culture and the mass audience, that provide

> accessible versions of avant-garde experiments, film "adaptations" of classic drama and literature, "popular arrangements" of classical music or "orchestral versions" of popular tunes, vocal interpretations of classics in a style evocative of scout choruses or angelic choirs, in short, everything that goes to make up "quality weeklies" and "quality shows" which are entirely organized to give the impression of bringing legitimate culture within the reach of all, by combining two normally exclusive characteristics, immediate accessibility and the outward signs of cultural legitimacy. (323)

But — and Bourdieu sketches this point but does not sufficiently emphasize it — the organs of middlebrow culture do not necessarily adopt a passive relation to their audience. In order to assert their role as cultural mediators, they enhance as they pretend to allay the cultural insecurity of the middlebrow reader; claiming to be neutral or "objective" translators of culture, they select, block, or critique elements of that culture even as they transmit it. We shall see this phenomenon more clearly in the social reception of *Trilby*.

But before I turn to that text, I need to put some pressure on Bourdieu's terms. I have been writing as if Bourdieu's delightfully circular argument about the relation of taste to class — that we have our tastes because of our social position and our social position because of our tastes — were indeed fully tenable; and as if the middlebrow were indeed a distinct and coherent social fragment. But neither is necessarily the case. For example, Bourdieu writes as if his categorizations were unitary and discrete — as if they were self-contained, autonomous systems. But common sense alone suggests that this model is inaccurate — and that it is most inaccurate when it attempts to account for middlebrow. One can imagine such a figure shuttling giddily between an abundance of "symbolic expressions of class positions" over the course of a single day: eating breakfast to *Good Morning America* (lowbrow?), then driving to work while listening to Mozart on a "Classical-Lite" radio station (high-middlebrow?), then driving home to rap heard on the local "soul" station (brow classification, significantly, breaks down altogether when inflected by questions of race), eating a steak for dinner (classic middlebrow) while drinking a fine Merlot (middle-highbrow?), then watching a baseball game (potentially every-brow), before retiring to bed, there to read a chapter of Dostoevsky (utter highbrow), Tom Wolfe (utter middlebrow) or John D. MacDonald (again, brow classification here is impossible).

Rather than see this lability as a sign of muddiness or confusion, I would like to take it as a key to definition. For it would seem to be the unique property of the middlebrow to be in a position to appropriate the greatest number of possible taste-positions at different moments of experience. This figure possesses on the one hand the grounding in the popular or low-brow culture and on the other at least the potential access to highbrow culture and hence is in a position to view all hues of the cultural spectrum. As a result, however, the middlebrow also possesses a particular uncertainty of self-definition in a consumer world that negotiates class identity through judgments of taste. Rooted neither in the assurance of the *grand bourgeois* highbrow nor in the contempt for high culture that mark the lowbrow, the middlebrow is constantly searching for a stable framework for their social identity; and the very plethora of taste-positions open to that figure only serve to confuse the middlebrow further, to heighten the insecurity which causes the cathexis to culture in the first place.

Confusions of a different sort need to be addressed before I continue: those involved in "applying" Bourdieu's model to the American scene. The limitations of this task may be best gleaned in a passage where Bourdieu attempts to establish a table of equivalencies between French and American cultures:

> One could replace *Les Temps Modernes* by *Partisan Review*, France-Musique by educational television (Channel 13, WQXR, WGBH, etc.) and perhaps ultra-leftism by sixties-camp, while the *New York Review of Books* would (alas) represent an unlikely combination of the weekly *Nouvel Observateur*, the review *Critique*, and, especially in its successive enthusiasms, the journal *Tel Quel*. As regards bourgeois taste, the American professionals, executives, and managers might ask of the film and book critics of the *New York Times*, *Time*, and *Newsweek* the same balanced, subtly diversified judgments which their French opposite numbers expect from *Le Monde*, *Le Figaro*, or weeklies like *L'Express* or *Le Point*. (xii)

Now, these parallels are spectacularly asymmetrical; and one can chart exactly the aberration of Bourdieu's own judgment by noting the kinds of mistakes he makes. For example, ahistoricism: *Partisan Review* and *Les Temps Modernes* possess different ethnic histories and class affiliations — to put it mildly.

And ignorance: Bourdieu's examples of educational TV stations reminds us that his knowledge of American culture extends no further than twenty miles beyond the Eastern seaboard. (To be fair, this is also the understanding of many American academics; but that hardly vitiates the point.) And anachronism: while it's true that *Le Figaro* may be increasingly looking like *Time* or *Newsweek*, *Time* or *Newsweek* are increasingly looking like *USA Today*. And, finally, the lack of a "feel" or intuitive sense of American culture: my own sense of the American professional-managerial class is that those who are looking for "balanced, subtly diversified judgments" turn elsewhere than *Time*; and those who do look there are probably searching for capsule summaries, not expansive critiques.

The point is not only that Bourdieu has a tin ear when it comes to American culture; it is also that his own schemas — which may not apply fully to the French situation — collapse entirely when applied directly to the American scene. But Bourdieu remains indispensable to this project, and for two reasons. The first is the sheer historical validity of his analysis: we shall see precisely this admixture of intense admiration for and anxiety at high culture coursing through American middlebrow responses of the 1890s and 1990s alike. Second, and perhaps even more important, is the distinction between the middlebrow *tout court* and middlebrow culture — a distinction that most American critics fail to note. For the organs of middlebrow culture help to generate this dual response as they guide its middlebrow audience in their cultural experience — act to enhance both the positive and the negative cathexes to "culture" in order to assert their own role as definers of what is and what is not legitimate in legitimate culture. Indeed, it is precisely the interplay between these three terms — an eager but conflicted middlebrow public, a high culture that condescends to them when it is not ignoring them, and a middlebrow culture that acts to aggrandize itself as it claims to referee the field of taste — that I see operative in recent controversies; and it is one we can trace to the origins of the middlebrow as a full-blown cultural consumer and of middlebrow culture as a fully articulated cultural formation in the late nineteenth century. And we can see both of these phenomena — and their problems — most visibly in the sensation that was *Trilby*-mania.

On 25 March 1889, Henry James recorded in his notebook that

> last evening, before dinner, I took a walk with G. du Maurier, in the mild March twilight... and he told me over an idea of his which he thought very good — and I do too — for a short story.... Last night it struck me as curious, picturesque and distinctly usable; though the want of musical knowledge would hinder *me* somewhat in handling it.[6]

The story Du Maurier told James was the tale that became *Trilby*, and in his notebook, James played with the idea of writing this story of a "servant girl with a wonderful rich full voice but no musical genius who is mesmerized and made to sing by a little foreign Jew who has mesmeric power, infinite feeling, and no organ . . . of his own" (97). Soon thereafter, however, he thought better of the project and handed it back to Du Maurier; five years later — just as James was beginning to despair over his attempted conquest of the London theatrical audience, and hence over his ability to survive at all in the brave new world of the fin de siècle marketplace — Du Maurier's novel began to appear in *Harper's Monthly*.[7]

To James's chagrin and Du Maurier's delighted embarrassment, *Trilby* rapidly generated precisely the enthusiasm that James had been hoping in vain to kindle. This was particularly true in that large and relatively untapped market, America. While British reviews were tepid and sales slow, American reviewers were ecstatic and sales extraordinary. It was not without reason that *Trilby* headed the first American best-seller list, published in *The Bookman* shortly after the novel's publication: over 100,000 copies were sold within the first two months of publication; over 2 million in two years.[8] And if anything, these figures understate the novel's popularity: 100 copies circulated at the Mercantile Library in New York, but still proved inadequate to readers' requests; public libraries in Boston and Chicago also reported unprecedented demand. A librarian from the latter reported, with the hyperbole that characterized all aspects of *Trilby*-mania, that "every one of our 54,000 card-holders seems determined to read the book." (20)

And the public excitement occasioned by *Trilby* was not confined to literary manifestations. Due to ill health, Du Maurier was not able to follow the likes of Dickens, Wilde, and Matthew Arnold onto the American lecture circuit; nevertheless the public appetite for *Trilby* led to numerous traveling companies of the theatrical version of the novel — twenty-four separate companies were simultaneously active at one point in 1896. And *Trilby*-mania did not end at the theater; other entertainments centered on the novel, and in many walks of social life. A New York society matron, Mrs. Charles Ditson, organized an evening at Sherry's restaurant for the benefit of the New York Kindergarten Association devoted to "Scenes and Songs from *Trilby*"; *tableaux-vivants* reproducing with painstaking fidelity Du Maurier's illustrations alternated with the performance of songs from the novel. ($2,500 was raised.) Meanwhile, at a burlesque house, the Eden Musée, a Miss Ganthony impersonated Trilby, as did Miss Marie Meers in Barnum's Greatest Show On Earth, "riding bareback . . . around the tan bark to the snapping of ringmaster Svengali's whip" (21). Literary and charitable societies devoted meetings to the novel; the Daughters of the American Revolution sponsored a *Trilby* evening to benefit the St. Luke's Home for Indigent Christian Females where "a literary criticism of the book was read . . . and the songs oftenest alluded to sung"; similarly, "An Evening with Trilby" was held in Omaha during which were read seven papers on the novel (e.g. "Could *Trilby* be Successfully Dramatized?" and "The French of *Trilby*"), and thereafter music associated with the novel was performed. Finally — but not the least significantly — a host of what we would call commercial tie-ins proliferated: it is to this cultural moment that we owe the origins of *Trilby* hats and overcoats, of course, but it also witnessed a proliferation of *Trilby* shoes, *Trilby* hearth-brushes, *Trilby* hams, and *Trilby* sausages which, its advertisers claimed in language perhaps not entirely unfamiliar to the current reader, "is something new, and fills a long-felt want; they melt in your mouth" (26).

The passing of "the germ" of *Trilby* from Du Maurier to James and back again, then, might appropriately symbolize the cultural situation of the novel at the end of the nineteenth century; and the explosion of this germ into a full-blown "mania" suggests some of its ramifications. If James was increasingly to learn the lesson of *Trilby* — that he was now thoroughly alienated from the genteel but not unremunerative readership whose affections he had seemed to win with the publication of *Daisy Miller* (1878) and which he had last successfully addressed with *Portrait of a Lady* (1881) — Du Maurier discovered the converse: that a new audience had risen from this earlier one, an audience similar in social aspiration, but different in size, lack of firm social variegation, and — perhaps most significantly — enthusiasm.

To a certain extent as L. Edwin Purcell has observed, this response was the product of transformations in the publishing industry — the rationalization of production, distribution, and advertising that generated the system of publishing whose vestiges we are still living with today. *Trilby*, as Purcell notes, illustrated the formula for the "new breed of 'sellers' that were at the heart of the new publishing system: secure copyright, promote well, supply the demand, and huge profits *might* be in store."[9] Thus the House of Harper serialized *Trilby* in its own magazine, *Harper's Monthly* (and made sure that it was edited to suit American sensibilities); printed additional copies when it was clear that the novel was a sensation; took advantage of the numerous forms of free publicity for the novel occasioned by the "*Trilby* craze" — including sending Mrs. Harper herself to the *Trilby* benefit at Sherry's restaurant; superintended the production of the play, whose very creation was more or less brokered by the *Harper* rights department, which read and approved it before sending it to Du Maurier for his approbation; and vigorously protected their property by suing parodists and performers of pirated versions of the play. And Trilby-mania also must be understood more broadly, as part of the construction of what Adorno and Horkheimer would call the "culture industry." The unabashedly commercial quality of *Trilby*-mania; its integration of multiple media of cultural production and distribution; the integral role of advertisement in the production of heightened demand for the novel; the seemingly spontaneous quality of this carefully cultivated frenzy of enthusiasm: all these lend themselves to analysis in the terms Adorno and Horkheimer establish with grim eloquence.

But it would be a mistake to view *Trilby* and *Trilby*-mania as part of a fully formed culture industry, in either Purcell's or Adorno and Horkheimer's sense.

The enthusiastic audience of *Trilby*-maniacs was not just called from the vasty deep; they came — and in droves — seeking something, and seem to have found whatever they were looking for. What this increasingly urban, upwardly-mobile, and culture-conscious audience was looking for was accessible knowledge of the world of European high culture — and the patina of cultural authority that came with it. But what they were also searching after was a way of dealing with the anxiety, the insecurity, that motivates this quest in the first place.

Trilby was perfectly suited to meeting the dual needs of this audience. The novel provided a painless thumbnail sketch — almost a taxonomy — of the European artistic and musical world, ranging from an idealized portrait of the Parisian *vie Bohème* to a thoroughly satirical representation of "the most bourgeois of bourgeois living rooms," and stopping just about everywhere in between.[10] The novel offered itself as a kind of cultural how-to kit; it provided a handbook to the facts and figures of the high-cultural experience. Indeed, with its grammatical lapses, its colloquial zest, its racy narrative, its violation of generic norms ("freedom of mind, freedom from artificiality, absolute freedom from conventionality," wrote Charles Dudley Warner in *Harper's*, conflating Du Maurier's authorial skill and his heroine's unconventional morals),[11] even in its abundant illustrations, the novel addressed its readers with an unpretentious immediacy enacted on all levels: language, grammar, plot, the book's physical appearance. But, more importantly, the text also offers a vivid account of the experience of being *truly* cultured, a reproduction of the inner processes of high-cultural response — and one that makes those processes not only available to a lower-brow audience, but also their property.

The novel performs this last task in those vivid and prolonged passages devoted to Trilby's musical performances — "the chapters, the wonderful chapters, in which the author gives a hint to all singers of the power there may be in the simplest song," as Warner wrote (636). Here Du Maurier's treatment of his musical culture is particularly significant: he offers the reader entry into the most privileged precincts of distinction. For, as Bourdieu acutely if somewhat sardonically observes,

> nothing more clearly affirms one's class, nothing more infallibly classifies, than tastes in music. This is of course because . . . there is no more 'classificatory' practice than concert-going or playing a 'noble' instrument (activities which, other things being equal, are less widespread than theatre-going, museum going, or even visits to modern-art galleries). But it is also because the flaunting of 'musical culture' is not a cultural display like any other: as regards its social definition, 'musical culture' is something other than a quantity of knowledge and experiences combined with the capacity to talk about them. Music is the most 'spiritual' of the arts of the spirit and a love of music is a guarantee of 'spirituality.' (18–19)

Music, in other words, is a site of particularly intense struggle on the battlefield of taste. Responses to music are defined by custom and the dominant discourse of Western aesthetics as expressions of an inner nobility of spirit which — ideally — depends on neither class nor circumstance, and is — at least in theory — free from the determinations of cultural capital. By affirming the power of their intuitive response to music, listeners claim a social éclat and value. *Trilby*'s vivid depictions of music, the lyrics, the effects of "even the simplest song," upon "all singers"; its use of the second person throughout these sections; its narrative depiction of an ordinary, tone-deaf woman transformed magically into a singer of genius: all these endow its audience with a powerful sense of their own aesthetic capacities and arm them for battle on the terrain of taste.

In these chapters, the novel offered its audience another gift as well: an uncannily precise guidebook to *Trilby*-mania itself. For in its musical sections, *Trilby* is nothing if not a novel about the public reception of art — and a spectacular, a frenzied, public reception of art at that. An audience, any audience, has only to hear Trilby sing to fall into a Bacchic delirium:

> When the song was over, the applause did not come immediately, and she waited with her kind wide smile, as if she were well accustomed to wait like this; and then the storm began, and grew and spread and rattled and echoed — voices, hands, feet, sticks, umbrellas! — and down came the bouquets, which the little page-boys picked up; and Trilby bowed to the front and right and left in her simple *débonnaire* fashion. It was her usual triumph. It had never failed, whatever the audience, whatever the country, whatever the song.
> (251)

Nor does the Trilby craze stop with her audience. The press is similarly infected — Trilby's performance is met with "a chorus of journalistic acclamation gone mad, a frenzied eulogy in every key" (269). In a striking anticipation of the mass marketing of Trilby (or is it *Trilby*?) shoes and boots, the novel tells us that "casts of her alabaster feet could be had at Brucciani's, in the Rue de la Souricière St. Denis. (He made a fortune.)" (280).

I want to designate this quality of the text as the most telling, and most problematic, aspect of its "middlebrow" status: the fact that the audience responding to *Trilby* learned the lineaments of their own behavior from the novel — learned, that is, how to respond to the cultural experience the text depicts in such vivid detail from that text itself. In so doing, the novel provided that audience with a critical perspective on their own conduct: the novel reflects on the nature and implications of *Trilby*-mania through an analysis of causes and consequences of "Trilby-mania." In a literalizing echo of fin de siècle cultural commonplaces and a remarkable adumbration of twentieth-century mass culture theory, those performances are portrayed as a kind of a mass mesmerism, a hypnotic spellbinding of the crowd which induces both fascination with and a slave-like dependence upon the figure of Trilby herself. In their experience of the novel, in other words, *Trilby*'s readers were both learning to act as *Trilby*-maniacs and invited to see themselves *as Trilby*-maniacs: simultaneously to act out their cultural enthusiasm and to see that enthusiasm as something lower or lesser.

Consider, for example, the positive and negative charges that accrete to the analogy between Trilby as hypnotic subject and the audience whom Trilby both cultivates and enthralls. When hypnotized, Trilby is told that she "shall *see nothing, hear nothing, think of nothing but Svengali, Svengali, Svengali*" (57; emphasis Du Maurier's); and similarly, after they encounter Trilby, her audience can see, hear, and think of nothing but Trilby, Trilby, Trilby. Indeed, we are shown that what we might want to call (in allusion but in contradiction to Brecht's "A-effect") Trilby's "T-effect" lasts not only for the duration of her performance but leaches into the very subsoil of her audience's psyche; following their exposure to Trilby's song, Taffee, the Laird, and Little Billee can quite literally dream of nothing else — when they can sleep at all. (In this, they are like Trilby herself, who dreams incessantly of Svengali after he hypnotizes her.) What is true of these characters is also the case with the audience which has not had the pleasure of knowing and loving Trilby since youth; the songs of Trilby affect them, too, on the most elemental of psychic levels. For, we are told in a lengthy description of Trilby's performance in Paris, just as Svengali's voice does to Trilby, so Trilby's voice "forces itself on you" until you feel as though "all your life is changed for you":

> Waves of sweet and tender laughter, the very heart and essence of innocent, high-spirited girlhood, alive to all that is simple and joyous in nature . . . all the sights and scents and sounds that are the birthright of happy children, happy savages in favoured climes — things within the remembrance and reach of most of us! All this, the memory and the feel of it are in Trilby's voice . . . and those who hear feel it all, and remember it with her. It is irresistible; it forces itself on you, no words, no pictures, could ever do the like! So that the tears that are shed out of these many French eyes are tears of pure, unmixed delight in happy reminiscence! (257)

But, as the conflation of the language of possession and domination with that of regressive soothing suggests, Trilby's hypnotic voice has a dual effect on the audience. On the one hand, the effect of Trilby's voice is therapeutic, cathartic. Just as Svengali's hypnotic voice heals Trilby of her migraine headaches, so Trilby's mellifluous voice cures her audience of their heart ailments: it brings even the jaded, misanthropic French public in touch with buried feelings and repressed memories, with, in short, "happy reminiscence." On the other, less benign, hand, however, her voice induces what can be called a species of collective insanity. Even "an audience made up of the most cynically critical people in the world" "burst into madness" on hearing Trilby; indeed, they regress all the way to a state of pre-human monstrosity: "the many-headed rises as one and waves its sticks and handkerchiefs and shouts" in acclamation (252, 257, 258).

It is this lability of the T-effect — its power to induce both intense anxiety and soothing, healing peace — that I want to cite as the prime example of the novel's own intense ambivalence on the question of the audience and the source of its extraordinary public effect on an equally ambivalent — or, more accurately, internally conflicted — middlebrow public. The novel evinces a fundamental conflict in attitudes towards spectatorship itself, suggesting both that a spellbinding artistic representation is to be understood from a perspective that valorizes the vision of the "highbrow" and from one that reinforces the vision of the "lowbrow" — to be viewed both *in bono* as a therapeutic dip into the daemonic, or *in malo* as a pernicious and terrifying species of mass madness. This multidimensional ambivalence is expressed — and sexualized — by the relation between Trilby's efforts and those of her ostentatiously Jewish "master," teacher, and common-law husband, Svengali. It is one thing to image intense audience response in terms of a beautiful young woman whose native purity of spirit, whose pristine and innocent spontaneity, speaks directly to the emotions of her listeners; it is quite another to think of that young woman as being merely an extension of the will of an evil genius. But such is the notion the novel compels us to entertain; in its later pages, it shows us increasingly that even in her guise as supremely captivating artist Trilby is merely the product of the twisted, domineering genius of Svengali. Since despite his extensive knowledge of the properties of the human voice Svengali has no independent powers of vocal production, Trilby is hypnotically induced to function as Svengali's "singing machine — an organ to play on — an instrument of music — a Stradivarius — a flexible flageolet of flesh and blood — a voice and nothing more" (357). And Trilby is subordinated to Svengali in a more powerful way as well. Under his hypnotic power, she is transformed into a walking extension of Svengali's own massive ego: she could produce only "just the sounds he wanted, and nothing else — and think his thoughts and wish his wishes — [and be] just his own love for himself turned inside out . . . and reflected back on him, like a mirror" (357).

The questions raised by Trilby's submissive relation to Svengali — a relation whose sexual dimensions shocked and titillated nineteenth-century audience — point increasingly and problematically beyond her to the audience itself: to that audience who, to follow this chain of argument through, is asked to experience through Trilby's manifestly beautiful voice neither an intensified version of their own repressed emotions, nor a purified version of Trilby's ennobled ones, but rather an odd and troubling reproduction of Svengali's least benign sentiments and impulses. They, too, are represented as hypnotized subjects compelled into mirroring back to Svengali his own narcissistic self-celebration — and hence rendered complicit, it would seem in a sexual as well as a musical enthrallment. For when Trilby sings,

> it was as if she said: "See! what does the composer count for? Here is about as beautiful a song as was ever written, with beautiful words to match, and the words have been made French for you by one of your smartest poets! But what do the words signify, any more than the tune, or even the language? The "Nussbaum" is neither better nor worse than "Mon ami Pierrot" when I am the singer, for I am *Svengali*; and you shall hear nothing, see nothing; think of nothing but *Svengali, Svengali, Svengali*"! (251)

This ambivalence — this increasing negativity — about the effect of public performance on the audience is, I think, the key to *Trilby*'s function at its historical moment. For if, as Levine has powerfully argued, the moment of *Trilby* is also the hour at which cultural hierarchy was fully crystallized, then the ideological work in which the novel and its own readership collaborate is both robust and overdetermined. Through its representation of that audience, the novel simultaneously endorses and problematizes the idea of cultural hierarchy itself; it sketches for its middlebrow audience a highbrow vision of a lowbrow audience response, but it does so, powerfully if paradoxically, in such a way as to render high and low indistinguishable from one another.

Thus on the one hand, the enthralled, hypnotized, but wildly enthusiastic audience in this novel resembles nothing so much as the American highbrow's dream of the once boisterous, now thoroughly tamed mass audience, a dream which, as Levine shows, late nineteenth-century conductors and concert impresarios struggled mightily to achieve, and in which the genteel audience seemed increasingly willing to collaborate. Indeed, the treatment of this crowd by Svengali and his instrument Trilby is of a piece with the behavior of those new cultural authorities who presented themselves as experts in the gentle arts of high-cultural crowd control. "Nothing seems to have troubled the new arbiters of culture more than the nineteenth-century practice of spontaneous expressions of pleasure and disapproval in the forms of cheers, yells, gesticulations, hisses, boos, stamping of feet, whistling, crying for encores, and applause," Levine writes, and to tame the savage audience, Theodore Thomas, John Phillip Sousa, Frederick Stock, and a group of martinet-cum-conductors following in their footsteps (usually European in origin and Germanic in demeanor) all deployed tactics ranging from the posting of regulations ("No spitting," "no hats") to sarcastic gestures from the podium, to the public humiliation of offenders. It was, for example, reported of Thomas that "when his audience relapses into barbarism on the subject of encores, he quietly but firmly controls them. I have seen him . . . leave the stand and quietly take a seat in a corner of the orchestra, remaining there until he had carried his point."[12]

Similarly, while Svengali and Trilby excite their audience into frenzies of emotion and paroxysms of enthusiasm, they also chasten and discipline their crowd — and they do so without resorting to the heavy-handed tactics their American contemporaries deployed. Contrary to custom, Svengali makes the audience stand enthralled for exactly one hour until he releases them into frenzies of approbation and, exactly like Theodore Thomas, sends them out into the night without benefit of the expected encore. But unlike Thomas, his efforts require no exceptional gestures, no extraordinary efforts; all he needs to perform this task is the melodious, mellifluous, and thoroughly enthralling voice of Trilby.

But if its representation of the crowd comports itself to the most extravagant highbrow dreams of social order-making, other elements in the novel enact a powerful subversion of the highbrow imaginary — just as, as we shall see, its labile popular reception undermines the picture Levine draws of disciplining authorities and self-punishing audiences. The crowd that this novel depicts is, surprisingly, not one composed exclusively of the lower orders: to the contrary. It is, rather, the elite that is most visibly infected by Trilby-mania — at least within the space of *Trilby* — a mania they conspicuously refuse to display under other circumstances. Du Maurier is quite unsparing in his representation of the boredom of the haute bourgeois salon or the snobbery of an aristocratic English cenacle. *Even* the most socially exalted, this text tells us, are susceptible to the effects of Trilby and Svengali, and when they are so affected, they adopt the mannerisms and the behavior of the lower classes; they become at once maddened and obsequious, frenzied and subservient. When a "famous composer" named Herr Kreutzer describes Trilby's acclaim in Vienna, he makes clear both that the crowd is of high — of the highest — social standing, and that their behavior works to strip them of the lineaments of aristocratic reserve even as they strip themselves of the signs of their status: "[z]e women all vent mad, and pulled off zeir bearls and tiamonts and kave them to her — vent town on zeir knees and gried and gissed her hands . . . Ze men schniffelled in ze gorners, and looked and ze bictures, and tissempled — efen I, Johann Kreutzer! efen ze Emperor?" (202) Not only does the diegetic Trilby-mania know no social bounds, it works actively to undo social difference, to level social hierarchies, to reduce all classes and orders to the same common denominator: madness, frenzy, in a word, mania.

The result is, however, overdetermined, if not confusing. The novel portrays the establishment of cultural hierarchy without endorsing the reification of social hierarchy; it speaks a classed discourse about taste without sanctioning, while in fact contesting, the class assumptions that underlie that discourse. It thus simultaneously moves in two directions, towards what we might call elitist and anti-elitist assertions about the effect of art on its audience. In what might be described as a populist move, the elite audience for culture is shown to act exactly like their lower-brow counterparts; but — in an anti-democratizing, indeed highly elitist move — the novel images both in the terms of hypnotic mind control, recapitulating both the imagery and the logic of class difference in the very means it uses to deny it.

The novel's message to its culturally insecure audience is equally dual. While its readership is theoretically empowered by the novel, the means of that empowerment are ultimately constraining. The novel's audience is endowed with a conceptual apparatus for thinking of their own response which leads to a sharply bifurcated vision of themselves as an audience, a position in which the readers of the novel are simultaneously asked to identify with the enthusiasm of the audience and the critique of that very enthusiasm — to participate vicariously in the response of the audience and to see that response from a critical position exterior to it. This knot of intensely contradictory subject positions is fully tied at the end of the novel, in the last scene of audience response it has to offer us. Trilby and Svengali are to debut their magnificent show in London; the increasingly unstable Svengali strikes Trilby in a rehearsal and is forbidden by his doctor from undergoing the strain of performance. Out of jealousy, anger, and pique, Svengali fails to hypnotize Trilby and (as we learn later) dies, leaving Trilby standing before an angry crowd, unable to sing or even to know why she stands before them. None of the seductive intimacy of the earlier scenes of audience response are evident in this scene; the audience, Taffee, the Laird, and Little Billee, and the reader all stand in incomprehending alienation from Trilby, as Trilby herself does to (the now dead) Svengali. At this moment of utter estrangement, the crowd is fully personified, and is represented in terms which bring to a dizzying climax the novel's play between high- and lowbrow:

> Then came a voice from the gods in answer [to Trilby's incomprehension, voiced not in French but in English]:
>
> "Oh, ye're Henglish, har ye? Why don't yer sing as yer *hought* to sing — yer've got *voice* enough, any'ow! why don't yer sing in *tune*?" (295)

When hypnotic control is withheld, in other words, Du Maurier's audience significantly speaks with one voice; and that voice possesses a distinctly lowbrow intonation. But the ostentatiously lower class and lowbrow identification of the crowd contrast utterly with its own words; the crowd's focus on Trilby's linguistic identity (a matter of mystery throughout the book) and its emphasis on vocal propriety ("sing as yer *hought* to sing") both stand in ironic contradistinction to its own demotic diction. Here the pattern of taste and class allegiances we have seen throughout the novel is significantly reversed. Instead of a highbrow audience acting with lowbrow frenzies, here a lowbrow audience acts with a highbrow concern for dictional and musical proprieties. But this reversal only indicates the true nature of the control to which the audience is now subjected; it reveals that that control is now, thoroughly, internalized. For, released from the gentle discipline of Trilby and the domineering mastery of Svengali, the audience demonstrates how well it has learned its lesson from them. At precisely the moment of freedom, the audience turns its own inner anxieties about cultural response outwards, and disciplines those figures who hitherto have disciplined them.

At this point in the text I would like to locate the full unfolding of what I am calling mania of the middlebrow — and a full unfolding of its labile dynamics. The switch from valorization to demonization is shown by the text itself to be not a moment of carnivalesque (or Levinean) populist critique but a thoroughly middlebrow response, a response which conjoins cultural squeamishness with cultural excess; a moment in which the critique of the embodiments of high culture like Svengali and even Trilby is shown to be predicated upon an impossibly idealized vision of high cultural propriety, and at which the response swings from adulation into revulsion at the sight of any deviation from a hyperbolized and over-invested norm. This moment has further significance for our current project. In the actual historical as well as the textual "Trilby-mania," we witness a "mania" not only in the sense of "enthusiasm" but also in that of "rage": a "rage" expressed simultaneously for and at the products and possibilities of high culture, a rage predicated upon the idealization of high culture that the negative moment of that response contests.

And it is this labile dynamic, I would suggest, that makes *Trilby*-mania so significant. It surfaces early and unfolds powerfully in both the novel and in its subsequent career in the world of mass or popular entertainment. As the audience switches from the idealization of Trilby to her denigration when her voice disappears, so too the audience of this text switched early and dramatically from their idealization of Trilby to the denigration of Svengali. To be more precise, the Trilby/Svengali doublet is also encoded in the very character of Svengali, which expresses in its acutest form the ambivalence that governs the text's response to high culture:

> Svengali playing Chopin on the pianoforte, even (or especially) Svengali playing "Ben Bolt" on that penny whistle of his, was as one of the heavenly host. Svengali walking up and down the earth seeking whom he might cheat, betray, exploit, borrow money from, make brutal fun of, bully if he dared, cringe to if he must — man, woman, child, or dog — was about as bad as they make'm.
> (45)

With Svengali, in other words, ambivalence about culture becomes definitional, structural; he is at once the cultural ideal and the cultural abject, the purest of the pure, the filthiest of the filthy. And here too the novel's ambivalence structured — or spoke to — the audience's own ambivalence on the subject of "culture." The career of the novel in the shifting spheres of public entertainment affords the best illustration of this lability; *Trilby*-mania soon merges into an odd fascination with Svengali, one which outlasts the early responses that centered with such cultural idealism on the figure of Trilby. We already see the figure of Svengali lurking behind the early stages of Trilby-mania — as the evil ringmaster, for example, snapping his whip in the Greatest Show On Earth. The enormously popular stage version of the novel, starring the illustrious Sir Beerbohm Tree, was entitled *Svengali* and focused its attention on that malevolent figure. As Trilby-mania faded into the mists of cultural memory, the figure of Svengali exerted an increasing force. The tale was made into two movies: a silent film of the twenties, entitled *Trilby* was followed by a (marvelous) 1937 film entitled *Svengali* and starring John Barrymore, a vehicle more or less carried by his remarkable performance (and one which, tellingly, was far more faithful to the illustrations and plot of the novel than its predecessor). When the novel is mentioned at all today it is usually remembered for the name "Svengali" — which has even entered, I was delighted recently to learn, the *Dictionary of American Slang.*

As the novel receded into cultural memory, then, it did so just as much as Svengali's text as Trilby's — and just as much as an emblem of the middlebrow's revulsion against the experience of high culture as a sign of their faith in it. Thus, far more that any of the other fin de siècle "manias" for "culture" (with the significant exception of that centering on Oscar Wilde's 1881–82 tour) *Trilby*-mania was accompanied by a spate of parodies — parodic songs, broadsides, burlesques, and other such ephemeral expressions of popular critique. And *Trilby*-mania was met with a significant degree of criticism from established cultural authorities:

> "Have you read 'Trilby'?" was the theme of the Rev. George Bicknell's sermon, and the topic crowded the [Boston] church. The Reverend Doctor declared that he had spent five hours reading the book, and had decided that it was a story of magnificent possibilities, but that its morality was "as one viewed it." He considered the tale far-fetched and over-drawn and lacking in healthful flavor, and placed it in the same class of art with the nude paintings at the World's Fair — a position to which, we presume, the author would not object. Then he launched into an emphatic declaration that it was time for the pulpit to speak out against art of this kind. (*Trilbyana*, 23–24)

But this negative response, like its positive counterpart, seems oddly grounded in the text. This thoroughly middlebrow preacher — seeking, one presumes, to enlarge attendance by delivering a sermon on a topic of cultural moment — resembles Svengali and Trilby in "crowding" his church with eager parishioners; and those parishioners in turn resemble the *Trilby*-maniacs by seeking from Bicknell instruction, guidance, counsel in proper responses to the mystifying world of high culture. Bicknell, in short, performs vis-à-vis *Trilby* the same maneuver that the novel performed vis-à-vis high culture; he serves at once as guide and judge, expositor and monitor towards his culturally insecure audience. This position places him in an oddly dual position vis à vis that text, one which uneasily conjoins imitation with competition. Bicknell moves from judgments of taste into those of morality (a conflation summarized by that wonderful phrase "healthful flavor") into a full-scale denunciation of the novel and the cultural order it represents — but in exactly the same way that the text itself switches between celebrating Trilby as an emblem of high-cultural perfection to demonizing, as emblem of a high culture gone horrifically wrong, the malevolent Svengali. And if Du Maurier establishes his own bona fides with the middlebrow audience by "speaking out" against the high culture his novel celebrates by representing that culture in the guise of a character "as bad as they make'm," Bicknell does the same thing both to high culture and his middlebrow rival by demonizing *Trilby* itself.

The persistence of Svengali-phobia and of the negative cathexis to culture that figure embodies is, I would suggest, the most enduring aspect of *Trilby*-mania. For — to move from the cultural manias of the fin de siècle to those of our own late-century moment — the same dynamics on display in *Trilby*-mania continue to be evidenced in the response of the middlebrow audience to the art and writing of its contemporary high culture — a culture, particularly in its avant-garde and academic phases, as exotic and esoteric to that audience as was the Left Bank to the American middlebrow at the end of the nineteenth century. The conflict that circulated in 1989 and still seems to circulate around the question of government funding of the arts, and especially the funding provided (indirectly) of the homoerotic art of Robert Mapplethorpe, provides a marvelous case in point. From the rather Olympian perspective of American academic culture it would appear that that controversy presents a classic collision between high- and lowbrow culture. But if we try to get outside our own structures of thought and read these events through what we have learned in *Trilby*-mania, we see that this hysteria registers a different version of the same dynamic I have been attempting to trace here. It reveals a public fear and resentment of the arts, to be sure, but one that rather paradoxically grants artist and art work a near-supernatural power to corrupt the minds of its audience. What makes this latter fear an expression of the middlebrow conflict, rather than, say, a lowbrow contempt for the arts, is the way that the anti-NEA sentiment deploys the figure of Mapplethorpe. Both the photographs and, by extension, the man who made them possess the magical power to corrupt, to destroy, if not to change the sexual orientation of, all those who come into contact with them. Mapplethorpe, in sum, has been made to serve as our culture's Svengali: as that hypnotic and hypnotizing object of fascination and fear onto which all the cultural insecurities and anxieties that mark the middlebrow can be loaded — and so loaded both by the efforts of the political and cultural right.

To conclude on an ominous note that brings this essay's concern up to the current moment, where Robert Mapplethorpe is made to stand, can the academic be far behind? Is it possible that when we refuse to sing the way we ought to, an increasingly resentful middlebrow culture led by an infuriated culture industry will rediscover their lowbrow origins, and boo us off the stage —

perhaps (to continue the analogy) for not speaking the right kind of English, for teaching the right kinds of texts? Certainly the frenzy in the middlebrow press on the subject of "political correctness" in the academy would suggest that we academics, hitherto students rather than occasions of public outrage, face a version of Svengali-phobia. For, as with Mapplethorpe, the attack on academic leftism centered, at a crucial moment, on the creation of a hypnotically endowed villain — the (like Svengali) implausible and (like Svengali, at the end of the novel) conveniently dead figure of Paul de Man.

I cite both in example and in conclusion the following, a letter published in the *New York Times Book Review* in response to a favorable review by Malcolm Bradbury of David Lehman's peevish critique of the academy, theory, Paul de Man, and just about anything else he can think of attacking: *Signs of the Times*.[13] Here, in toto, is the letter, from George Wellwarth of Binghamton, New York:

> Malcolm Bradbury's excellent review of David Lehman's "Signs of the Times" neatly deconstructs the claims of deconstruction. It fails, however, to make clear the pernicious influence that Paul de Man still exercises on the academic profession despite his (alas!) posthumous disgrace. Departments of literature in American universities continue to teach the moronic theories of deconstruction and continue to turn their curriculums upside down, making what they call criticism superior to creation by requiring courses in deconstruction and making courses in primary sources elective.
>
> I never met de Man because I carefully avoided several opportunities to do so. Those who did know him cannot be blamed for having been taken in by that manipulative and conscienceless opportunist and intellectual fraud. No decent person can have any defences against the former; unfortunately, only another can be taken in by the latter.

There's much both to amuse and alarm here from a purely intellectual standpoint: the collapse of "theory" into the term "deconstruction," for example, as if the hopes of the most fervent deconstructor could be realized and the two could be seen as identical. But what most fascinates and appalls in the current context is the way that this letter moves farther into middlebrow mania the closer it gets to the figure of De Man. That figure is rendered, in the hands of Wellwarth, as hypnotic as he is malignant — hypnotic, indeed, precisely because he is so unimaginably malevolent that "no decent person" can have any defences against his wiles. (De Man, like Svengali, is "as bad as they make'm" — and "bad" precisely because he is so prodigiously gifted.) Indeed, the author tells us that he has carefully avoided the seductions of this "manipulative and conscienceless opportunist" by the expedient of never meeting him, as if to do so would be to be seduced as inevitably as was Trilby by her own hypnotic teacher. ("You will hear nothing, see nothing, feel nothing, but *deconstruction, deconstruction, deconstruction*!!!") Further enhancing the connection between Svengali-phobia and (what else can it be called but) DeMania, the *Times* punctuates the letter with a picture of the fearsome De Man himself, exercising his seductive wiles in his very own concert arena: the classroom. De Man — a charismatic presence in the classroom, current neo-conservative dogma has it; I myself found him only slightly less off-putting than my other teachers of the time — De Man sits at the head of the seminar table leering at once toothily and awkwardly at the camera, while the audience he has so thoroughly enthralled sits just out of camera range, represented only by disembodied arms: faceless puppets, one assumes, controlled by the master mesmerist.

The analogy between the image of De Man constructed by the *Times a*nd that constructed of Svengali by Du Maurier, the House of Harper, and the fin de siècle middlebrow readership is not, I hope, fanciful or factitious. In the *Times's* version of DeMania — a mania as carefully cultivated as was Trilbymania (not a single negative word, for example, has been allowed in the *Times* about Lehman's book, nor a positive one about De Man or deconstruction) — we see middlebrow medium and middlebrow reader match and reinforce each other's prejudices with uncanny accuracy. This juncture is perhaps best demonstrated, again, by Wellwarth's letter, which safely confirms what the *Times* reviewers (Michiko Kakutani and an unsympathetic academic, Malcolm Bradbury) both affirm as well: a hopelessly naïve notion of such thoroughly problematical notions — even to us non-Demaniacs — as culture, origin, morality, truth, interpretation, literature, art, value, reading. And in so doing, audience and medium confirm each other's roles with an unerring precision. The reader is confirmed in all of the common-sensical notions (Bourdieu calls them, after Barthes, *doxa*, received and unquestioned truths) that both academic and avant-garde discourses have sought to examine, challenge, and complicate. And, more importantly, the experience of the common, ordinary reader — that figure's comfortably unmediated, common-sensical response to literary works — is validated and affirmed. Meanwhile the organs of middlebrow culture define *themselves* as true dispensers of cultural enlightenment by playing upon (and playing up to) precisely these readerly sentiments. Through their management of this issue, institutions like the *Times* and individuals like Lehman (a book critic for *Newsweek* and a poet of modest achievement) proclaim that they, rather than those wacky academic Demaniacs, are the true purveyors of cultural truth, the genuine arbiters of aesthetic standards and artistic value.

These most recent examples of middlebrow outrage provide only the latest in a series of interlocking conflicts that have structured and defined both the experience of the middlebrow and of middlebrow culture in America since their rise to full articulation and partial hegemony in the late nineteenth century. These conflicts have different embodiments — the split between pure "original source" and polluted "theory"; between ideal "art" and Mapplethorpian "obscenity"; between commonsensical journalistic critics and toothy tweedy academics — but, I am trying to suggest, all originate in the conflicts about "culture" we have seen in *Trilby*-mania. For in all these sites of contestation, we note both idealization of cultural experience — culture imaged as being as innocent and beautiful and ideal as a Trilby — and the creation of a primitive, sexualized, alternative to it — culture imaged as being as malevolent and hypnotic as Svengali. Both responses generate and enhance each other within the middlebrow public; they play volatilely off against each other, causing cathexes and decathexes, bursts of enthusiasms and antagonism towards, the high culture whose acceptance the middlebrow reader both seeks and resents. And both responses are carefully shaped by the organs of middlebrow culture, who seek thereby to establish themselves as commonsensical guardians of the high-culture tradition — the true source of cultural knowledge, the true arbiters and interpreters of cultural value and distinction.

From Du Maurier to David Lehman, from the House of Harper to the *New York Times*, and from the nineteenth century fin de siècle to our own, the middlebrow public, middlebrow culture, and those of us who would seek to establish our autonomy from both — the cultural avant-garde and/or the academic — all find ourselves enmeshed in the ambivalence with which the middlebrow responds to the contradictory terms of its own social compact — its own desire to affirm social status through a cathexis to the ephebes of a high culture that, by its very nature and definition, defines itself against just such middlebrow audiences. Or such at least is what I have tried to show in this essay, which attempts to argue to the only audience I can reach — this audience of fellow-academics — that our fate is wholly caught up in the experience of the middlebrow we would marginalize, whose rage *for* culture we find literally indispensable for our own efforts, and whose public outrage, whose raging out *at* the very cultural arrangements that that public by the very same logic and with the very same energy so thoroughly idealizes, we should properly and prudently fear.

University of Michigan

Notes

Generous audiences at the University of North Carolina, Michigan, and Emory University provided thoughtful responses to versions of this essay; I'd like to thank James Thompson, Walter Reed, and June Howard for asking the right questions at the right time. Richard Brodhead, Stephen Tifft, and Adrienne Donald commented on incessant drafts of the essay. I thank them for their patience and perceptiveness.

[1] For the former points, see Peter Burger, *Theory of the Avant-Garde*, tr. Michael Shaw (Minneapolis: U of Minnesota P, 1984), and Andreas Huyssen, "The Search for Tradition: Avantgarde and Postmodernism in the 1970s" in *After the Great Divide: Modernism, Mass Culture, Postmodernism* (Bloomington: Indiana UP, 1986), 160–177. For the latter, see Marshall Berman, *Modern Culture and Critical Theory: Art, Politics, and the Legacy of the Frankfurt School* (Madison: U of Wisconsin P, 1989), esp. 27–53 and 70–98; and Dwight MacDonald, who, in 1962, wrote "*Pour épater les bourgeois* was the defiant slogan of nineteenth-century avant-gardists but now the bourgeoisie has developed a passion for being shocked," in *Against the American Grain: Essays on the Effects of Mass Culture* (New York: Random House, 1962), 57. This last point, adumbrated by Lionel Trilling, has recently become a crucial tenet of the neo-conservative right (Hilton Kramer is a particularly egregious example), members of which routinely condemn contemporary bourgeois-phobes but celebrate their nineteenth-century versions.

[2] See Gerald Graff, *Professing Literature* (Chicago: U of Chicago P, 1987) and Jonathan D. Culler, *Framing the Sign: Criticism and its Institutions* (Oxford and New York: Blackwell, 1988).

[3] Lawrence Levine, *Highbrow/Lowbrow: The Emergence of Cultural Hierarchy in America* (New York: Oxford UP, 1988); Neil Harris, *Cultural Excursions: Marketing Appetites and Cultural Tastes in Modern America* (Chicago: U of Chicago P, 1990) and Joan Shelley Rubin, *The Making of Middlebrow Culture* (Chapel Hill: U of North Carolina P, 1992). Janice Radway's work on the Book-of-the-Month Club is forthcoming.

[4] Virginia Woolf, "Middlebrow" in *Collected Essays*, 4 vols., (London: The Hogarth Press, 1966), 2: 196–203.

[5] Pierre Bordieu, *Distinction: A Social Critique of the Judgement of Taste*, tr. Richard Nice (Cambridge: Harvard UP, 1984), 323. Further citations refer to this edition.

[6] F. O. Matthiessen and Kenneth Murdock, eds., *The Notebooks of Henry James* (New York: Oxford UP, 1947), 97. Du Maurier's recollection of this incident are in *Trilbyana*, a special issue of the journal *The Critic* (separately published, New York, 1895), 3. Further citations refer to these editions.

[7] The relation between James and DuMaurier's plot was already somewhat vexed, since DuMaurier's device of a woman who can achieve effects of genius only when hypnotized is lifted from James's *Bostonians*. But, although James did not fail ruefully to contemplate his own failure to achieve a similar public success, his attitude towards

DuMaurier was always generous, perhaps best evidenced by the *hommage* he pays to his friend's novel in his text which comes closest to depicting bohemian Parisian life, *The Ambassadors*. It is no coincidence that one of the most winsome and sympathetic characters of that novel, the "little artist-man" Little Bilham, seems to be named after DuMaurier's prodigious if modest artistic genius, Little Billee. While Little Billee pines for Trilby and dies of grief after her death, Little Bilham ends happily, by winning the affections, and perhaps the hand, of Mamie Pocock.

[8] The novel was published first in America by Harper's, subsequently in England by Longman's. The figures for sales are from *Trilbyana*, 13.

[9] To these ingredients, we add another: charge a lot of money. Passage of the American Copyright Act of 1891 guaranteed that no cheap editions from reprint houses would threaten the profits of established publishers, so Harper's felt free to print a lavishly illustrated edition of the novel — more lavish than the one Du Maurier's British house, Osgood, Mcilvaine and Co., produced — at the extravagant price of $1.75 per volume. These efforts guaranteed that *Trilby* would prove remunerative as well as popular: although Du Maurier signed away the initial copyright for a much-needed $10,000, Harper's volunteered sufficient royalties to allow Du Maurier to realize the princely sum of $135,000 — enough, he gratefully recorded, to allow him to build a new house overlooking Hampstead Heath. Harper's could afford such a generous gesture; they made $600,000 on the book in 1895 alone, and even more in licensing fees for theatrical productions. All told, the House of Harper was estimated to have realized about $1,000,000 dollars on Du Maurier's novel — a tidy sum even in our day, a fortune in Du Maurier's. For additional details, see Purcell, "Trilby and Trilby-Mania: The Beginnings of the Best-Seller System," *Journal of Popular Culture* 11 (Summer 1977): 62–77; quotation 74. Further citations to Purcell refer to this publication.

[10] George Du Maurier, *Trilby* (1931; London: Dent, 1978), 35. Citations refer to this edition.

[11] Charles Dudley Warner, "Editor's Study," *Harper's Magazine*, September, 1894, 636. Citations refer to this publication.

[12] As quoted in John Mueller, *The American Symphony Orchestra* (Bloomington: Indiana UP, 1951), 132–33, 356–57, reproduced by Levine, 192.

[13] *New York Times Book Review*, 31 March 1991, 86.

KATHLEEN L. KOMAR

Whatever Happened to the Lyrical Novel? Madness and the Lyrical in Bessie Head's *A Question of Power* and Ingeborg Bachmann's *Malina*

I began rereading my well-fingered copy of Ralph Freedman's *The Lyrical Novel* in anticipation of writing a piece for this *Festschrift*.[1] One of my young colleagues in East Asian literature spotted the volume and commented that it had been a crucial critical text in her graduate studies in Hong Kong. My mind began to journey to African texts that could be better understood by thinking in the critical terminology of *The Lyrical Novel*. Ralph's work has traveled well both geographically and temporally, I thought. At the same time, I was reading a paper by one of my graduate students on madness in the work of a contemporary Chinese woman writer.[2] And I began to mull over the connections between the lyrical novel as it is defined in Ralph Freedman's work and the issue of madness in the works of twentieth-century women writers from diverse cultural backgrounds.[3]

It occurred to me immediately that many of the "purely lyrical" novels Freedman mentions contain a central consciousness (or consciousnesses) who is either on the brink of madness or descends into it full force. Rilke's Malte Laurids Brigge, for example, seeks psychiatric help; in Djuna Barnes's *Nightwood* several characters flirt with madness; many of Virginia Woolf's characters maintain only a precarious balance on the borders of sanity; the same could be said of Hesse's heroes. Why is this the case? And does the pattern continue into lyrical novels by contemporary women writers? These are questions I would like to explore in two novels from the 1970s: Austrian Ingeborg Bachmann's *Malina*[4] and South African Bessie Head's *A Question of Power*.[5] These two texts display a particularly intense interaction of madness and the lyrical and may serve as examples of lyrical strategies employed by recent women writers to tap non-rational domains of understanding.

Both Bachmann and Head feature intense, female, first-person narrators whose experience of the world is enacted through a progression of images that renders the narrating self as a symbolic vision. Both works have been read (perhaps too often) as closely autobiographical because of the distinct impression that the narrator embodies the author's "I" or a lyrical persona, thus conflating experiencing self and experienced world into a lyrical inwardness captured in an aesthetically objective form. All of this description is familiar, of course, from Freedman's defining chapters on the lyrical novel. Interestingly, both Bessie Head's Elizabeth and Bachmann's (unnamed) first-person narrator have bouts of insanity, of such intense experience of a painful internal life that it fragments their consciousnesses and threatens to destroy the self.

Perhaps this proximity of insanity and the lyrical should not be so surprising in novels where the lyrical self is an extremely sensitive experiencing consciousness whose rhetoric is that of images and the creative imagination. Indeed, many of our definitions of madness have to do with the inability to disentangle the visions of the mind from what we experience in the outside world; it is precisely this purposeful confusion of the external world and internal experience that marks the lyrical novel. Tracing the roots of the lyrical novel back to the idealistic epistemology of Romanticism (and particularly the works of Novalis), Freedman describes this interaction:

> This process of telescoping self and world is based in the main on the idealistic epistemology of the time. The artist represents himself in an object. He portrays his inner experience and by this act transmutes the object that expresses him into a manifestation of his "infinite self" — the visible work of art. The perceived object becomes part of the poet's experience while rendering his private sensibility public, but, in mirroring the poet's inner state, it loses its separate, independent character. In this way, perceived objects become manifestations of the poet's spirit — features of his self-portrait — as they are portrayed symbolically in the form of art. The "object" is the catalyst through which a finite, individual self is transmuted into an infinite, aesthetic self. (20)

The difficulty for contemporary women writers lies in the fact that the infinite, perfected, transcendent self is rather hard to achieve nowadays. Bessie Head's protagonist can still, with extreme struggle, reach such a self; Ingeborg Bachmann's narrator cannot. In Bachmann, the self is rather absorbed into the world of objects, walled up in an external physicality that eliminates the internal and poetic.

But it is striking that two women writers from such different cultures would produce such similar literary embodiments of their experience. In both *Malina* and *A Question of Power* a female narrator is positioned psychologically between two male personalities who represent differing sets of experience. The female character spends some time transmuting the outside world into an internal, lyrical comprehension in order to choose a male with which to align herself and who would provide some stability upon which she could define a coherent self of her own. In both novels, the female characters are for some time absorbed or smothered by the male character, kept from finding a voice — and a self — of their own. The moments at which the female characters can break loose to speak and explore their fragmented selves are those passages which are most lyrical and least plot oriented. They are also the passages in which insanity most intensely threatens.

Malina

To begin with the earlier of the two novels, *Malina* (which alludes several times to two other lyrical novels, Rilke's *Malte* and Novalis's *Heinrich von Ofterdingen*) actually begins in a dramatic rather than lyrical mode. It presents a list of characters as well as designating a setting and a rather vague time frame, "Heute" (today), which immediately calls up all the yesterdays that preceded it. But the drama in the novel occurs on what the narrator calls a "Gedankenbühne" (thought stage),[6] thus linking what would appear to be a form in the external world back to a subjectively experiencing consciousness. As Bachmann suggests in her *Vorrede* to *Der Fall Franza* (The Case [or Fall, as in ruin] of Franza), the real setting of the action of her stories is "in dem Denken" (in thought) and "[dem] Innen" (the internal);[7] the external *Schauplätze* (stages or theaters) simply provide a physical space in which to work out or "perform" the work of the mind. Bachmann's description here comes remarkably close to Freedman's analysis of the lyrical novel itself in which:

> many contemporary novelists have dissected a self — their own or that of their protagonists — and have turned it into a stage on which plot and themes are enacted . . . . A poetic design rather than an external world describes the limits of that stage . . . . (18)

Bachmann, then, sets precisely the stage that Freedman foresees in his discussion.

In fact, it is often impossible to disentangle the internal and external in *Malina*. Much of the text takes place on the borderlands where consciousness and event merge to produce patterns of imagery not easily comprehended rationally. It is impossible to tell if events and even characters (particularly Malina himself) exist in the "real" world or as projections of the nameless female narrator's tortured psyche — or both. This aesthetically productive confusion of internal states of consciousness and external experience is the perfect ground for the lyrical novel.

One area in which that lyrical narration becomes immediately evident is the treatment of the male characters, and specifically of Malina. Bachmann's unnamed first-person narrator is torn between the rational and practical Malina and the passionate Ivan, who invigorates her imagination but remains largely indifferent to her needs. The two male characters can be read both as discrete characters and as fragments of the narrator's own mind.[8] Malina, in particular, seems to function as a part of the female narrator's lyrical imagination. The narrator projects Malina into a number of fairy-tale settings, seeing him as "'Eugenius' . . . weil 'Prinz Eugen, der edle Ritter' das erste Lied war, das ich zu lernen hatte und damit auch den ersten Männernamen" (17) ("Eugenius" . . . because "Prince Eugen, the noble knight" was the first song that I had to learn and also the first male name). Malina thus exists in song and legend — and in the narrator's projections into the lyrical mode — as much or more than he exists in reality.

This enveloping of male characters in an inner projection applies also to the narrator's remembering of her father in the novel's central dream (or nightmare) section. The dreams open in the "Friedhof der ermordeten Töchter" (cemetery of murdered daughters) (182 ff.) and contains a holocaust-like vision of torture and abuse (both psychological and sexual) at the hands of a relentlessly cruel father. These are the pages in which the narrator most forcefully descends into an insanity of which she is conscious: "Wenn es anfängt, ist die Welt schon durcheinandergekommen, und ich weiß, daß ich wahnsinnig bin" (183) (When it begins, the world is already in chaos, and I know that I am insane). The most intense inner experience can only be expressed in a series of images, of disjointed recurrences of fire and ice, of figural embodiments of the father's destructive force (as in his crushing underfoot the blossoms of the narrator's life force).

The lyrical here allows the narrator a voice of symbols when she is pointedly unable to provide a logical narrative thread in the text's rational surface. In fact, much of the text is precisely about finding a way to narrate that which is much too personal, internalized and painful simply to emplot. The narrator must enact her memories through lyrical symbols in order to confront experiences so traumatic that they render the narrator mute on the rational level.[9] The lyrical mode allows the narrator to temper information too excruciating to brave directly.[10] Only by passing through the cauldron of the intensely internal experience embodied in the veiled symbolism of the lyrical can the narrator finally begin to find a voice and face the painful struggle and endless battle to create a self.[11] The struggle is not triumphant in *Malina*, but the first step in the war is waged in the lyrical center of the text.

But the lyrical also appears in those few moments in the text when the narrator is liberated from the male world and finds, at least temporarily, a center within herself not defined by men. While contemplating herself in a mirror when trying on clothing, the narrator comes to a moment of stability and coherence of self:

> Ich möchte aber beim Anprobieren Ivan nicht hier haben, Malina schon gar nicht, ich kann nur, weil Malina nicht da ist, oft in den Spiegel sehen, ich muß mich im Korridor vor dem langen Spiegel mehrmals drehen, meilenweit, klaf-

tertief, himmelhoch, sagenweit entfernt von den Männern. Eine Stunde lang kann ich zeit- und raumlos leben, mit einer tiefen Befriedigung . . . (139)[12]

[While trying on clothes, I don't want Ivan here, and certainly not Malina, only because Malina isn't there can I look in the mirror often, I have to turn around several times in the corridor before the tall mirror, miles away, fathoms deep, sky high, fabulously distant from men. For an hour I can live without time and space, in a deep satisfaction . . .]

This momentary liberation is followed by a lyrical venture into a fairy-tale realm of the not-yet-achieved future world of women who are whole.[13] "*Ein Tag wird kommen, an dem die Frauen rotgoldene Augen haben, rotgoldenes Haar, und die Poesie ihres Geschlechts wird wiedererschaffen werden*" (140; italics in the original)(*A day will come on which women will have red-golden eyes, red-golden hair, and the poetry of their sex will be re-created*). This wholeness is generously extended to "Die Menschen" (mankind) as a whole very quickly as the opening line becomes "*Ein Tag wird kommen, an dem die Menschen rotgoldene Augen und siderische Stimmen haben, an dem ihre Hände begabt sein werden für die Liebe, und die Poesie ihres Geschlechts wird wiedererschaffen sein*" (142; italics in the original) (*A day will come on which mankind will have red-golden eyes and sidereal voices, on which their hands will be gifted for love, and the poetry of their race will be re-created*). What seems to be a gendered wish-fulfillment fairy tale immediately expands to become a vision for mankind as a whole, a vision in which the struggle between gender roles and split selves is resolved into a unity.

However, the fairy tale rapidly takes on an apocalyptic tone as a vision of the final destruction of our world and a rebirth into a new realm is described:

Ein Tag wird kommen, an dem unsere Häuser fallen, die Autos werden zu Schrott geworden sein, von den Flugzeugen und von den Raketen werden wir befreit sein, den Verzicht leisten auf die Erfindung des Rads und der Kernspaltung . . . , wir werden tot sein und atmen, es wird das ganze Leben sein.

(144; italics in the original)

[*A day will come on which our houses will fall, automobiles will become scrap metal, we will be freed from airplanes and rockets, we will forgo the invention of the wheel and the splitting of the atom . . . , we will be dead and breathe, it will be all of life.*]

(One is reminded here of Malte Laurids Brigge's distaste for the distractions of technology in Rilke's novel.) In the narrator's vision in *Malina*, the old world of technology and scientific thought will be replaced by a more poetic (and ecological) unity with nature, "*die Diamanten werden im Gestein bleiben und uns allen leuchten, der Urwald wird uns aus dem Nachtwald unserer Gedanken übernehmen, wir werden aufhören, zu denken und zu leiden, es wird die Erlösung sein*" (145; italics in the original) (*Diamonds will remain in the rocks and shine for all of us, the primeval forest will take possession of us from the night forests of our thoughts, we will cease thinking and suffering, it will be deliverance*). Only when the poetry of the race overcomes our valorization of rational and scientific — as well as individuating and isolating — thought can we find a kind of lyrical salvation. For Bachmann, then, the lyrical can embody a unifying salvation (somewhat reminiscent of Novalis's *Heinrich von Ofterdingen*) as well as a threatening world of the subconscious.

This more benevolent lyrical moment is short-lived, however. The narrator remains split and doubled; she cannot finally create an integrated self that can comfortably accommodate both her masculine and feminine components.[14] She disappears at the end of the text into a symbolic wall that suppresses her voice and her being. Only the male persona of Malina remains as the text closes with the words, "Es war Mord" (It was murder).[15] The lyrical may hold out some hope and may lead the narrator through otherwise untraversable territory, but in the end, the relentless domination of the rational, male world overpowers all remaining symbols of the narrator's internal vision. Malina carefully crushes and discards the narrator's eyeglasses as well as her writing as he moves to occupy the whole of the textual world. The lyrical passages finally give way to a matter-of-fact and rational assertion of exclusive male identity that is verified by a numerical identification number via a piece of technology: "Meine Nummer is 723144. Mein Name? Malina." (356) (my [telephone] number is 723144. My Name? Malina). The male-dominated technological and rational world has swamped the salvation fleetingly envisioned in the female-aligned lyrical passages.[16]

A Question of Power

Bessie Head's *A Question of Power*, on the other hand, depicts women's withdrawal into their own minds and the lyrical projection of that experience into symbolic writing as a therapeutic gesture that allows women to make a space within the larger, rationalist-dominated culture for more non-rational contemplations. Head's main character, Elizabeth, hallucinates through much of the text in order to find her way back to a unified identity and a stabilized outside world. The lyrical and symbolic that Bachmann fleetingly suggests might be a move in the direction of salvation becomes for Head a full-fledged redemption.

Elizabeth's re-vision of her life in the interior space of her mind not only involves her own psychological space, but the space of literature and culture as well. In a distinctly lyrical mode, Elizabeth calls up and literally "re-members" the male and female figures of African, Western European and East Asian cultural tradition in order to create a reunification not just of her own identity, but of the world at large. Figures from Greek mythology and philosophy, Buddha, the biblical David, Egyptian and Hindu mythological figures, and a host of African deities interact and merge in Elizabeth's tortured mind as she struggles to return to sanity.[17]

The process Elizabeth works through is illuminated by Freedman's comments in *The Lyrical Novel* on the technique of mirroring which is tied to the German Romantic roots of the genre:

> Since the self is the point at which inner and outer worlds are joined, the hero's mental picture reflects the universe of sensible encounters as an image. The "world" is part of the hero's inner world; the hero, in turn, mirrors the external world and all its multitudinous manifestations. He *distorts* the universe or dissolves it into hallucination or dream in which its "true" (infinite and organic) nature is revealed. Thus, the magic of spiritual awareness unfolds a picture of infinite reality which is hidden to the ordinary glance. (21)

If we substitute heroine for hero and she for he, we have here a precise description of the progress of Head's protagonist, who does dissolve the world into hallucination in order to come to understand its implications and its ultimate unity. Much more consequently "romantic" in her unifying and idealist vision than Bachmann, Head comes very close to embodying Novalis's description of the successful transcendent hero who reunifies the external and internal worlds through the aesthetic.

I must be careful here not to give the impression that Head is "romantic" in any soft or idyllic sense. I quite agree with Kolawole Ogungbesan in "The Cape Gooseberry Also Grows in Botswana: Alienation and Commitment in the Writings of Bessie Head" when this critic asserts that:

> Miss Head, perhaps more than any other African Writer, has dwelt on the poverty of rural Africa. She is no Romantic, celebrating the superiority of rural life over the urban. Instead, she examines at length the reality of life in the remotest village in Botswana, paying the minutest attention to the poverty and the grim struggle for survival faced by the most lowly villager.[18]

Head does indeed depict poverty, alienation and torment. I compare her to the German Romantic Novalis here only in her capacity to create a unifying vision from her intense internal experience that transcends that individual involvement by raising it to a unity with the universal. And for Head the universal unity is found in the brotherhood of mankind on earth, not in a divine being beyond it. Or as Head puts it, "God is people. There's nothing up there. It's all down here" (*A Question of Power*, 19).

Being a mixed-race woman in the twentieth century rather than a white male in the eighteenth, Head has visions that are much more troubling and dark than Novalis's unifying and transcendent "blue flower." Head's character must fight her way through the hallucination in order to glimpse a larger unseen truth rather than being led forward by the dream imagery toward a goal that is clearly suited to the character's personality as in Novalis's *Heinrich von Ofterdingen*. As Arthur Ravenscroft puts it:

> In *A Question of Power* we are taken nightmarishly into the central character's process of mental breakdown, through lurid cascades of hallucination and a pathological blurring of the frontiers between insanity and any kind of normalcy. It is precisely this journeying into the characters' most secret interior recesses of mind and (we must not fight shy of the word) of soul, that gives [Head's] three novels a quite remarkable cohesion.[19]

But the hallucination does at least lead to that larger unifying vision in Head's text; it only leads to paralysis in Bachmann's. Where Bachmann's narrator is reabsorbed into a deadening outer world, Head's character absorbs and transmutes that threatening external world to produce a reunification of humanity through her symbolic vision.

Like Bachmann's narrator in *Malina*, Bessie Head's Elizabeth in *A Question of Power* is torn between two male characters, the spiritual and mythic Sello and Dan, who represents masculinity and physicality. Even more intensely than is the case in *Malina*, in Head's text, the male characters are a symbolic projection of Elizabeth's mind. They are a symbolic composite of shards of cultural traditions that have been internalized and intermixed by Elizabeth to produce a powerful dichotomous pair of dominating males. The interaction of these symbolic males with Elizabeth in the most lyrical — and most hallucinatory — sections of the novel creates a pattern of imagery that overshadows the linear plot line in the text's rational surface.

In many ways, Elizabeth is forced into her internal world by being a displaced person in the outer one. She is doubly marginalized by her mixed racial heritage. Her mother was white, and her father black; Elizabeth is thus "colored" rather than "African," and thus belongs nowhere. This interaction and conflict of white and black, light and dark is reemphasized in Elizabeth's hallucinations as she is torn between Sello, who is associated with the moon and darkness, and Dan, who is aligned with the sun and light.[20] Having been taken forcibly from her white mother (who was sent to a mental institution in punishment for her racial transgression) at birth,[21] the partially black Elizabeth is psychologically wrenched from her a second time by a heartless teacher who informs Elizabeth that her mother was insane and that Elizabeth, therefore, must be on her guard against inherited insanity. This externally instilled fear of insanity helps to precipitate Elizabeth's breakdowns. Insanity, however, becomes a new means of apprehending a confusingly hostile outer world. The irrational world of symbols rather than the rational world of logical thought provides the way for Elizabeth to reinvent a unified self and world.

After several years of her own psychological torment, embodied and aesthetically solidified in the symbolism of her hallucinations, Elizabeth survives and emerges as a self who has progressed beyond suppression and isolation. In a gesture opposite to that of Bachmann, Head gives her character a parting vision of unity beyond the insular and silenced self. Returning at the end of the novel to the engendering of life in her symbolic garden plot, Elizabeth realizes that she is part of all humankind and that she stretches beyond either of the male personae that battled for control of her mind.[22] The lyrical reemerges into a newly aestheticized external world where inner meaning informs outer object.

The creation of that aesthetic object provides a salvation for Head herself as well as for her character Elizabeth. She describes the writing of the book as follows:

> Oh, I was able to look back and realize that I had been involved in something diabolical. My anxiety was to explain it but to step to one side. I feel, in most situations which you are doubtful of, once you've assessed that something is wrong, if you may not end it or destroy it, you may step to one side. If something is intent on destroying you, it may, but it will not do so without your cooperation. A person with a nervous breakdown is co-operating with the forces that are destroying him. In writing *A Question of Power* I tried to communicate something about evil — the horror that exists behind the every day affairs of man — and in this way I was able to lever myself out of it. (Marquard, 54)

Bachmann's narrator's exploration of the irrational and nightmare leads back to the solidly external world of male dominance and suppression embodied in the socially constructed wall of male language and patriarchal social exclusion, but the trek by Head's Elizabeth through the lyrical landscape of madness allows her to reappropriate language and the external world for a unified human community. Head's ending is a vision of hope amidst the extreme threat of personal and social madness; Bachmann's text is a lament over loss of both language and social coherence for women.

Conclusions

Entering into the lyrical domain, then, is no guarantee of achieving the romantic transcendence envisioned by Novalis and outlined by Freedman as part of the tracing of the roots of the lyrical tradition in the novel. The lyrical novel as realized in the works of contemporary women writers can depict the failure of the internal world to accomplish unity with the external as intensely as it can illustrate success in doing so. But the need to employ the lyrical in the contemporary female novel seems quite acute. The problem of expressing non-rational experience and the insights it can produce in a form that is comprehensible (even if symbolically very complex) may underly the extensive use of the lyrical by contemporary women writers.

The need to find a means by which madness and the irrational can speak to the rational world drives the exploration of lyrical narration by many women writers. Earlier philosophers such as Descartes emphasized thought as the exercizing of reason in order to attain truth. Since madness is outside of reason, philosophy has tended to exclude it from the process of thought that arrives at truth. But women writers (particularly in the nineteenth and twentieth centuries) have come to realize that truth is approachable through other than rational means. Experiences of the body and of the emotions and of the irrational can also lead one to a comprehension of truths. The difficulty is finding a way to express those non-rational experiences in language without being trapped in a wall of reason. The lyrical provides one means by which madness — and the women who experience it — can find a voice.

This voice is not heeded in the external rational world; it cannot speak itself directly. But when embedded in a narrative fiction, the lyrical voice can find expression. This combination of lyrical and narrative allows madness — and women within it — to speak again. After their objectification as "mental illness" in the early twentieth century, madness and the irrational had to regain a footing as accesses to truth, which could be used effectively by women; they had to find a way to escape the discourse of psychiatry that reasoned about madness in order to regain a voice of their own, which women could employ. The lyrical novel affords just such an opportunity.

Shoshana Felman makes a similar point in *Writing and Madness* when she suggests that literature provides an arena in which madness can speak. She says:

> On the idea that literature, fiction is the only possible meeting place between madness and philosophy, between delirium and thought, Foucault would doubtless agree with Derrida. It is in fact *to literature* that Foucault turns in his search for the authentic voice of madness . . . it thus seems that literature is there to *re-place* madness: metaphorically and metonymically. (48)

I would add that the lyrical novel provides an especially suitable ground for madness to find expression that can illumine truth. In the lyrical novel an author can explore the depths of delirium or the imagination and reemerge to proffer truths that can be rationally comprehended by readers. The lyrical novel allows irrational and non-linear perception to be embedded within an otherwise traditionally linear narrative, thus allowing madness an aesthetic reification that can precipitate rational comprehension.

That contemporary women writers would be especially attracted to this possibility is perhaps to be expected when cultural tradition has so often connected madness and women. Ranging from the etymology of the term "hysteria" (deriving from "hystera" or womb) to the common symbols that link feminity and madness (the moon, for example),[23] women and madness have shared a common lot of being imprisoned and silenced by the dominant rational discourse. The need to focus on madness becomes especially pressing for women writers who can use the language of irrationality for particularly seditious ends. As Carol Margaret Davison puts it in a discussion of Bessie Head, "madness may be described as the most potentially subversive subject in women's fiction, for the reassessment of female insanity necessitates its corollary — the reappraisal of patriarchal sanity."[24] The lyrical novel provides one language in which women and madness can find a voice in the late twentieth century.

With its particular suitability for writers concerned with exploring a self and often doing so by fathoming the depths of insanity, the lyrical novel offers contemporary women a genre in which they can investigate both the social and the psychological constructions that condition definitions of gender, madness and self. This form affords women the opportunity to explore understanding itself, or, as Freedman puts it, "The lyrical process expands because the lyrical 'I' is also an experiencing protagonist. The poet's stance is turned into an epistemological act" (271). By scrutinizing this epistemological act in their lyrical novels, women can question the means by which we are constrained to know — or as the patriarchal philosophical tradition demands, to *reason* — in order to arrive at truths appropriate to women's lives. The lyrical novel allows women to act out an epistemology different from that valorized by the Western male tradition. As Freedman rightly asserts, "Few other forms allow the author, or his *persona*, to penetrate so directly into the very act of knowledge and to represent it in immediately accessible portraiture" (283). It is precisely this penetration into the act of knowledge that women authors such as Bachmann and Head are appropriating for their own writing.

Perhaps, then, the somewhat eclipsed future significance that Freedman predicted for the lyrical novel when he was writing in the early 1960s,[25] as the women's movement was just beginning to come into prominence, can be modified in the late 1990s as women have discovered the aptness of this particular genre for their considerations as the twentieth century draws to a close. And perhaps Ralph Freedman's work on the lyrical novel may itself help shed light on some of the more complex narratives of women authors today.

University of California, Los Angeles

Notes

[1] Ralph Freedman, *The Lyrical Novel: Studies in Hermann Hesse, André Gide and Virginia Woolf* (Princeton: Princeton UP, 1963).

[2] Stephanie C. Zhong, "The Madness of the Thinking/Speaking Subject: Exploring the Intersectionality of Madness, Gender and Writing in 'The Golden Cangue,'" unpublished paper June 1996.

[3] Madness and women writers has become a popular topic over the past several years. Witness Sandra Gilbert and Susan Gubar's now classic *The Madwoman in the Attic: The Woman Writer and the Nineteenth-Century Literary Imagination* (New Haven: Yale UP, l979) as well as Shoshana Felman's *Writing and Madness* (Ithaca, NY: Cornell UP, 1978) among others. See also Janet Hadda's discussion of psychological stresses for women in *Passionate Women, Passive Men: Suicide in Yiddish Literature* (Albany: State University of New York P, 1988). A good many texts by women psychologists have focused on avoiding madness by exploiting specifically female possibilities of understanding. Among other studies, see: Nancy Chodorow, *The Reproduction of Mothering: Psychoanalysis and the Sociology of Gender* (Berkeley: U of California P, 1978); Carol Gilligan, *In a Different Voice: Psychological Theory and Women's Development* (Cambridge: Harvard UP, 1982); and Jean Baker Miller, *Toward a New Psychology of Women* (Boston: Beacon, 1976).

I would like to focus here specifically on the embodiment of moments of "madness" in lyrical expression within novels.

[4] Ingeborg Bachmann, *Malina* (Frankfurt am Main: Suhrkamp Verlag, 1971). Translations from the novel are my own.

[5] Bessie Head, *A Question of Power* (London: Heinemann, 1974).

[6] "Für mich ist nie jemand gestorben und selten lebt jemand, außer auf meiner Gedankenbühne" (301)(For me no one ever dies and seldom does anyone live, except on my thought stage). On the topic of a *Gedankenbühne*, see also Monika Albrecht's article, "Kriminalfälle auf einer Gedankenbühne," in *Kein objektives Urteil — nur ein lebendiges: Texte zum Werk von Ingeborg Bachmann*, ed. Christine Koschel and Inge von Weidenbaum (Munich: Piper, 1989), 555–68.

[7] *Ingeborg Bachmann: Werke*, ed. Christine Koschel, Inge von Weidenbaum, and Clemens Münster, 3 vols. (Munich: Piper, 1984), 3:342.

[8] For a discussion of the "aufgelöste Figur" and the "geistige Dreieck" in *Malina*, see Ellen Summerfield's *Ingeborg Bachmann. Die Auflösung der Figur in ihrem Roman "Malina"* (Bonn: Bouvier, 1976).

[9] For more on memory and narration, see Dirk Göttsche, *Die Produktivität der Sprachkrise in der modernen Prosa* (Frankfurt am Main: Athenäum, 1987), 188 ff.

[10] See Sigrid Weigel's discussion of the withholding or obscuring of information in *Malina* in Weigel's *Die Stimme der Medusa. Schreibweisen der Gegenwartsliteratur von Frauen* (Dulmen-Hiddingsel: Tende, 1987), particularly 143 ff.

[11] For a more extensive discussion of female identity in *Malina*, see Gabriele Bail, *Weibliche Identität: Ingeborg Bachmanns "Malina"* (Goettingen: Edition Herodot, 1984) and Saskia Schottelius, *Das imaginäre Ich: Subjekt und Identität in Ingeborg Bachmanns Roman "Malina" und Jacques Lacans Sprachtheorie* (Frankfurt am Main and New York: Peter Lang, 1990).

[12] For a more problematizing reading of the mirror passage, see Sigrid Schmid-Bortenschlager, "Spiegelszenen bei Bachmann: Ansätze einer psychoanalytischen Interpretation," *Modern Austrian Literature* 18.3/4 (1985): 39–52.

[13] For an enlightening discussion of fairytales in Bachmann's work, see Karen Achberger, "Beyond Patriarchy: Ingeborg Bachmann and Fairytales," in *Modern Austrian Literature* 18.3/4 (1985): 211–22.

[14] For more commentary on male/female relations, see Kurt Bartsch, "'Es war Mord': Anmerkungen zur Mann-Frau-Beziehung in Bachmanns Roman *Malina*," *Acta Neophilologica* 17 (1984): 71–76.

[15] In her 1984 comments on Bachmann entitled, "Der Krieg mit anderen Mitteln" in *Kein objektives Urteil — Nur ein lebendiges*, 311–20, Elfriede Jelinek points up the feminist implications of Bachmann's text and the struggle between male and female needs and social demands.

[16] The reception of Bachmann's work by feminist critics has varied over the years — ranging from seeing Bachmann as too resigned and depressing to seeing her as a powerful voice of protest. For a summary discussion of this reception, see Sara Lennox, "The Feminist Reception of Ingeborg Bachmann," *Women in German Yearbook 8: Feminist Studies in German Literature and Culture*, ed. Jeanette Clausen and Sara Friedrichsmeyer (Lincoln and London: U of Nebraska P, 1993), 73–111.

[17] For a more detailed discussion of Head's use of various mythologies, see Joyce Johnson, "Metaphor, Myth and Meaning in Bessie Head's *A Question of Power*," *World Literature Written in English* 25.2 (1985): 198–211.

[18] Kolawole Ogungbesan, "The Cape Gooseberry Also Grows in Botswana: Alienation and Commitment in the Writings of Bessie Head," *Présence Africaine* 109 (1979): 92–106, quotation 95–96.

[19] Arthur Ravenscroft, "The Novels of Bessie Head," in *Aspects of South African Literature*, ed. Christopher Heywood (London: Heinemann Educational, 1976), 175. The volume was reissued in 1978 in New York by Africana Publishing Corporation; the essay is on 317–29.

[20] For a more extended discussion of the significance of Sello and Dan, see Joyce Johnson, "Structures of Meaning in the Novels of Bessie Head" *Kunapipi* 8.1 (1986): 56–69.

[21] This extremely traumatic birth story in fact corresponds to Bessie Head's own life. See her interview with Jean Marquard, "Bessie Head: Exile and Community in Southern Africa," *London Magazine*, 18.9/10, December 1978/January 1979, 48–61.

[22] For more discussion of Elizabeth's insight born of madness, see Femi Ojo-Ade, "Bessie Head's Alienated Heroine: Victim or Villain?" in *Ba Shiru: Journal of African Languages and Literature* 8.2 (1977): 13–22.

[23] I thank my student Stephanie Zhong for pointing me to M. Esther Harding, *Women's Mysteries Ancient and Modern: A Psychological Interpretation of the Feminine Principle as Portrayed in Myth, Story and Dreams* (New York: G. P. Putnam's Sons for the C. G. Jung Foundation, 1971) which provides more detailed examples of this kind.

[24] Carol Margaret Davison, "A Method in the Madness," in *The Tragic Life: Bessie Head and Literature in Southern Africa*, ed. Cecil Abrahams (Trenton: Africa World Press, 1990), 19. For an extended discussion of madness in Bessie Head and other African women writers, see Mary Lederer's unpublished dissertation, "Becoming A Prophet: Representations of Madness in Bessie Head's Novels" (UCLA, 1996).

[25] In 1963 Freedman suggests that:

> At present we confront a paradox in the fortunes of the lyrical novel. At a time when narrative has evolved toward a greater penetration of the self, the lyrical novel, which has fostered this condition, has undergone a decline. This is not to say that the lyrical novel is finished. It is merely to suggest that following its great importance in the first half of this century as a response to the naturalistic novel, a hiatus in its influence has occurred. (279)

I would argue that contemporary women writers have emerged on the other side of that hiatus.

MARTINE WATSON BROWNLEY

Atwood on Women, War, and History: "The Loneliness of the Military Historian"

> "In the evenings the news seeps in
> from foreign countries,
> . . .
> We listen to the war, the wars,
> any old war."
> — Margaret Atwood,
> "Two Headed-Poems"

> "History cannot be erased, although we
> can soothe ourselves by speculating about
> it."
> — Atwood,
> "Marrying the Hangman"[1]

A devoted recycler, Margaret Atwood seldom wastes literary effort. Commentators on her work have long noted themes, characters, and even images from her poems and short stories that subsequently reappear in her novels. The example most often cited is *Bodily Harm* (1981), which reflects the story "A Travel Piece" in *Dancing Girls* (1977) as well as a number of poems in the collection *True Stories* (1981).[2] Peter Klappert has described those poems as "notes for" or "outtakes from" the novel,[3] and his attitude is typical of most U.S. critics, who in general value Atwood's novels more highly than her poetry.

In many cases, however, these poems of Atwood's are far more than minor preparatory drafts, in effect ur-leavings, of novels, and they deserve to be considered on their own textual grounds. Over a decade ago George Woodcock noted that the wider recognition given to Atwood as a novelist was making her role as a poet more difficult to evaluate,[4] and nowhere is his point illustrated more clearly than in her poems related to novels. In the context of Atwood's developing poetic oeuvre some of them reevaluate long-term concerns of hers with new complexity and comprehensiveness, concerns that in many cases the novels have not treated as directly or effectively. A good example is "The Loneliness of the Military Historian" (1990), a dramatic monologue by a character who is a prototype of Tony Fremont, the military historian who appeared three years later in *The Robber Bride*.[5]

What is surprising about a comparison of the two literary relatives is how little the poem's persona illumines the protagonist of the later novel. As good historians who are also women, they naturally enough share certain traits and experiences — thorough professionalism, a commitment to accuracy, a distaste for dissecting motives, and the suspicion of associates because of what they study. Their sex may or may not play a role in the emphasis of both on what Tony terms the "more lowly" elements of war — lice, disease, food shortages, military clothing (even including in Tony's case the "technology of fly-front fastenings" [23]) — rather than grand martial exploits. It is amusing enough to recognize minor poetic details that resurface in the novel, such as the flowers each woman picks from battlefields and presses in hotel Bibles ("Loneliness," 53; *Robber Bride*, 17), and the lavender scent in the poem (49) that becomes Tony's lavender-filled satin sachet from the siege of Lavaur (460). But these details function similarly in each text (the lavender, for example, suggesting something slightly old-fashioned about each woman),[6] and their juxtaposition yields no additional analytical insights.

After writing the poem Atwood apparently decided that she needed a livelier protagonist to carry her novel. The military historian, with her "dresses of sensible cut" in "unalarming shades of beige" (49) and her mildly depressed air, is a pale shadow of bouncy and energetic Tony in her "floral-wallpaper print" frocks (17). Tony's more colorful appearance reflects her substantially stronger attraction to the romantic and exotic (and for her, escapist) elements of warfare. Indeed, the poem is in general more strongly anti-war than the novel.

More significant are the different approaches to history and historical writing taken in the two texts, in part because of the more detailed development of character inevitable in a novel as compared to a lyric poem. *The Robber Bride* focuses primarily on the meanings of personal histories, and Tony's skills are therefore applied mainly to reconstructing and understanding the pasts of herself and her friends. The novel emphasizes history as a human construct, and particularly the difficulty, even the futility, of writing it — "the impossibility of accurate reconstruction" (458). The poem is focused, as its opening line indicates, on the historian's "profession" (*pro*, "forth," and *fateri*, "to confess," "to acknowledge"),[7] and although recognizing the multiple impediments to historical work, it ultimately affirms the value of such work.

Fredric Jameson, following Louis Althusser, writes that "as old-fashioned narrative or 'realistic' historiography [becomes] problematic, the historian should reformulate her vocation — not any longer to produce some vivid representation of History 'as it really happened,' but rather to produce the *concept* of history" (italics Jameson's).[8] With the novel's capaciousness allowing more lengthy and particularized discussions of events, *The Robber Bride* produces more "representation," depictions of historical actions, than "concept"; the poem, in contrast, produces mainly "concept," the idea of what history itself is and should be. Questioned in an interview about the differences between novels and poems, Atwood commented: "novels are about change, living in time. But poetry, lyric poetry anyway, is more likely to be about the out-of-time experience" (Ingersoll, 223). Not diachronic event but synchronic perspective on the mind of a military historian is the poem's concern; it explores the parameters rather than the ultimate viability of historical thought and language about war.

I

In her early poetry war served Atwood as a source of metaphor more often than as a subject. Despite her concern with political atrocities, which stemmed from her work with Amnesty International and was reflected in many of the poems in *True Stories,* and despite isolated poems such as "1837 war in retrospect" (*The Journals of Susanna Moodie*) and "Projected slide of an unknown soldier" (*Procedures for Underground*), Atwood's early work usually subordinated public martial concerns to personal struggles. Typical was *Power Politics*, which in poems such as "They are hostile nations" and "My beautiful wooden leader" figured relationships between the sexes in military imagery.

However, in an address to the Harvard Consortium in Inter-American Relations in 1981, Atwood emphasized "the study of human aggression" as "the most important field of study at the moment."[9] Over the next decade or so she wrote several powerful poems and prose poems on the subject of war, from "Machine. Gun. Nest" in the mid-1980s to "Poppies: Three Variations" and "Epaulettes" in the collection *Good Bones* (1992).[10] "The Loneliness of the Military Historian" takes its place among these poems as a part of Atwood's increasing concern with and exploration of war as a subject.

At about the same period that Atwood began to write poems on war, she also in her "Historical Notes" appended to *The Handmaid's Tale* began to focus directly on the problems of writing and interpreting history.[11] Her personal interest in history dated from childhood. Describing her father as "a history nut" with a basement full of historical works, she noted in an interview that one of the things that she "grew up on . . . was a lot of history." She particularly recalled reading "Second World War stuff" in her early teens, including a biography of Rommel when she was twelve and Churchill's five-volume history two or three years later (Ingersoll, 182, 216).

History itself entered Atwood's work in various ways. The overt statements about history in her poetry tended to be passing, somewhat unsatisfactorily orphic utterances: "history / breeds death but if you kill / it you kill yourself"

(*Selected Poems II*, 32). But she excelled in interpreting and re-creating historical material in both prose and poetry. During the decade of the 1970s, in *Survival*[12] Atwood deftly surveyed literary and symbolic manifestations of Canadian history, while in *The Journals of Susanna Moodie* she focused on the pioneer past and in "Four Small Elegies" wrote on the reprisals around Beauharnois after the failed 1838 uprising. *The Handmaid's Tale* in the mid-1980s imaginatively reworked New England's Puritan history.

The lonely military historian takes her place in a long line of what one critic describes as Atwood's "unsympathetic central characters," who force readers "beyond identification into speculation and self-criticism."[13] A woman who chooses military historiography as her profession is an incongruous figure, given the traditional associations between masculinity and militarism.[14] As Micaela di Leonardo points out, "gender is at the center of recurrent contradictions in the militarization process."[15] Many of these contradictions have been highlighted in hotly contested contemporary debates over women and the military. From conscription to combat, male military space has been staunchly defended. A 1983 U.S. Army reclassification project, for example, went so far as to redefine carpenters, electricians, and plumbers as combat positions, exclusively for males.[16] Barred from the battlefield, women and their views have been equally unwelcome in the study of armed conflict. Cynthia Enloe writes that "a woman who presumes to theorize about militarism is too frequently dismissed, as if she had wandered uninvited into the men's locker room" (39), while Carol Cohn, after participating for a year in seminars with defense intellectuals, concluded that "There was no evidence that feminist critiques had ever reached the ears, much less the minds, of these men."[17]

With men identified with war, the figure of the military historian is also disturbing because of equally strong traditions linking women and peace.[18] Again and again commentators have pointed out the lack of historical grounding for this long-standing popular association. From the mythical Amazons and the Biblical Deborah to Joan of Arc, Nicaraguan women in Sardinista militias, and U.S. servicewomen in the Gulf War, women have fought in wars, and fought well. Even more important has been women's support of wars, from Plutarch's Spartan mothers to pre-World War I women peace advocates who recanted once war broke out and women workers in defense industries.

The persistence of the belief in women's natural pacifism despite overwhelming historical evidence suggests that it serves some crucial psychological as well as social needs. The tendency to explain this pacifism in terms of women's roles as mothers locates the origins of the construction not only in sexist sentimentality but in deep human fears and compensatory wish-fulfillments that underlie refusals to accept constructions of women as violent or aggressive. Social needs also supplement personal ones. As the capacity for nuclear destruction proliferates, peace becomes more imperative even as it becomes more difficult to achieve. Under such conditions, Diane Eyer points out, "As so often happens in avoiding a complex, cultural problem, it is projected onto women, who are then required by the tenets of their sex role to perform a symbolic redress."[19]

Various feminist theorists, particularly those connected with the peace and nuclear disarmament movements, have repeatedly tried to draw on the association of women and pacifism, with predictably mixed results. The 1980s marked a high point for such theories, culminating in the publication of Sara Ruddick's *Maternal Thinking: Toward a Politics of Peace* (Boston: Beacon, 1989). But by the time Ruddick's study appeared, the emerging anti-essentialist emphasis in feminist theory had fairly thoroughly deconstructed the stereotype of the naturally peaceful woman. With her demise, questions about the relationship between women and militarism emerged as yet another aspect of the ongoing equality-versus-difference debates between liberal and radical feminists. Liberals insisted that women's equal access to and opportunity in every area included military service, while radicals insisted that any such integration inhibited the substantive transformations of values and institutions for which they believed feminism should stand. Questions about war's reinforcement or subversion of male dominance proliferated as women gained greater access to the armed forces:

> Do [women soldiers] subvert the military by depriving it of its historic claim to masculinity, thereby also demasculinizing the state which it serves? Or do these battles won by women stalking the corridors of state power have the effect of relegitimizing the military at a time when it was about to seem an anachronism? (Enloe, 60)

It is within these kinds of contexts that Atwood's figure of the military historian functions to problematize the relationship of women to war. Atwood's previous poetry had reflected the stereotypical military gender equivalencies:

> The history of war is a history of killed bodies. That's what war is: bodies killing other bodies, bodies being killed.
> Some of the killed bodies are those of women and children, as a side effect, you might say. . . . But most of the killed bodies are men. So are most of those doing the killing.[20]

Women and war are separated: "No woman can imagine this," the gunner in "Machine. Gun. Nest" asserts (*Selected Poems II*, 138). The depiction of women as war's victims inevitably accompanied the association of men and violence, even though in other poems Atwood had depicted women's implication in men's power games.

"The Loneliness of the Military Historian" marks an important change of focus in Atwood's treatment of militarism, with a more complex construction of the relationship between women and war than in the earlier poems. Women are still shown as war's victims. Indeed, one of the images of female victims in the poem, that of women who, "having been raped repeatedly, / hang themselves with their own hair" (50), is presaged in her earlier poem "Christmas Carols," where a

> woman with her hair cut off
> so she could not hang herself
> threw herself from a rooftop, thirty
> times raped & pregnant by the enemy
> who did this to her.
>
> (*Selected Poems II*, 70)

But "The Loneliness of the Military Historian" also depicts women's complicity in men's wars. They appear as supporters of war, engaged in various forms of "moral cheerleading" (50). Through juxtaposition Atwood highlights the mixed historical record of women's responses to war: "Women should march for peace, / or hand out white feathers to arouse bravery" (49). The movement in Atwood's poetry from women as war victims to women as both victims and abettors of conflict parallels the evolution of feminist theory away from the figure of the naturally peaceful woman. Here Atwood's poetic stance on women and war also catches up with her theoretical treatments of victimhood in other works. She has long been interested in what she calls in *Survival* "Victor/Victim games" (39), and from the ending of *Surfacing* on — "This above all, to refuse to be a victim"[21] — most of her work has valorized refusals of victimhood.

II

Atwood in her poetic character sketch of the military historian in "Loneliness" is delineating a certain cast of mind, the perspective and attitudes necessary for good historical writing. Her historian directly addresses what some would see as the problematical gender demands of her profession:

> In general I might agree with you:
> women should not contemplate war,
> should not weigh tactics impartially,
> or evade the word *enemy*,
> or view both sides and denounce nothing. (49)

Her word choice — "contemplate," "weigh impartially," "view both sides and denounce nothing" — reflects the discourse of reason, traditionally defined in terms of men and denied to women. This language is in stark contrast to the rest of the stanza that follows, which portrays both women victims and accomplices during war behaving with passion — with the feeling and, from the Latin root *patior*, the suffering traditionally connected with women.

In deconstructing this stereotype of women, feminist theory in focusing on misuses of reason (overly narrow conceptions of reason, reason as rationalization for male power and desire, etc.) has too often veered into overstatement, with totalizing denigrations of reason itself, rather than asserting women's own claims to participate in rational discourse. Atwood's poetry, as opposed to her novels, has always focused on intelligent women, and part of the appeal of "Loneliness" is the historian's firm assertions of her rationality in her work. Her strong feelings against war surface in various ways in the poem — for example, she comments that "Grand exploits merely depress me" (52) — but professionally she contains them. Their displacement is reflected in the "flower or two" she picks at each battleground she visits for research and presses in the hotel Bible (53).

The historian's commitment to the realm of reason is clear in her rejection of both romance and speculation in her work. Dominick LaCapra has noted "the tendency of traditional narrative to romanticize events"[22] and has detailed some of the resulting problems for historiography. Recognizing the difficulties, the military historian relegates the "glamour" of war to her dreams in an effective passage in which the poetry itself conveys the attraction of the color and power of certain aspects of war and their pull on the imagination. The stanza ends, however, with the historian firmly — and ironically — rejecting what "A poet might say," because of the taint of romance (51).

Speculation about the reasons for war are also avoided: "I don't ask *why*, because it is mostly the same. / Wars happen because the ones who start them / think they can win" (50). Significantly, in "Alien Territory," another of Atwood's poems that deals with war, the persona offers a detailed answer to the question "Why do men want to kill the bodies of other men?":

> Here are some traditional reasons: Loot. Territory. Lust for power. Hormones. Adrenaline high. Rage. God. Flag. Honor. Righteous anger. Revenge. Oppression. Slavery. Starvation. Defense of one's life. Love; or, a desire to protect the women and children.
>
> (*Good Bones and Simple Murders*, 100)

The questions of poetry, however, are not the questions appropriate for historical writing, and the military historian refuses to engage them.

"The Loneliness of the Military Historian" itself enacts several of the analytical and linguistic processes that contemporary critics have identified as crucial to historical writing. Following Bakhtin, LaCapra has emphasized the importance of dialogism in historiography. He notes, for example, "the way the 'voice' of the historian may be internally 'dialogized' when it undergoes the appeal of different interpretations" (36). Such dialogism permeates the poem. As the military historian discusses the representation of war, qualifying conjunctions, adverbs, and adjectives introduce different viewpoints to widen the scope. "Despite," "true," "though," "sometimes," and "but" qualify and enlarge the historical perspective as she enumerates factors influencing the course of wars, from technology to food supplies, disease, and, on occasion, "being right" (52). Metonymy dominates the section: "But rats and cholera have won many wars. / Those, and potatoes / or the absence of them" (52). In Hayden White's well known tropological system of historiographical analysis in *Metahistory*, metonymy is the trope connected with the tragic mode of emplotment, which would of course be appropriate for military history.[23]

But tragic potential is contained within Atwood's poem by irony, the great trope of negation and the perfect embodiment of the skepticism necessary for effective historical reconstruction. Significantly, White emphasizes that irony has "continued to flourish as the dominant mode of professional historiography, as cultivated in the academy," since the end of the nineteenth century (xii). LaCapra includes among the methods of dialogizing historical writing moments when the historian's voice "employs self-critical reflection about its own protocols of inquiry, and makes use of modes such as irony, parody, self-parody, and humor, that is, double- or multiple-voiced uses of language" (36). Self-conscious about the limits of her methods and ironic in her expressions of her insights, the voice of the historian in the poem reflects this kind of dialogic approach to history. Various forms of irony — litotes and understatement, along with occasional sarcasm — recur in the poem. Limiting herself to "What [she] hope[s] will pass as truth," she refuses to provide "a final statement," insisting that she deals only in "tactics" (50, 53). Kathy Ferguson has pointed out that "the recognition of limits" that irony invokes is a virtue "historically associated with women."[24] Joan Riviere's famous formulation of womanliness as masquerade, when juxtaposed with the *eiron*'s traditional position as a dissembler, a weak person or an underdog who survives through clever manipulation, also has suggestive gender ramifications.[25] Particularly in view of the female military historian's position as a minority within a minority — not only does the field of military history attract few women, but history itself still remains male-dominated — the ironic stance is an especially appropriate one for her. At the same time, the traditional critical categories of tragic irony and cosmic irony are reminders that gendering irony, while of some use in particular textual contexts, if carried too far may ultimately restrict the wider human ramifications of the trope and limit readings.

III

The qualities of mind that the female military historian in "Loneliness" represents can be clarified by juxtaposing her with Atwood's other representation of an academic historian, Professor James Darcy Pieixoto in *The Handmaid's Tale*. Pieixoto's speech analyzing historical contexts of the Handmaid's story at a scholarly symposium comprises the bulk of the "Historical Notes on *The Handmaid's Tale*" appended to the novel (379–395). Pieixoto is the nightmare Other of the military historian; through him, Atwood produces a savage and brilliant satire on certain kinds of male academic historians.

The military historian's approach is dialogic, self-consciously critical, and non-sexist. Pieixoto's is just the opposite. A pompous pedant, condescending to his audience and his material, he represents positivistic historiography at its worst. The title of his address, "Problems of Authentication in Reference to *The Handmaid's Tale*," reflects his emphasis on method and technique, in his case not very critically applied, rather than interpretation. Peripheral evidence — for example, "a metal footlocker, U.S. Army issue, circa perhaps 1955," which even Pieixoto has to admit "need have no significance" (381) — is more carefully scrutinized than the Handmaid's surviving text. His concerns center on old-fashioned political history and its great men; dismissive of the Handmaid's story, he longs instead for "even twenty pages or so of print-out" from the Commander's home computer (393).

LaCapra has noted the historian's problem of "coming to terms with 'transference' in the psychoanalytic sense of a repetition/displacement of the 'object' of study in one's own discourse about it" (40). Because of such transference in the process of historical writing, he warns that "considerations at issue in the object of study are always repeated with variations — or find their displaced analogues — in one's account of it" (72). In Pieixoto's account of Gilead, this kind of transference is reflected in his replication in his address of the sexism and the objectification of women that characterized Gilead itself. Along with his sexist jokes, his euphemisms — "birth services" for childbearing and "serial polygamy" for late twentieth-century marriage (386) — reflect his androcentric biases and misogyny.

With his narrow conception of what constitutes historical fact, Pieixoto misreads the Handmaid's text, when he bothers to consider it at all. Raising questions about matters on which the Handmaid is silent, Pieixoto comments:

> We may call Eurydice forth from the world of the dead, but we cannot make her answer; and when we turn to look at her we glimpse her only for a moment, before she slips from our grasp and flees. As all historians know, the past is a great darkness, and filled with echoes. (394)

Yet another of Atwood's poems that has ramifications for a subsequent novel puts the professor's ornamental rhetoric into perspective. In "Orpheus (1)," published in *Interlunar* a year before *The Handmaid's Tale*, Eurydice explains why she had to leave Orpheus on the way out of Hades. Orpheus viewed her only in terms of his own desires — "the image of what you wanted / me to become." Eurydice was his "hallucination." The poem ends: "You could not believe I was more than your echo" (*Selected Poems II*, 106–107). Like Orpheus, Pieixoto can see only himself, and he imposes himself and his views on the past. The result is a historical monologism that silences the Handmaid and those like her in Gileadic culture.

Academic critics have savaged Pieixoto for his excesses, in most cases accurately.[26] But if Atwood's depiction of the military historian offers an alternative to Pieixoto, in the process she also corrects a widespread critical misreading of him. For no statement has Pieixoto been more excoriated by critics than his refusal to take a moral stand on his material: "Allow me to say that in my opinion we must be cautious about passing moral judgment upon the Gileadeans. . . . Our job is not to censure but to understand" (383). In this connection one critic goes so far as to say that any scholar who fails to assert moral or political positions on issues like totalitarianism "will necessarily become an apologist for evil."[27]

However, the response to immoral human beings and events appropriate for a novelist, a reader of novels, or a poet is not necessarily useful for a historian. Pieixoto's statement actually reflects proper historical practice. Atwood's military historian, too, several times in the poem firmly asserts her refusal to deliver moral judgments. She "evade[s] the word *enemy*"; she "denounce[s] nothing." Describing her "trade" as "courage and atrocities," she "look[s] at them and do[es] not condemn" (49–50).

The military historian chooses instead to "write things down the way they happened" (50). The "way they happened" is reminiscent of Leopold von Ranke's famous "wie es eigentlich gewesen."[28] Ranke's remark occurs in the introduction to his first historical work in 1824, signaling his revolutionary break with earlier conceptions of historiography: "History has had assigned to it the office of judging the past and of instructing the present for the benefit of the future ages. To such high offices the present work does not presume: it seeks only to show what actually happened" (58). Atwood, always aware of the human construction of historical writing and therefore its contingency, updates Ranke with an important qualification; the military historian adds that she writes things down "the way they happened, / as near as can be remembered" (50). Nevertheless, the echo of the famous break with classical and Renaissance conceptions of history as moral monitor and political instructor remains.

In the process of historical writing, overt moral judgment is often the easiest path, and almost always an unnecessary one. Herbert Butterfield almost half a century ago discussed why historiography does not require moral interpolations: "those who do not recognise that the killing and torturing of human beings is barbarity will hardly be brought to that realisation by any labels and nicknames that historians may attach to these things."[29] Thus moral exhortation within historical texts becomes simply pointless rhetorical posturing. In Butterfield's view the one way that the historian can reinforce her initial moral judgment and thereby serve general morality is through her representation of events, "merely describing, say, the massacre or the persecution, laying it out in concrete detail, and giving the specification of what it means in actuality." He sees this kind of representation as crucial because

> One of the causes of moral indifference is precisely the failure to realise in an objective manner and make vivid to oneself the terrible nature of crime and suffering; but those who are unmoved by the historical description will not be stirred by any pontifical commentary that may be superadded. (123)

As with all texts, the construction of histories is inevitably shaped by ideological perspectives and moral ones, as Butterfield's own comment about "the terrible nature of crime and suffering" suggests. Interspersing overt moral judgments, in contrast, is a matter of conscious authorial choice, one that creates various textual difficulties. Indulging in direct denunciation, the historian turns preacher, in the process distorting the focus on the material that he or she is ostensibly treating. In the case of Atwood's military historian, her adamant refusal to take sides works against transference into her own texts of the conflicts she chronicles. Her strong personal feelings against war are displaced into her pressed flowers rather than into her text.

The problem with Pieixoto, then, is not what he says about moral judgments in historiography but what he actually does in his own historical text. There, in violation of his stated principle, he affirms and supports immoral positions. Sometimes he does so overtly, as when he attempts to exculpate Gileadic tyranny: "Gileadean society was under a good deal of pressure, demographic and otherwise" (383). In addition to what Annette Kolodny terms his "discourse of exoneration,"[30] by projection Pieixoto reads his shabby personal standards into his text. For example, he suggests that the Handmaidens must have enjoyed the Particicution or that Nick might have been wiser to assassinate the Handmaid himself (390, 394). His evaluative language also conveys moral viewpoints, as when he speaks of Gilead's "genius" in connection with the savage Particicution and Salvaging rituals or praises the Commanders for their brilliance and ingenuity (389, 391).

Ranke's "wie es eigentlich gewesen" now reads more like naively wishful thinking than a viable goal, and even Butterfield's slightly less demanding "merely describing, . . . laying it out in concrete detail, and giving the specification of what it means in actuality" seems somewhat dubious. Writing in the early nineteenth and mid-twentieth centuries, Ranke and Butterfield naturally enough showed greater confidence in the ability of language to re-create the past than most contemporary theorists would. For Pieixoto there is no such excuse.

IV

Atwood's military historian is sensitive to language and particularly to its limitations. Her comment that each of the battlefields she visits for research "has inspired a few good quotes in its day" highlights the inadequacy of language for coming to terms with the events she studies, as does her reference to the ubiquity of the word "glory" on gateways (52–53). That words themselves have histories whose reverberations are often unknown to and beyond the control of those who use them is ironically reflected in the historian's closing demurral, when she insists that she deals in "tactics. / Also statistics" (53). The word "statistics" evokes the ordered objectivity of numbers, but it is actually derived from the German *Statistik*, "political science," via the Neo-Latin *statiscus*, "of state affairs," to the Latin *status*, meaning "state" or "position." Its ultimate root is the Latin *stare*, "to stand." Etymologically, then, behind the putative detachment of modern mathematical data lurks the unruliness of ideologies, dominions, and politics — essentially, the very forces fueling the militarism that the historian seeks to study and understand.

One of the comments that best sums up the kind of historian the persona is, the subtlety of her understanding of both the tenuousness of historical evidence and the instability of the language used to describe it, occurs as she discusses the battleground cemeteries she sees in the course of her research. Describing their marble angels as "Sad," she parenthetically notes that they "could just as well be described as *vulgar*, / or *pitiless*, depending on the camera angle" (52–53). The key is her reference to the camera and its perspectives. Photographs are popularly believed to directly reflect and reproduce what Roland Barthes terms "literal reality," and for this reason he notes their "special credibility."[31] Barthes's decoding of this "myth of photographic 'naturalness,'" however, has increased understanding of how connotations of various kinds shape a medium that seems to be purely denotative, "exclusively constituted and occupied by a 'denoted' message, a message which totally exhausts its mode of existence" (44, 18). The historian's adjectival alternatives emphasize her recognition of the variability and fallibility of the camera's eye in any given situation. At the same time, within its own limits the camera is of course much less fallible than the human eye and its repository of images, the memory. The historian's sensitivity to how perspective shapes description under the most seemingly unmediated conditions highlights her general awareness of the provisionality and contingency of any historical construction.

Finally, Atwood's deployment of language in the poem suggests that the tendency on the part of some contemporary critics to dismiss earlier commentators like Butterfield because of their lack of attention to linguistic limitations may be in some cases excessive. Butterfield's call was for "merely describing" atrocities, "laying [them] out in concrete detail" in order to render precisely their moral impact. In her poem Atwood depicts the atrocities of war using two different modes of expression. Simple language and straightforward description such as Butterfield prescribes are used about women who

> spit themselves on bayonets
> to protect their babies,
> whose skulls will be split anyway,
> or, having been raped repeatedly,
> hang themselves with their own hair. (50)

In contrast, Atwood moves to simile to describe death in battle: "Sometimes men throw themselves on grenades / and burst like paper bags of guts / to save their comrades" (52). The poetic image not only obscures but in a sense diminishes the impact of the deeds.

Overwriting is not a poetic sin unknown to Atwood, and it could be objected that the simile is simply an unfortunate one. However, a more elaborate series of metaphors in another battleground description ends up producing roughly the same effect. She describes fields "that once were liquid with pulped / men's bodies and spangled with exploded / shells and splayed bone" (52). Attention focused on the images themselves and the way they work detracts from the stark reality of the events being recalled; the passage thus lacks the "specification" which Butterfield demanded. In dealing with such horror, when history strains toward poetry, even the little that one can hope to recapture of the past becomes lost. Susan Schweik has noted that war poetry generally tends to be a bad subgenre, and she connects its shortcomings to its tendency towards excessive historicism, its failure "to entirely transcend its time" (13). The example of Atwood suggests that the subject of war also involves another kind of difficulty with specificity because of the abstraction of poetic language and its self-referentiality. Singing about arms and the man too often becomes focused at the level of the song rather than the arms.

Though Butterfield was more optimistic than we that any language could be capable of re-creating "what [any event] means in actuality," the example of Atwood's practice suggests that the plain style he commends is more effective than elaborate alternatives. The linguistic shortcomings that limit Butterfield's theoretical viability do not ultimately vitiate the practical usefulness of his formulations as a working guide to historical style.

Although Atwood's historian speaks with both straightforward and metaphorical description in the poem, given the depiction of her mindset, her attitudes and perspectives, it is not difficult to guess which kind of language would predominate in any history that she might write. Moreover, Atwood makes it clear that the specialized case of the military historian has broader ramifications. As the closing lines of the poem point out, "for every year of peace there have been four hundred / years of war" (53). Under such circumstances almost every historian is in some sense a military historian.

Thus Atwood's poem offers a penetrating analysis of the demands of historical writing and the kind of mind that can meet those demands. The requirements are unusual ones, and some of the positions that Atwood has previously taken in her poetry shift accordingly. In general she has insisted on ambiguity and on human thralldom to fictions intentional and unintentional, asserting the impossibility of "True Stories":

> The true story is vicious
> and multiple and untrue
>
> after all. Why do you
> need it? Don't ever
>
> ask for the true story.
>
> (*Selected Poems II*, 58)

She has also consistently criticized the stance of "uncommitted independence," questioning the ability of anyone to remain unaligned (McCombs and Palmer, 337). Skeptical about human memory and human language, refusing transference and moralism but encouraging dialogism, the military historian is fully aware of the limitations of any "truth" — "A blunt thing, not lovely" (50) — that she can reconstruct. But her perseverance despite the implied criticism to which her poetic monologue is a response asserts the value of that truth and of the informed detachment required to recreate it.

At a time when the kind of rationality the military historian represents is often disdained, and when even the limited kind of objectivity that she creates from her dialogism and refusal of transference is considered by many illusory, the persona in Atwood's poem is a challenging figure. Her uncompromising assertion of impartiality as a proper academic stance and refusal to function as a moral arbiter also have resonance given the sloughs of ideology and political commitment in which contemporary literary studies flounder. Noting the "prompt politicization of empirical differences" in some current criticism, Howard Horwitz finds that it risks becoming "a new moralism, in that disputes about evidence and its interpretation are subordinated to the rush to judgment and recast as sanction or censure."[32] In such circumstances the modest but compelling claims of Atwood's military historian are a salutary reminder of the kinds of validity that rigorous intellectual inquiry — work which recognizes its own limitations, the liabilities of language, and the different roles that are appropriate for the historian and the critic as opposed to the preacher — can retain.

Emory University

Notes

[1] Margaret Atwood, *Selected Poems II: Poems Selected and New, 1976–1986* (Boston: Houghton Mifflin, 1987). The first quotation is on 34, the second on 19.

[2] See Atwood's comments in Earl G. Ingersoll, ed., *Margaret Atwood: Conversations* (Princeton: Ontario Review, 1990), 170.

[3] Peter Klappert, "I Want, I Don't Want: The Poetry of Margaret Atwood," *Gettysburg Review* 3 (1990): 217–30; quotation 226.

[4] George Woodcock, "Canadian Poetry: The Emergent Tradition," *Yearbook of English Studies* 15 (1985): 239–55; quotation 252.

[5] "The Loneliness of the Military Historian" first appeared in 1990 in *Times Literary Supplement*, 14–20 September, 976, and was printed again in *Harper's* in December of that year (17–18) with credit to *TLS*. In 1995 Atwood included it in *Morning in the Burned House* (Boston and New York: Houghton Mifflin, 1995), 49–53. See also Atwood's *The Robber Bride* (New York: Doubleday, 1993).

[6] Jack Goody in *The Culture of Flowers* (Cambridge: Cambridge UP, 1993) prints a Renaissance lyric connecting lavender with "lovers true." However, he notes that in the lyric "significances attached to each flower are clearly ruled by the desire for assonance," concluding that the "written code is largely a literary conceit in which the meanings are shaped or constructed to fit the poem's form" (181). Any connections between lavender and love would probably be somewhat more ironic in Atwood's poem than in her novel.

[7] Etymologies in this essay are from the *American Heritage Dictionary* (*Second College Edition*) and the *OED*.

[8] Fredric Jameson, "Periodizing the 60s," *The 60s Without Apology*, ed. Sohnya Sayres et al. (Minneapolis: U of Minnesota P, 1984), 178–209; quotation 180.

[9] Margaret Atwood, *Second Words: Selected Critical Prose*, 1982 (Boston: Beacon, 1984), 391.

[10] Margaret Atwood, *Good Bones and Simple Murders* (New York: Doubleday, 1994).

[11] Margaret Atwood, *The Handmaid's Tale*, 1985 (New York: Ballantine, 1987).

[12] Margaret Atwood, *Survival: A Thematic Guide to Canadian Literature* (Toronto: Anansi, 1972).

[13] Judith McCombs and Carole L. Palmer, eds., *Margaret Atwood: A Reference Guide* (Boston: G. K. Hall, 1991), 322–23.

[14] Cynthia Enloe notes that "Investigations of women's relationships to militarism have been pouring forth during the last decade" (*The Morning After: Sexual Politics at the End of the Cold War* [Berkeley, Los Angeles, London: U of California P, 1993], 19). Susan Schweik offers a useful short survey of available material in *A Gulf So Deeply Cut: American Women Poets and the Second World War* (Madison: U of Wisconsin P, 1991), 300–1, n. 40.

[15] Micaela di Leonardo, "Morals, Mothers, and Militarism: Antimilitarism and Feminist Theory," *Feminist Studies* 11 (1985): 599–617; quotation 615.

[16] Ultimately, carpenters were reclassified as noncombat (Enloe, 59).

[17] Carol Cohn, "'Clean Bombs' and Clean Language," *Women, Militarism, and War*, ed. Jean Bethke Elshtain and Sheila Tobias (Savage, MD: Rowman and Littlefield, 1990), 33–55; quotation 35.

[18] The bibliography on women and peace is as extensive as that on women and war; most treatments of one topic include the other. Three good surveys of the issues are Adrienne Harris and Ynestra King, eds., *Rocking the Ship of State: Toward a Feminist Peace Politics* (Boulder, San Francisco, and London: Westview Press, 1989); Linda Rennie Forcey, "Feminist Perspectives on Mothering and Peace," in Evelyn Nakano Glenn, Grace Chang, and Linda Rennie Forcey, eds., *Mothering: Ideology, Experience, and Agency* (New York and London: Routledge, 1994), 355–75; and Lynne Segal, *Is the Future Female? Troubled Thoughts on Contemporary Feminism* (London: Virago, 1987), 162–203.

[19] Diane E. Eyer, *Mother-Infant Bonding: A Scientific Fiction* (New Haven and London: Yale UP, 1992), 14.

[20] Margaret Atwood, "Alien Territory," *Good Bones and Simple Murders*, 99–100. See also Atwood's "Liking Men," in *Murder in the Dark: Short Fictions and Prose Poems* (Toronto: Coach House, 1983), 54.

[21] Margaret Atwood, *Surfacing* (New York: Simon and Schuster, 1972), 222.

[22] Dominick LaCapra, *History & Criticism* (Ithaca and London: Cornell UP, 1985), 120.

[23] Hayden White, *Metahistory: The Historical Imagination in Nineteenth-Century Europe* (Baltimore and London: Johns Hopkins UP, 1973).

[24] Kathy Ferguson, "Interpretation and Genealogy in Feminism," *Signs* 16 (1991): 322–39; quotation 338.

[25] Joan Riviere, "Womanliness as a Masquerade," *International Journal of Psychoanalysis* 10 (1929): 303–13.

[26] One of the best treatments of the "Historical Notes" is Arnold E. Davidson's "Future Tense: Making History in *The Handmaid's Tale*" (Kathryn VanSpackeren and Jan Garden Castro, eds., *Margaret Atwood: Vision and Forms* [Carbondale and Edwardsville: Southern Illinois UP, 1988], 113–21) — although practically no critic who writes on the novel fails to take a shot at Pieixoto.

[27] Amin Malak, "Margaret Atwood's 'The Handmaid's Tale' and the Dystopian Tradition," *Canadian Literature* 112 (Spring 1987): 9–16; quotation 15.

[28] Leopold von Ranke, *The Secret of World History: Selected Writings on The Art and Science of History*, ed. and trans. Roger Wines (New York: Fordham UP, 1981).

[29] Herbert Butterfield, *History and Human Relations* (New York: Macmillan, 1952).

[30] Annette Kolodny, "Margaret Atwood and the Politics of Narrative," *Studies on Canadian Literature: Introductory and Critical Essays,* ed. Arnold E. Davidson (New York: MLA, 1990), 90–109; quotation 107.

[31] Roland Barthes, *Image — Music — Text*, trans. Stephen Heath, 1977 (New York: Farrar, Straus, and Giroux, 1992), 17, 21.

[32] Howard Horwitz, "'I Can't Remember': Skepticism, Synthetic Histories, Critical Action," *South Atlantic Quarterly* 87 (1988): 787–820; quotation 803.

LORE METZGER

Atwood's *Robber Bride*: At the Borders of Feminist Narrative

In recent decades feminist novels have established themselves in remarkable multiformity: lesbian, utopian, dystopian, autobiographical, science fiction, hard-boiled detective novels, gothic (or non-gothic) romances and anti-romances — and, most frequently — postmodern fusions of these genres. Moreover, postmodern writers have responded to a sociopolitical challenge: at a time when news of ethnic cleansing, racial paranoia, lethal epidemics, terrorist attacks on abortion clinics, and welfare reforms that punish the poor dominate our social texts, what salutary role can fiction play without becoming enmeshed in the violent discourse? Not surprisingly, some feminist novels, like their masculinist counterparts, have come to question the validity of fictional narratives altogether. "Years ago," observes DeLillo's novelist, who is caught in a web of terror, "I used to think it was possible for a novelist to alter the inner life of the culture."[1] But now writers are "giving way to terror, to news of terror, to tape recorders and cameras, to radios, to bombs stashed in radios." And he concludes: "News of disaster is the only narrative people need. The darker the news, the grander the narrative" (41–42). Threatened by this usurpation of narrative energy, the contemporary novel frequently tries to contain, incorporate, or problematize the violence that permeates our social discourse.

I

I focus on one such effort at foregrounding the forces of destabilization: Margaret Atwood's *The Robber Bride*, a daring "borderwork."[2] Like DeLillo, Atwood acknowledges the fact that real events have outstripped fiction "in absurdity or ghastliness" and that "serious writers these days don't write uplifting books because what they see around them is not uplifting."[3] And like DeLillo, Atwood incorporates into her fiction the question of the validity and value of the construction of fictional lives. In *The Handmaid's Tale*, for example, her darkest vision of what the future holds, the Swiftian projection of the totalitarian institution of what we would like to think of as extremist family values, Atwood ironically questions the factual foundation and moral implication of the central narrative. The novel's postscript, "Historical Notes," delves into the archival origins of the tale recorded on thirty tape cassettes (shades of *Krapp's Last Tape?*) which have challenged the industry of historians, archivists, and anthropologists to establish the identity of the narrator and other principal characters.

Resorting to a Grimm fairy tale instead of a dystopia, *The Robber Bride*, like *The Handmaid's Tale*, constructs a realistic-surrealistic fictional landscape filled with gothic images, nightmarish repetitions, moral ambiguity, and victimization of women. Atwood, however, now integrates into her central narrative the issue of the authenticity and moral value of both fiction and history. She replaces the peripheral caricature-historian of *The Handmaid's Tale* with the principal narrator, the diminutive female academic, Tony Fremont, an expert in medieval warfare and carnage. Possibly she was a reincarnation of Julius Caesar "sent back in the body of a woman, to punish him. A very short woman, so he can see what it's like to be powerless!"[4] Tony's expertise in martial strategies informs her narrative efforts to reconstruct her personal encounters with a catastrophe called Zenia who invades not only Tony's life but that of two other female protagonists as well.

The impact of *The Robber Bride* is similar to that which Anca Vlasopolos ascribes to antigeneric drama: "destabilizing our certainties, making us uneasy, giving us a glimpse of the violent processes in which we participate daily without recognizing them for what they are so long as violence is kept from affecting us directly."[5] From the beginning, Atwood's narrative raises two disturbing questions, the first of which is posed by one of its epigraphs: "A rattlesnake that doesn't bite teaches you nothing." Zenia is nothing if not snakelike — when she dies someone quips, "Dead? Of what? A self-inflicted snakebite?" (449) — but what does she teach us by destabilizing our certainties about good and evil, truth and lies, body and mind?

The Robber Bride raises a second disturbing question: why does Atwood choose to embody the turbulent, seductive, and destructive force that impinges on every other character in the form of the archetypal femme fatale? Why *The Robber Bride* rather than *The Robber Bridegroom*, as in the title of the Grimm fairy tale? Given the fact that Atwood has exposed the insidious ways in which social institutions victimize women, especially in *Bodily Harm* and *The Handmaid's Tale*, it is puzzling to a feminist reader why she now gives center stage to this destructive female figure whose many roles include that of scheming enchantress and vampiric revenant and recall the archetypal Lilith, Eve, Circe, Jezebel, and Delilah. Seeking answers to these two preliminary, intertwined questions quickly involves us in broader moral, political, and aesthetic issues that place this novel at the borders of feminist fiction.

II

What does Zenia teach us through her multiple identities, her false passports, her fictitious origins, her guerrilla tactics? Tony tries to find some clue by investigating possible etymological connections with Zenia. She discovers many ethnic strands — Greek, Russian, Hebrew, Syrian, Hindu, Japanese — though she finds no record of the name *Zenia* itself. Cognates, such as *Xeno, Zenana, Zenobia*, range from signifying a stranger, women's quarters or harem, to the name of a Syrian warrior queen and suggest the contradictory private and public personas assumed by this consummate contriver. As Tony observes, "out of such hints and portents, Zenia devised herself. As for the truth about her, it lies out of reach, because — according to the records, at any rate — she was never even born" (457). Even her death is dubious: she stages one fake death as victim of terrorism in Lebanon; she finally acts out a second death, which remains open to three possible interpretations — that she is indeed the victim of dark conspiracies and is murdered, that she has exhausted her resources for survival and chooses to leap to her death, or that she has taken a drug overdose and dies accidentally. She remains even in death an accomplished equivocator.

Tony is daunted by the impossibility of reconstructing such a life. She knows that she can never demystify Zenia's overdetermined identity. Nevertheless she persists in her project of historical reconstruction, because Zenia cannot be controlled unless Tony shapes her into history; the fragments of her existence are in Tony's hands (457). And yet Tony has deep doubts about the whole historical task, doubts about the claim that history is a purveyor of wisdom and truth. Echoing DeLillo's sentiments about fictional narrative being replaced by the narrative of catastrophes, Tony, speaking here for Atwood, recognizes the chaos which we try to bridge with our narrative constructs. "History was once a substantial edifice, with pillars of wisdom and an altar to the goddess Memory, the mother of all nine muses," Tony notes to herself. "Now the acid rain and the terrorist bombs . . . have been at it, and it's looking . . . more and more like a pile of rubble." It no longer teaches anything beneficial through its "tales of greed, violence, viciousness, and lust for power." Historical actions (like fictional narratives) cannot resolve questions of good and evil, which are inextricably intertwined. This is why Tony prefers battles: "in a battle there are right actions and wrong actions, and you can tell apart by who wins" (458).

Zenia's life, which Tony tries to construct, encompasses "tales of greed, violence, viciousness, and lust for power," centered on Zenia's compelling fictions about herself across a wide spectrum of marginal personas — war orphan, victim of sexual abuse, terrorist, spy, drug dealer. Like the exotic Other that has become a commonplace in literary and cultural criticism since Edward Said's *Orientalism*, Tony's Zenia is an object of both revulsion and fascination, both fear and desire. She represents the negative Other to Tony's secure bourgeois sphere. Zenia's actions, like her words, are uncensored, unlicensed, unfettered, chaotic acts of violence. Her female victims experience the full force of her anarchic aggression but they also, despite themselves, admire her daring exploits. Zenia calculatedly evokes these ambivalent emotions by playing the role of arrant outsider and elicits sympathy by presenting herself as homeless waif. Tony, for example, finds that despite Zenia's betrayal, "a part of her has wanted to cheer Zenia on . . . . To participate in her daring, her contempt for almost everything, her rapacity and lawlessness" (184). And, assimilating Zenia into her professional agenda, Tony frequently casts her in the role of a cunning warrior. Whoever, whatever, wherever Zenia has been in her life, she has been at war: "An unofficial war, a guerrilla war, a war she may not have known she was waging, but a war nevertheless," comments Tony, the expert on war (465). What side she was on in her guerrilla warfare finally no longer matters to Tony, who comes to see that "although she was many other things, she was also courageous" (466). Tony can create a history for Zenia but Zenia herself has left no record other than the eventful texts inscribed in the memory of others.

Tony knows the unreliability of chronicles. She knows that every beginning and every ending is arbitrary: "nothing begins when it begins and nothing's over when it's over" (4); "the end of any history is a lie in which we all agree to conspire" (461). In reading the arbitrary text of Zenia's history, we agree to conspire in Zenia's "malign vitality" (10). Her lethal energy represents not just personal but global aggression: "waves of ill will flow out from her like cosmic radiation" (33). Atwood superimposes an intercontinental map on the local site of Toronto and contains both levels of narrative between two definitive moments: 23 October 1990 (a beginning) — the Soviet bloc is crumbling, the United States is preparing for war in the Gulf — and 11 November 1991 (an ending) — Armistice Day. There's famine in Africa, ethnic feuding in former Yugoslavia but the war in the Gulf is over and "both sides claim to have won, both sides have lost" (461).

This year-long "present" of crises encompasses defining moments — past and present — in the lives of the three female protagonists, Tony, the historian, Roz, the business executive, and Charis, the spiritualist; their stories all turn on their momentous encounters with Zenia, which despite distinctive differences replay key features of a single scenario. Frequently Atwood introduces their horrific stories through a fairy tale formula — "the story of Roz and Zenia began on a lovely day in May . . ." (294); "once upon a time Roz was not Roz . . ." (315) — which emphasizes our inability to learn from archetypal stories. Each of the three protagonists mistakes Zenia for a victim when she is a victimizer; each welcomes Zenia into her home, thinking that she is coming to her rescue when she is really facilitating her entrance into a disruptive triangular relationship. Each offers hospitality to this double agent a second time, even though each has not only experienced her betrayal for herself but also has learned of

Zenia's predatory sexual power over the men in the lives of the others. Each is forewarned by the stories of the others and yet each remains disarmed in the face of Zenia's lures, becomes a complicit partner in her merciless acquisition of their men. And each of them is enchanted and ensnared by Zenia as a more courageous, uninhibited, ebullient alter ego.

Zenia's strategies and designs form a vertiginous pattern that constantly threatens yet energizes the master narrative of Atwood's *Robber Bride*. She appears not only as a specific, unsettling persona whom Tony, Charis, and Roz encounter at specifically defined times and places but she also functions as *la belle dame sans merci*, an overcondensed fantasy of disquieting indeterminacy. To consider some specific psychological, political, and aesthetic implications of this enigmatic persona, I focus on the section entitled the "Robber Bride," with some side glances at two other mythic markers, "Black Enamel," and "Remembrance Day."

III

Within the long section of the novel entitled "Robber Bride," which constitutes Roz's psychobiography, we find a deceptively simple explanation of how the brothers Grimm's robber bridegroom is transformed into a bride.[6] It is created to satisfy Roz's young twins, who demand that all characters be female. Tony reads them the gruesome tale in which a rich and handsome stranger who victimizes innocent girls is outwitted by his bride, who survives because she is given the voyeuristic opportunity to observe the robber bridegroom dismember and devour another maiden.[7] Tony gets barely beyond the opening sentence when the twins interrupt with the demand that the cannibalistic bridegroom be "she." When Tony asks them whom "she" will murder, men or women victims, "the twins do not flinch. They opt for women, in every single role" (292). Years later, after Zenia has, with Roz's assistance, ensnared Roz's husband Mitch in her web of fatal lies, Roz muses over the transformed fairy tale, which she in turn transforms to match her private bitterness and anger: "Let the grooms take it in the neck for once. The Robber Bride, lurking in her mansion in the dark forest, preying upon the innocent, enticing youths to their doom in her evil cauldron. Like Zenia" (292). Thus Roz casts Zenia in the role of man-eater, who preys on weak but not so innocent male victims. The twins, however, delete *all* male roles.

Changing the pronoun, inverting the gender in the fantasy of victimizer and victim, exploiter and exploited, the powerful and powerless, produces a Brechtian alienation effect but proves efficacious neither as daily gender politics nor as strategic resolution of violent conflict. Tony, the historian, insists on giving Roz's children the authentic, unbowdlerized version of fairy tales with "all the pecked-out eyes and cooked bodies and hanged corpses and red-hot nails intact" because they were "more true to life" (292).

A fantasy in which all roles are played by women results not in a utopian community of peace and love; in Atwood's fairy tale, women are not exempt from feeling murderous impulses, from participating in the world's violence, even though they control only a minute number of socioeconomic institutions. Roz, who as a corporate executive is the most powerful of the three women, reminds herself that if public recognition is the measure of power, then "Mickey Mouse is a million times more powerful than she is, and Mickey Mouse doesn't even exist" (88). Moreover, Roz knows only too well that everything in the public and private realms is controlled by male fantasies. "Even pretending you aren't catering to male fantasies is a male fantasy" (388). Male fantasies are readily internalized by women: "You are a woman with a man inside watching a woman. You are your own voyeur" (388). The three women's obsessive interest in Zenia is indeed driven by this internalized voyeurism. They feel a fatal attraction for their lawless alter ego, a desire for libidinous escape from society's internalized limits, laws, taboos. Roz, for example, fantasizes about cutting loose and committing "some great whopping thoroughly despicable sin" (388). She is attracted by extremes of good and evil. And sometimes she would like to be Zenia (389). Whereas she sees through Zenia's exploitation of what the sex industry has to offer, from nose jobs to silicon breast implants, as she redesigns herself into the perfect erotic construct, Roz fails to recognize her calculated appropriation of men's fantasies. Zenia works her magic power over men, steals their souls, and then discards them. Tony's, Roz's, and Charis's men are all enchanted by this siren because they are all fundamentally hollow men. Zenia openly flaunts her magic tricks, but the men are tricked by their own fantasies. And the women are caught in the same web. Charis, the most intuitive of the three women, recognizes that one way of "succumbing to Zenia would be believing her, . . . letting her take them in, letting her tear them apart" (439). This knowledge does not, however, prevent the three female protagonists from being taken in by Xenia, by her self-engendered male fantasy: the ultimate delusion of self-empowerment.

Through Zenia's agency Atwood makes visible some of the threads in the complex web of gendered subject formation, threads from which women cannot escape by seceding from the community at large or by seeking to escape from the historical present into private desire and fantasy. The twins' insistence that all the characters in every story had to be female may be an appropriate stage in the development of their identity as they try to gain control over the plots, the stories of their own lives. Their experiments go beyond those of the Wordsworthian (masculinist) child who tries out "some little plan or chart, / Some fragment from his dream of human life" before rehearsing another part, "As if his whole vocation / Were endless imitation."[8] Atwood's twins are not merely imitating the adult roles but are transforming the inherited gendered scenarios. They are precociously exposing the novelist's tool for social change: they have glimpsed how language traps us, despite efforts to liberate ourselves, in given assumptions, in ideologically conditioned ways of defining our moral and political universe. "The Big Bad Wolf fell down the chimney, right into the cauldron of boiling water, and got his fur all burned off. *Her* fur! It's odd what a difference it makes, changing the pronoun" (291).

It makes a difference: we have to adjust our fantasies to the possibility that even if the guileless victim is inevitably female, the victimizer, the big bad wolf, is not inevitably male. And yet neither the robber bridegroom nor the robber bride can suffice as guides to moral choices. Both the Grimm's cautionary tale (women must guard against seduction by handsome princes or risk the fate of becoming dead meat for their lovers) and the twins' version (the innocent maiden is lured to her doom by a female woman-eating predator) are equally grotesque.

Nevertheless the twins' prescription that women play the roles of victims and victimizers alike comes close to the insight of their godmother, Tony, who responds to the suggestion that she should teach her course Merovingian Siege Strategy in a less Eurocentric way by teaching it from the point of view of the victims: "They were all victims! They took turns! Actually, they took turns trying to avoid being the victims. That's the whole point about war!" (21). And, as Atwood shows, that is also the whole point about life. Tony, Charis, and Roz try to avoid being victims while Zenia victimizes them as part of her commitment never to be a victim. She feels contempt for those who passively suffer. In this respect Atwood aligns Zenia with the protagonists of *Bodily Harm* and *Surfacing* who ultimately refuse to identify themselves as victims. The *Robber Bride* complicates this view by implicating in evil the persona who chooses never to be a victim, except as part of a ruse designed for her own survival. Through the figure of Zenia Atwood makes us confront a positive view of evil, which destabilizes our familiar cultural text.

IV

Atwood's world is not painted in black and white, though Zenia indeed stages a black backdrop for her own radiantly white presence at the "bash" at which Tony, a socially inexperienced university student, first catches sight of her. In a room whose walls, floor, ceiling, and even windows, have been painted a glossy enamel black, and which is filled with people dressed in trendy black — in the center of this room, in which Tony feels out of place, is Zenia in her place. Dressed in a seductive white shepherd's smock, she stands out against the black background of walls and people: "her face and hands and torso swim against the darkness," glowing like the moon (126). Tony feels obliterated by her.

Zenia, however, does not relegate her to the faceless darkness but sweeps her up into her own orbit. The decisive moment, the beginning of their story, is Zenia's asking Tony, "What's your obsession?" And to her own surprise, Tony answers candidly, "raw," having reversed the intended word: "I want to study war." Zenia is delighted, touches Tony's arm lightly, eerily, "as in a game of tag played with cobwebs. 'Let's have coffee,' she says. And Tony smiles" (129).

In this moment of recognition and complicity the die is cast. As Tony comes to understand in time, "people like Zenia can never step through your doorway, can never enter and entangle themselves in your life, unless you invite them" (114). As in Coleridge's narrative about the vampiric Geraldine who invades and usurps the innocent Christabel's existence, the usurper enters through an act of hospitality, a gesture of recognition, as host and parasite enter into a symbiotic relation. At this decisive moment Tony forsakes the security of her "beetle-like little armoured carapace" (130), the familiar confines of the "various little well-worn runways that got her through the weeks, like mice through a field" (114) to become the confidante of a free, amoral spirit. She has always experienced herself as marginal, as approximate, whereas Zenia "has never been *almost*, even at her most fraudulent. Her fakery was deeply assumed, and even her most superficial disguises were total" (36–37).

As Tony is caught in Zenia's trajectory she remembers "the sensation of having lost her footing, of being swept out into a strong current" (130), into "perilous waters" (134). Perilous, because she has been swept beyond the safe borders of her intellectual universe to be challenged to explore extreme scripts of Zenia's invention. "What would it take to kill yourself?" and "What would cause you to kill someone else?" are typical, unsettling, personal questions with which Zenia confronts Tony, inventing graphic contexts: "What if you knew you were going to die slowly, in unbearable pain? What if you knew where the microfilm was, and the other side knew you knew, and they were going to torture you to get it out of you and then kill you anyway?" (131). No imaginary scenarios are off limits for Zenia, as she tests Tony's moral limits and delights in undermining the norms by which Tony timidly orients herself. She confronts her with a choice between love, respect, or fear, and asks her which she would rather have from other people. Tony hesitates between respect and love. Zenia claims "I'd choose fear . . . . It works better . . . . It's the only thing that works" (188).

Zenia opens up a brave new world for Tony, in which dormitory curfews, academic decorum, and other institutional proprieties are contemptuously dismissed, though Zenia has a reputation for being brilliant because she gets high grades without even trying. The judgment of the women in Tony's residence hall is that Zenia, whom they do not know, is beautiful, brilliant, and brutal: "Wolfish, feral, beyond the pale" (133). Zenia's voyeuristic explorations into experiences "beyond the pale" resonate with Tony's historical instinct for reenacting in gruesome detail some of the bloodiest battles of early medieval Europe. She wants to see how war works. "There's an element of mischief in history, thinks Tony. Perverse joy. Outrageousness for its own sake" (169). Unlike Zenia, Tony confines her own enjoyment of outrageousness to her historical reenactments, staging, for example, Otto the Red's fateful battle in which he and his army were ambushed by the Saracens. Tony imagines the setting on the west coast of Italy as "impetuous, brilliant Otto" and his warriors push ahead in their ill-starred expedition, "buoyant with adrenaline, high on the prospect of bloodshed and loot, dizzy with imminent winning" (112). She knows that Otto's defeat will engender "uprisings, rebellions, a return to the old cannibal gods. Brutality, counter-brutality, chaos" (190).

Zenia does not limit her love of outrageousness to imaginary exploits: the actual usurpation of others' lives provides the underpinnings for all her schemes. Thus she appropriates, for example, Tony's intellectual capital (along with some of her monetary inheritance) by inveigling her to write her term paper for her. Playing the helpless waif, Zenia produces a melodramatic sketch of herself, "rented" out at an early age by her mother, a White Russian refugee trying to survive in wartime Paris. (This is one of four different family scenarios Zenia persuasively fabricates.) And Tony comes to the rescue by providing a high-caliber paper on the Slavic slave trade with the Byzantine Empire, not recognizing that she has herself traded her freedom to be her honorable self for bondage to what she regards as a braver alter ego. Endowing Zenia with the potency of male fantasies, Tony sees Zenia as displaying "steely courage in the face of adverse destiny" (165), a victorious warrior: she "pictures her on a horse, cloak flying, sword-arm raised" (165). Tony herself comes to identify with the kings who had enemies' skulls made into wine cups (14). Zenia has an uncanny gift for tapping into unacknowledged feelings, enchanting Tony, as well as Charis and Roz, precisely by offering them a libidinous alter ego while at the same time appropriating some of their energy and power.

Through the figure of Zenia Atwood explores the contradictory effects of an individual who disrupts, wrenches out of shape, all personal and social relations on which she impinges. If we wish to call such a persona evil, Atwood shows us that evil is both a negative and a positive force, that it comes embodied in ever shifting identities, that it is never fixed in time and place, that it has no determinate shape, and that, unlike Tony's battles, it produces no clear outcome. Like toxic fallout, it permeates our atmosphere; we're never outside its field of force. Evil is like power, which, as we have learned from Foucault, "is everywhere; not because it embraces everything, but because it comes from everything."[9] The multiplicity of force relations that constitute power manifests itself in "ceaseless struggles and confrontations"; "where there is power, there is resistance, and yet, or rather consequently, this resistance is never in a position of exteriority in relation to power" (95). *The Robber Bride* shows us in dramatic specificity the complex manifestations of the force of evil that inescapably generates "ceaseless struggles and confrontations." It also generates war. Tony has Zenia in mind when she notes that "the personal is not political . . . : the personal is military. War is what happens when language fails" (39). If the personal is the military, then maybe von Clausewitz's doctrine translates into the thought that war is the personal pursued by other means. Atwood's novel places the personal and warfare not in opposition (women as victims of war) but in apposition (the personal as war). It is not surprising, for example, that each of the three protagonists secretly plots a lethal final showdown with Zenia only to retreat from the battle, having been outwitted by superior tactics.

Even the scene of writing is the scene of warfare: Tony's cellar with its sandtable map on which she stages devious ambushes and bloody massacres, a fitting setting for constructing the story of Zenia who thrives on wreckage and also practices the art of fiction. Writing, said Atwood in 1987, "is exploration. Exploration is going into a territory without knowing what you may find. It is then recording as accurately as you can what you find rather than what you think you should find."[10] The writer-explorer is an alter ego of Zenia, going into uncharted territory, disturbing the artifacts, impinging on the lives of native inhabitants. And isn't the writer-explorer's recording of what she finds as patchy, arbitrary, and problematical as the historian's recreations of past events? Tony, the historian as explorer, muses about the relation of the chronicler to the actual participants in the chronicled events. "They are long gone; at the same time, they are in our hands. Like Roman gladiators, they are under our thumbs. We make them fight their battles over again for our edification and pleasure . . ." (109). And are such historical reconstructions or records of explorations true? Are they edifying? "Every sober-sided history is at least half sleight-of-hand: the right hand waving its poor snippets of fact, out in the open for all to verify, while the left hand busies itself with its own devious agendas, deep in its hidden pockets" (457–58).

Not least of such devious agendas is the writer-explorer's vampiric feeding on the lives of others. Like Zenia, who renews herself by uncannily usurping what strength and what little power the other three women possess, the artist exploits for her own purpose the joys and sufferings of other lives. Like Tony, the writer-explorer voyeuristically participates in conflicts and battles. Tony can discourse on the specific instances of genocide through the ages as if brutal mass murder were just a matter of words. But what if the vampiric artist also usurps the empathic energy of Charis, who feels interconnected with all living beings, and for whom words turn into pictures of suffering, and then screams, and then "the smell of rotting meat, and . . . of burning flesh, and then physical pain, and if you dwell on it, you make it happen" (64)? If then by dwelling on the catastrophic experiences of others the artist becomes complicit with the violence inflicted on others, what possible justification is left for creating narratives vampirically nourished by terror? What traditional apologies for art hold for our time with its daily fare of narratives about the victims of starvation, rape, bombings and shellings, acid rain and tidal waves? Is there indeed any viable justification for the artistic re-creation of these catastrophes?

The Robber Bride broaches these ethical and aesthetic questions even as it defiantly weaves together the strands of its postmodern fairy tale. Significantly it is Tony, the most skeptical of the three protagonists, who attempts to construct Zenia's story out of the fragments of the collective memories of the three survivors, hosts to Zenia's exploits, complicit in her violent disruption of their lives. Though she insists that all choices are arbitrary when it comes to writing history, Tony believes there are "definitive moments, moments we use as references.... We can look at these events and we can say that after them things were never the same again" (4).

Tony's reconstruction of the intersection of Zenia's life with her own, Roz's, and Charis's lives focuses on such "definitive moments," as does the larger fictional construct of the entire text of the *Robber Bride*, weaving these moments into plausible narratives. In the face of profound doubts about the value of such construction and reconstruction, Tony offers one possible motive that drives her to carry on this morally dubious enterprise. Maybe it is an

> act of defiance: these histories may be ragged and threadbare, patched together from worthless leftovers, but to her they are also flags, hoisted with a certain jaunty insolence, waving bravely though inconsequently, glimpsed here and there through the trees, on the mountain roads, among the ruins, on the long march into chaos. (458)

V

Remembrance Day: the three women invent their private armistice ritual, a rite de passage, their own act of commemoration of a dead warrior. They consign Zenia's ashes to the waves from the back of a ferry, creating the final "definitive moment" in Zenia's existence. She has no history, is relegated to oblivion, apart from the re-membrance of the three protagonists who had tried to purge themselves of her polluting presence. Now that the "Other" is condemned to silence, they no longer see her as a menace. They have passed through an enlightening process of welcoming, repulsing, and even demonizing the "other," and have come to recognize how deeply enmeshed their lives have been with her. Tony utters the unutterable in her final question about Zenia: "Was she in any way like us? . . . Or, to put it the other way around: Are we in any way like her?" (466).

Their final act of commemoration is not the ritual cannon shot Tony would like to accord Zenia, but a verbal tribute: "Tonight their stories will be about

Zenia" (466). This moment of conviviality and communality does not, however, open up a final utopian space in this dark novel. It does not mark a new Eden. The community of three women ("how long before we are three genuine certified batty old crones," wonders Roz [440]) encompasses the turbulent female presence whose benign-malign vitality informs their stories. They are re-enacting Zenia's dubious battles though they are unable to map her battlefield. "Where was her battlefield? Not in any one place. It was in the air all around, it was in the texture of the world itself" (465). And it is in the very texture of *The Robber Bride*.

Significantly, Zenia's death — whether by accident or design, — does not restore a stable moral world, as do the expulsion of scapegoats in traditional plots. There is no Fortinbras to come on stage and restore stability in the face of violent disruption. Atwood refuses to offer such a consoling closure, marked by the banishment of anarchic forces. The world she depicts is even in its most secure moments threatened by the eruption of violence; it is the world Tony experiences: "a thin iridescent skin held in place by surface tension." This is a world of "willed illusion of comfort and stability," invested with the energy of words and the routines of love. "But underneath is darkness. Menace, chaos, cities aflame, towers crashing down, the anarchy of deep water" (35).

As in the case of the historical massacres that Tony superimposes on each other on her sand-table map of early Europe, the boundary between the forces of evil and the forces of good, between the material and the spiritual, between form and chaos, between the body politic and the embattled self, has become unstable. This narrative palimpsest of arbitrarily chosen moments leaves us contemplating the shifting boundaries of our moral universe.

VI

The Robber Bride is a feminist "borderwork": it is not centered on the current debates about feminist ideologies and agendas though it touches peripherally on such issues as women's victimization (including the "backlash" of the beauty industry) and gender identity as well as the relation between private and public spheres. Is Atwood's robber bride, who entraps her bridegrooms by first gaining the trust of their wives or lovers, merely a playful spoof to turn the tables not only on robber bridegrooms but also on robber barons? For while Zenia appropriates other women's men along with other women's intellectual and material property, the scale of her exploitation is always limited by the fact that she is a woman. Her biggest catch is Roz's husband Mitch and her biggest fraud is forging checks to collect fifty thousand dollars from the magazine *Woman*, owned by Roz, and on the staff of which Roz had installed her in ever more authoritative positions. That's a puny accomplishment by capitalist robber baron standards. Even outside the law women's access to power remains minimal, whether on the local, national, or international stage.

Atwood's attempt to extend the allegory of the Robber Bride to a global scenario — Zenia's battlefield was "in the texture of the world itself" (465) — is arguably the weakest part of this novel. The imminent Gulf War and the breakup of Yugoslavia as global markers of the beginning and end of this narrative remind us that while we annually celebrate Armistice Day we live in a world ruled by never-ending violent confrontations. Nevertheless the global catastrophes form nothing more than a vivid backdrop for the regional scenarios featuring Zenia as robber bride. In this more limited sphere, Atwood turns a searing searchlight on the roles of women as victims and victimizers.

Emory University

Notes

[1] Don DeLillo, *Mao II* (New York: Viking/Penguin, 1991), 41–42.

[2] I am borrowing Margaret Higonnet's suggestive title *Borderwork* from a volume of essays she edited that aims at meeting the challenge of "reading at the crossroads, reading along the borderline of silence" (*Borderwork: Feminist Engagements with Comparative Literature* [Ithaca and London: Cornell UP, 1994], 16).

[3] Atwood, *Conversations*, ed. Earl G. Ingersoll, (Princeton: Ontario Review P, 1990), 55, 126.

[4] Atwood, *The Robber Bride* (New York: Doubleday, 1993), 65–66.

[5] Anca Vlasopolos, "Emotions Unpurged: Antigeneric Theater and the Politics of Violence," in *Borderwork*, 120–43; quotation 143.

[6] Margaret Atwood has repeatedly commented in interviews on her early, influential reading of the unexpurgated *Grimm's Fairy Tales*. "I had pretty well memorized them by the time I was six. One of the interesting things was that there were a lot of quite active female characters, whereas if you get the watered-down version, you just get Cinderella and Sleeping Beauty" (*Conversations*, 224; see also 46, 70, 147, 152). It is worth noting that Atwood's original working title for what became *Bodily Harm* (New York: Simon and Schuster, 1982) was *The Robber Bridegroom* (Helmut Reichenbächer, "Von *The Robber Bridegroom* zu *Bodily Harm*: Eine Analyse unveröffentlicher Entwürfe Margaret Atwoods," *Zeitschrift für Anglistik und Amerikanistik* 41 [1993]: 54–65; reference 55) and that her 1984 volume, *Interlunar*, included a poem entitled *The Robber Bridegroom*, which explores the bridegroom's "red compulsion" as his need to ravish and appropriate the bride's soul (*Selected Poems II: Poems Selected and New 1976–1986* [Boston: Houghton Mifflin, 1987], 110). She also painted a watercolor sketch entitled *The Robber Bridegroom*, picturing a man holding an axe and a blond head (Sharon Wilson, "Sexual Politics in Margaret Atwood's Visual Art," in *Margaret Atwood: Vision and Forms*, ed. Kathryn VanSpanckeren and Jan Garden Castro, [Carbondale: Southern Illinois P, 1988], 205–14; see 209).

[7] Jacob Grimm and Wilhelm Grimm, *Kinder- und Hausmärchen* (Munich: Winkler, 1987), 239–42.

[8] William Wordsworth, "Ode: Intimations of Immortality," ll. 90–91, 106–07.

[9] Michel Foucault, *The History of Sexuality*, trans. Robert Hurley, (New York: Vintage Books, 1980), 93.

[10] Jan Garden Castro, "An Interview with Margaret Atwood. 20 April 1983," in *Margaret Atwood: Vision and Forms*, 233–43; quotation 241.

GAYATRI CHAKRAVORTY SPIVAK ©

Foucault and Najibullah

Foucault's *Discipline and Punish* opens with a public hanging. Foucault contrasts this with the Panopticon.[1] The book traces the story of our times as the story of the rationalized individual and of the development of (the) discipline(s). "The carceral network does not cast the unassimilable into a confused hell; there is no outside" (DP 301). It is the story of the emergence of "man as object of knowledge" (DP 24). It is indeed the story of our time. The book was first published in 1975. Today we might say that the narrative was to produce the "wo/man" of Human Rights, in the name of which power legitimizes itself repeatedly. Here is a summary of Foucault's narrative by way of two passages from the book: "In the ceremonies of the public execution, the main character was the people, whose real and immediate presence was required for the performance"(DP 57). This is the initial moment. And then:

> It is as if the eighteenth century had opened up the crisis of this economy and, in order to resolve it, proposed the fundamental law that punishment must have "humanity" as its "measure," without any definitive meaning being given to this principle, which nevertheless is regarded as insuperable. We must, therefore, recount the birth and early days of this enigmatic "leniency"
>
> (DP 75)

"I shall choose examples from military, medical, educational and industrial institutions. Other examples might have been taken from colonization, slavery and child rearing," writes Foucault.[2] It appears from the body of the book that he has in mind the establishment of penal colonies overseas or the deportation of "delinquents, undisciplined soldiers, prostitutes and orphans . . . [to] Algeria, . . . Guiana . . . New Caledonia" (DP 279). But even if we give Foucault the benefit of a doubt here, the application of the analysis to colonialism would trace the production of the colonial subject, whose best examples, in the French case, would be Ho Chi Minh, Frantz Fanon, and Assia Djebar. I have attempted to trace a counter narrative here .

In an earlier essay, I faulted Foucault and Deleuze for a romantic populism. Here too Foucault puts the reason for his enterprise in the hands of "prisoners," confined to France and the Western world (although he speaks of "the world" in general), assigning, one cannot help feeling, a meaning to their actions that would suit his argument. There is little discussion of the actual prison revolts, certainly nothing like the loving documentation that the "past" receives; the lesson of the book

> is a lesson that I have learnt not so much from history as from the present. In recent years, prison revolts have occurred throughout the world.... What was at issue was not whether the prison environment was too harsh or too aseptic..., but its very materiality as an instrument and vector of power... that of the educationalists, psychologists and psychiatrists.... I would like to write the history of this prison... if one means writing the history of the present. (DP 31)

Whatever Foucault might have intended, it has led readers to embrace his critique of governmentality without regard for its sphere of study. We who are interested in alternative Development propose an ab-use (not abuse) of the Enlightenment (understood in shorthand as "the public use of reason"), a use from below. Marx had tried, but he was too much the organic intellectual of industrial capitalism to have broken through to the question of agency; his proletarian remained a straw figure when Communism became a form of government. This allowed intellectuals like Foucault to throw Marx out with the Enlightenment, although in this relatively early book he articulated his narrative in terms of "the bourgeois revolution" and made certain connections:

> If economic exploitation separates the force and the product of labour, let us say that disciplinary coercion establishes in the body the constricting link between an increased aptitude and an increased domination. (DP 138)

Today's solution in the Development lobby (including United Nations universalist feminism) is simply to make the world multiculturalist American. It is ignorant of Foucault of course; when necessary, it knows to be against "postmodernism," whatever that might be. Its unacknowledged prophet is Cecil Rhodes: "I contend that we are the first race in the world, and that the more of the world we inhabit the better it is for the human race.... If there be a God, I think that what he would like me to do is to paint as much of the map of Africa British red as possible."[3] (*Mutatis mutandis*: territorial imperialism is no longer convenient; economic restructuring for exploitation will do. By contrast, attempts at learning to alter the history of the future anterior are minor indeed.)

In *The Sunday New York Times* for 6 October 1996, there is an item called "Afghanistan Reels Back into View." There is a picture of "[t]he bodies of Najibullah, left, and his brother hang[ing] from a Kabul traffic post." There is a crowd of peering men from behind, looking as much at the cameramen as at the backs of the bloody bodies, as far as one can tell. What is the lesson of this public spectacle?

In the months before Afghanistan's new rulers marched him from a United Nations compound in Kabul and summarily beat, shot and hanged him, Afghanistan's last Communist President, Najibullah, spent much of his time preparing a translation into Pashto, his native language, of a 1990 book about Afghanistan, "The Great Game," by the English writer Peter Hopkirk.[4] Mr. Najibullah told United Nations officials that he wanted Afghans to read the Hopkirk text because of what they would learn from it of the 19th-century struggle between imperial Britain and imperial Russia for influence in Afghanistan. "They can see how our history has represented itself," he said. "Only if we understand our history can we take steps to break the cycle."

Here is ab-use of the Enlightenment. "The Great Game" is, of course a reference to Kipling's *Kim*.[5] A child plays spy for industrial capitalist imperialism, as if it is a feudal game. The particular scene is a Russian and a Frenchman in the Himalayas, where the Russian points at the monstrous colonial subject (my ancestor, M.A. from Calcutta University), and says that they, the Russians, know the Orient and can govern them. Hopkirk tells us that the term was invented by "Lieutenant Arthur Conolly of the 6th Bengal Native Light Cavalry . . . [who], aged 16, . . . [had] joined his regiment as a cornet" (GG 123–124). Najibullah, no doubt waiting for a violent death, knew these books and thought that reading them might help. This is the kind of ab-use of the Enlightenment that we learn from. And behind reading is literacy. Islam is not just a People of the Book, but a People of the letter; literacy. *Al-Quran* earns its name by the injunction to read: *qra*.

The Great Game is a book of riveting popular journalism. What it does demonstrate in as narrative a mode as *Discipline and Punish* (albeit with fewer theoretical pyrotechnics) is that Afghanistan (as part of Central Asia) was a pawn in a game between the Russians and the British — both eager to win a passage to India. He suggests that the Game began in Russia's reaction to "the 'lost' Mongol centuries" (GG 16; ca 1206–1553). This is to plot the story not by economic modes of production (as in Marx and DP's Foucault) but by great movements of people (as in Samir Amin).[6] Today this seems altogether persuasive.

The production of the colonial subject in order to administer a settled colonial possession could not appear on the agenda in this region. The examples I have chosen — Mohandas Karamchand Gandhi, barrister, also comes to mind — support the truism that it is in this class that nationalist resistance took root. But Afghanistan was never "colonized," and, it can be surmised, that Najibullah, by translating this book, was trying to produce something like that subject in his country; a subject that will know that to take sides in that theater is simply to agree to be a plaything in a game that neither began nor ended with the Cold War. In the event, he became a public spectacle in a discourse — military, political, economic — that he could not signify. In the New World

Economic Order of electronic capitalism, the separation "between force and the product of labour" has become aporetic, displaced itself into operative virtuality. That Afghanistan, the only part of Central Asia that was not a member of the USSR, had a role in the consolidation of the end of the Cold War and thus the establishment of the New World Economic Order cannot be doubted. Yet the separation between its failed nationhood and the success of globality is so vast, that in this public spectacle, the people do not countersign the "super-power" of a monarch, as in Foucault's Early Modern France. They face the photographer of the super-power, furtively, once again providing evidence of an archaic violence.

In this theater, the masters masqueraded as the native. As in *Kim*, the Great Game was almost invariably played in disguise. Hopkirk's pages are strewn with pictures of British and Russian soldiers in Afghan, Persian, Armenian dress. If in Foucault's story, the transformation of the soldier into a docile body "could become determinant only with a technical transformation: the invention of the rifle" (DP 163), the rifle clinched no great narrative in Najibullah's. Plate 35 in GG shows a British officer in native dress surrounded by Afghans. " . . . [M]any minor players," the caption runs, "were involved in the Great Game. An anonymous political officer (rifleless), hardly distinguishable from his companions, is seen here with friendly Afghan tribesmen," who all carry rifles, but are not called "soldiers." This picture is outside of Foucault's beautifully organized system, so beloved by the disciplines, but also "inside," for this is the wild counter-narrative, rifle-toting tribesmen and rifleless white soldier, that keeps the story of efficiency and leniency going in the metropolis.

If Foucault ignores the colonial subject and Kipling (like Rushdie) constructs him as monstrously comic, Hopkirk cannot understand him. Like Kipling's Hurree Mookerjee, Mirza Shuja is part of

> an élite group of handpicked and highly trained Indians . . . [who were sent] into these forbidden regions[.] They were far less likely to be detected than a European, however good the latter's disguise. If they were unfortunate enough to be discovered, moreover, it would be less politically embarrassing to the authorities than if a British officer was caught red-handed making maps in these highly sensitive and dangerous parts. (GG 329–330)

"Just what drove men like Mirza Shuja to face such hardships and extreme dangers for their imperial masters has never been satisfactorily explained" (GG 332). I see in him my intellectual ancestor, fooled by "white mythology," serving intellectual ambition rather than his imperial masters. Afghanistan was not a locus of the large-scale production of such trained subjects, male in the Great Game, but male and female in the disciplines.

How did Islam become such a tremendous oppressor of women? Here is the *Times*.

> Last week, . . . the Taliban . . . began constructing their new state along strict Muslim fundamentalist [islamist nationalist] lines — complete with the closing of girls' schools and beatings for improperly dressed women, as well as at least one public display of a man punished with amputation. . . . [The US State Department] voiced American concerns about the protection of human rights, "especially women's rights," but added, "We will have to judge them by their actions." . . . There is logic in thinking that Washington will not be unhappy with the prospect of a government in Kabul that may limit Iranian influence in central Asia . . .

Universalist feminism will take up the cause of these women and congratulate itself on being radical and, once again, with various photo opportunities, make the world safe for capitalism recoded as democracy. Not much will change for the woman at the bottom.

Already in 1975, at the inception of today's electronic capitalism, and in the year of publication of *Surveiller et punir*, the Report of the World Conference of the International Women's Year declares: "True peace cannot be achieved unless women share with men the responsibility for establishing a new international economic order."[7] Twenty years later, the Women's World Bank is busy breaking up long-standing gendering arrangements in the interest of "negotiating with the commercial sector," telling them that there is a "huge untapped market" among the world's poorest rural women.[8] Just as the British had secured their colony by promising India for the Hindus, and Russia's countermove was to have been "that they had come to restore Muslim rule under the Moguls to its former glory" (GG 21), a general female will for economic restructuring is being constructed in this brutal way. Afghanistan will be brought to stability by the gendered subject of globalization.

Let us ask again: How did Islam become such a tremendous oppressor of women? Of course, one cannot answer such questions with correct narratives, but I am trying to follow in Foucault's footsteps; he seemed to think late eighteenth century governmentality could be held responsible for policing the body. My question: how did Islam . . . has been asked by many contemporary Muslims. I know no Arabic, and little history. I can make a footnote.[9] And offer, first, a model as fantasmatic as Foucault's: Melanie Klein.

Klein suggests that when a group of men is oppressed by another group, against whom it can do nothing, Envy makes it turn against women, especially the imago of the Mother.[10] This is a complicated argument, and I will not try to lay it out here. But it is a good working hypothesis against the racist argument that Islam is essentially oppressive. Indeed, Foucault offers certain developments in rather a simpler cause and effect model: "It was against the new régime of landed property — set up by the bourgeoisie that profited from the Revolution — that a whole peasant illegality developed" (DP 274). He also gives the itinerary of the production of "the delinquent" as we could of "the terrorist," "serv[ing] as a support for the 'great fear' of a people who were believed to be criminal and seditious as a whole...." He argues at the same time that "the new forms of law . . . threw to the other side of the law many individuals, who, in other conditions, would not have gone over to specialized criminality" (GG 274–275).[11]

Something like a second argument comes from colonially settled areas: that the conquered civilizations were not put to respectful rest, were not mourned, when the culture of imperialism brought the nation to a new frontier. I offer a poem and a bit of a novel. Can poems and novels argue? Remember, I am following Najibullah's conviction, as Foucault claimed to follow that of the world's prison rioters. Can there ever be more than "half-mourning?" (*demi-deuil*)?[12] I do not believe so. But let the glass be half-full, so that it can continue to produce quenching, rather than be crushed under the boot of imperialism as development.

My third position: the largest part of the electorate in these places is non-urban children. You start at the bottom, for the long haul; you don't just adopt wholesale and make new Americans, as a policy; or practice thoughtless cultural intervention in the interest of finance capital; that's Cecil Rhodes and beyond. Hence rural literacy. Some years ago, I was appalled by these sentiments uttered by a "feminist" intellectual:

> This challenged giant [the United States] . . . may, in fact, be on the point of becoming a David before the growing Goliath of the Third World. I dream that our children will prefer to join this David, with his errors and impasses, armed with our erring and circling about the Idea, the Logos, the Form: in short, the old Judeo-Christian Europe. If it is only an illusion, I like to think it may have a future.[13]

I should like to propose that the real David (if I may ab-usively appropriate that West Asian story for a lesson) is in the camps of the alternative development activist, and literacy is their littlest project; who has time for the painstaking long haul of little changes? Only the Gramscis and Najibullahs of the world, with all the leisure that governmentalist confinement produces.

Point four: the argument for teaching reading/writing/numeracy to the non-urban landless is embedded in an argument about academic freedom in a postcolonial situation. The body of the piece was written for Cape Town. I have done nothing to change it, because I hope it will give a sense of the sheer heterogeneity of the narratives of emancipation in the postcolonial world. No invocation of prison riots all over the world will teach you anything if all you visit is the library.

Ab-use of the Enlightenment, then. Patriarchal Envy in the policy-making men of the colony. Absence of mourning rites for the lost civilization. Academic freedom at the top bound by the cry for literacy at the bottom. I hope this context will allow me to launch myself *in medias res*, with the following pronouncement:

You cannot keep a rational politics "free."

The risk of necessary contamination involved in binding reason to a politics — however "good" in the liberatory intuition "now" — *cannot be avoided*. Yet this risk must be taken, for reason is made possible not only by unreason, but by the radically irrational, which it can neither encompass nor indeed, perhaps, touch. The risk is in the possible future, always around the corner, *that we feel we can bet on*, and it will not have been avoided by any deconstructive caution, any "tortuous prudence [,any] . . . severe economy of writing holding back declaration within a discipline of severely observed markers" — hyphens, parentheses, — if freedom is not only granted but exercised.[14] The fight for freedom before it is granted is also an exercise of it; by means of stating a freeing that we now perform as resistance. What is it to perform a freedom that has not been granted? Who can grant freedom? And this moment, here, today, is that future that was always around the corner. And what future is it that has slipped around a corner in its turn that we have trouble glimpsing? It is with that question in mind that I invoke this necessary but impossible philosophy of "rural" literacy, so difficult because the task itself has always seemed so easy.

From my own experience of India, Algeria, and Bangladesh, it seems to me that the postcolonial state, based on the seemingly originary idea of a new nation opposed to the imperialist politics of racism, has proved particularly susceptible to the terrifying contaminations of having avoided contamination, for the battle seemed won.

(Again, and it bears repetition, Afghanistan is ex-orbitant to this narrative, thanks to the Great Game. Hence Najibullah's translation project.)

We who are within the heritage of imperialism, are still failing to demand and exercise freedom as an absolute *means* to guard an end that is necessarily contaminable. In invoking learning to learn from the ignored "rural" base even as we teach the majority of the future electorate the intuitions of "democracy," some of us are attempting to guard and defend the hope that this model of freedom as absolute means to a responsibility may be more easily available from the compromised and hardly salvageable "below" than the rampant European Enlightenment alone, as the policeman of human *rights*. Yet that model is so terrifyingly open to political sloganeering, to abuse of trust! And its subject, the rural underclass, is unconstituted for academic freedom, so that the bridge between ethno-cultural notions of responsibility and a modern education still rests on air!

Makeup on the dead face of the past. It is the past as the unburied dead that calls us in postcoloniality. It is in response and responsibility to that call that the postcolonial must strain to gain access to cultural responsibility. Farhad Mazhar, a Bangladeshi poet, contrasts the contemporary Bengali archaeologists — working in the restricted arena of academic freedom, more "British" than the Royal Asiatic Society, — to the poet-persona forever guarding the unburied corpses of the Sepoy Mutiny (1857), the first battle of independence on the subcontinent:

> Lord, Dhaka's mosque is world-renowned
> Much varied work on pillar and cloister. In British days
> the Whites, right or wrong, put in place
> th'Asiatic Society and researched it all
> Here. In the white eyes
> Of whites the new Bengalis dig now
> And look for things we see.
> I wish them good luck. But doctor's degrees,
> Make them twice
> As wily as their White forebears.
>
> Lord, I'm an unlettered fool,
> Can't grasp the art of architecture, paint,
> Yet my heart aches empty
> As I stand by the old Ganga.
> The Sepoys seem to hang still on hangman's ropes
> Waiting for last rites, the ropes uncut,
> Their bodies still aloft, none to mourn,
> To perform *zannat*.
> Don't you mock me with minaret and arcade,
> Me, the corpse-keeper of revolt.[15]

Foucault never quite tells us what we should do about Damiens the regicide. For this poet, a task remains undone; as it is for Najibullah.[16]

Assia Djebar complicates the metaphor with the double difficulty of regaining an active perspective for women in the unperformed burial rites for the dead old culture when the colonial culture seemingly gave access to the new. (Part of the legacy of that colonial culture is, precisely, an "academic freedom" which may become unmindful of the dishonored past or, alternatively, invoke ethnic material as a cosmetic upon its face, even as it uses that "freedom" to find more and more theoretically sophisticated ways to *describe* the mechanics of violence without the responsibility of setting it to work.) The men fighting, the women mourning is all that Djebar stages as a recovery: "the body, not embalmed by ritual lamentations, is found dressed in rags. As an echo the cries of our ancestors, unhorsed in forgotten battles, return; and the dirges of the women who watched them die, accompany them."[17]

It is well-known that most sub-Saharan African cultures had a more active role for women. Yet, if we are reckoning with colonialism, and Enlightenment-model liberatory struggles, and the constitution of the subject of academic freedom, what percentage of female *subalternity* will be able to deploy this or a simulacrum of this, within the enclosure of the University? and can this be seamlessly sutured to the European tradition of academic freedom?

These passages should make clear that I am not attempting to bring the dead to life, but rather to be haunted by the ghost of one past so that we can reasonably (ab)-use another. I am suggesting that the unlamented corpses of colonized cultures must be lamented anew as we attempt to (ab)-use their un-affiliated living after-runners (not their "proper inheritors"). I have never been at all interested in designating "proper" inheritors of anthropologized older cultures so that they can be distanced from the advantages of the unaffiliated after-running colonizing culture and its indigenous collaborators.[18] Hence ethnic identitarianism is rather far from my concerns. I am, however, profoundly interested in the persistent performance of those funeral rites by bringing the question of academic freedom down, in postcolonial countries, to the constitution of the subject for academic freedom, in the primary education of the subaltern, even as the already-constituted subject of academic freedom deconstitutes and unravels itself by learning to learn the responsibility-ethics of subaltern culture so that it can perhaps be preserved through the teaching of learning, which after all is the substance of literacy.[19] That is where the resources of the (ab)-use of the Enlightenment are located, where the majority of the future electorate can be otherwise mobilized by the mere mouthing of democracy as vote control.[20] Later I will suggest that this is also the growing new front where the resistance to Development-as-alibi-for-exploitation is growing its globe-girdling network.[21]

Sometimes the possibility of progress is infinitesimal. This should neither discourage nor discredit the urgency of the need. (After all, lavish international conferences on "Decolonizing the Imagination" — for the world's best-educated people, of course — or "Global Civilization/Local Cultures" — from the European Universalist perspective, of course — remind us often, at great length and with much subtlety that, even after many years of quality education, sufficient progress is not achieved, and we tend to find these reminders cathartic.)

Here, then, David; or, if I may appropriate Woolf, David's sister; via Sukumar Ray, *pāglā jagai*.

The night-schools in the remoter rural areas of Bangladesh meet out of doors. They cannot afford to have more than thirty students at each school, and not more than two hurricane lanterns. No blackboards. One teacher. At best five levels of students. Teachers with minimal basic training but considerable goodwill and real dedication, never participants in the university level playing fields of academic freedom.

The schools meet at night because the boys must work by day. Field labor, any sort of hired work. It is clear how the boys would gain through knowledge of reading and numbers. The girls do not often return after the third year. In support of the future-enlightenment-of-children argument, local men say that if the girls get more education, they would have to find matriculate husbands. Well-placed critics should appreciate that this creates a problem for poor parents.

This is not immediately unreasonable. Just as primary health care, related to change in life habits, is not identical with (though related to) clinical support in case of disease, so also the constitution of the subject for academic freedom, in the long-term slowest-motion careful drive for the agency of lasting social change, is not identical with legal aid when patriarchy leads to visible violence.

The men's argument is an example of patriarchy assigning responsibility (as duty) from above, even in subalternity, and successful gendering convincing the woman to be inferior in public status to her husband. This bit of internalized gendering can be broken, and it is part of the task of the constitution of the subject for academic freedom. In this arena, the (ab)-use of the Enlightenment has led indigenous female activists to persist with rural mothers over months to win one female child to schooling, convincing them with obviously sincere expression of physical affection for the children. These activist women, however, are also totally separated from that enclave of urban radicalism which can think academic freedom. In postcoloniality, especially in gendering, it is facts of this kind that lead me to repeat: the issue of academic freedom begins with the gender-sensitive style of rural literacy.

If we are gender-sensitive, we must be able to imagine the very long haul, and think of constituting the future subject for academic freedom for a much-delayed opening of access to the University. (Alas, the short haul epistemic violation is in the powerful hands of the Women's World Bank.) What follows is an extended example:

Winning over rural girl-children one by one is obviously not an achievement commensurate with the large-scale systemic change necessary for people in general not to offer the need for matriculate husbands as a reason against women's education.[22] In the mean time, the devising of small survival techniques can happen only if we who celebrate full academic freedom in a new nation expand the area of our concern. The long term and the rhythm of day to day can perhaps coexist.

In these remote night-schools, literacy is focused on reading. Considerable importance is attached to memorizing — the alphabet, multiplication tables, poems and so on. It fits in with the rote learning emphasized in all but the best schools in the colonies because of the anterior richness of orality even within so-called "literate" cultures. (In the colonial period, and within the general framework of what I have elsewhere called "epistemic violation," the emphasis on rote learning in the lower reaches of society is an example of the desiccation of the old culture as it is unmoored from the dynamics of upward mobility and the theatre of robust historical change.)[23] As a result, the children will often "read" something different from the page they are following with finger and eye. To "correct" them from above is a total undermining of the entire delicate effort. Yet those interested in the eventual subject for academic freedom must devote some of their energies to these sorts of details because there are not enough resources at this ground-level for the kind of individual attention for which one might agitate under more favorable circumstances. And the Enlightenment cannot be (ab)-used by rote. Arrived here, it is the class-separated (though not necessarily race-separated) universitarian who must learn and change: the task is not to make the schoolchild terrified. We are, after all, speaking of the countryside after nightfall — not the children of the urban underclass who have frequently had to learn counter-warfare too soon. What one is testing is a teaching system compromised by dead tradition, not the child.

If the girl-child is asked to write her own message to someone, the emphasis on memory and reading does not come to her aid. And yet, when after three years she is confined to home, yard, and perhaps field and stream, soon to be married, she finds no books in her rural household. If in those three years, emphasis had been laid on writing a free-style sentence every day, it is at least remotely possible that, when deprived of her education and yoked to household labor and childbirth, she would have had a companion, in the secret skill of writing. We have examples of slave narratives and women's secret writing to corroborate this. The patriarchally severed minute effort at the constitution of the gendered subject for the long term of the narrative of history may perhaps (there is no guarantee) find shelter in this small sustained change in the teaching of female children. And yet the change is not easy to make. For once again, we must remember that these limitcase teachers, themselves from the rural subaltern order and seldom with more than inferior secondary education, are conditioned by the obedience-to-authority to which responsibility is reduced by its delegitimation in colonial as well as postcolonial education; the former with its fantasmatic base in Enlightenment principles which are ideally (though not ideologically) in conflict with the practice of colonial administration, and the latter finding its energy in the abstract subject that was the bye-product of the conflict and that can now seek redress only as the resolution of that conflict in terms of the discourse of rights. As a result of this, the imperative towards drawing out freestyle writing itself runs the risk of reduction to a from-above formula. To "train" the subaltern teacher without the all-too-easy coercion and yet without loss of authority, is itself part of the training-in-learning of the already constituted subject of academic freedom, if she cares to involve herself in these different dynamics of rural literacy.

To offer another example: organizing in Indian villages against wife-beating, women workers agitate on the side for a supply of teachers at the supposedly free inactive State primary schools. If our imagined activist suggests to these organizers that it is still possible for them to mark the time of survival by teaching "the practice of writing and reckoning," even if for fifteen minutes a day, all of what I have written above has to be kept actively in mind.

It is in such small ways that we make provision for a continuity of the potential for freedom until the patriarchal or political system changes sufficiently, also through our efforts, in other spheres. A poor provision at best. Yet not necessarily less important than the inspirational prose of culturalist academics confined to a colonial/anticolonial historical scheme in euphoric postcolonial space.

(These words were written five years ago. This sort of slow work is now hopeless. The non-governmental organizations that are enthusiastic about women's micro-enterprise with no commitment to building infra-structure will soon produce the globalized subject; the literate woman, out from cultural gendering with no ideological base, signing her way into the general will for economic restructuring. The statistics will be persuasive. Yet one cannot give up training for resistance.)

This essay has been uneasily shuttling between the two foci of resistance: the aggregative apparatus of the postcolonial state; and the *pouvoir/savoir* of the rural girl-child in literacy. The two meet in the arena of "Development." Najibullah and his brother seem to be hanging in some other space. But they are casualties of a Game that consolidated the narrative of conquest / colonialism / postcoloniality / globalization; itself serving to consolidate the emergence of the Foucauldian "man as object of knowledge." This narrative also leads to "Development" as the history of the present.

In the New World Order, where there is only North and South rather than East and West, it is impossible for a new state to escape the constraints of a "neo-liberal" world economic system which, in the name of Development, removes all barriers between itself and fragile national economies. As I have stated above, the real front against these forces is located in a subalternity condemned (or celebrated, depending upon your politics) as a mere enclave of tradition. In fact it is upon this terrain that the resistance to "Development" has been organizing. Since resistance to "Development"-as-an-alibi-for-exploitation is by no means a refusal of development as such, its connection with the (ab)use of the Enlightenment — reconstellation from below and in the interest of gender equity — should by now be clear. The only bulwark against the insanity of unrestricted competition which is reflected in the three controlling global agencies — the World Bank, the International Monetary Fund, and the General Agreement on Tariffs and Trade — is a reinvention of the old responsibility-based ethics, without which the well-meaning arrogance of enforcing human *rights* is a pathetic reliance upon the Enlightenment notion that an ennobled sense of self will not be able to brook the suffering of the other. This effort at reinvention animates the persistent short-term initiatives of local self-management that run interference against the financialization of the globe, which become possible through a politics that brings subalternity to crisis.[24] This is where we locate the long-term double-sided effort of rural literacy, building not only for struggle against political oppression, but for a sustainable future as well. It is thus that we place together the concept that in the New World Economic Order the new state is obliged to veer away from any redistributive functions, and the metaphor that postcolonial culture must actively mourn the precolonial, which has remained so long without funeral rites. In my fancy, Najibullah was trying to provide a means to educate the people of Afghanistan to want a civil society, and to mourn a violent past.

Just as in the case of academic freedom we are not proposing to turn our backs on the Enlightenment but rather to learn how to revise and recycle it through lessons learned from below, so also in this area there is no question of a refusal of development. It is a question of sustaining development through local self-management. Because these local initiatives in fact run interference with transnational capitalism and are therefore of global impact, it is not possible for the postcolonial state in the New World Order to take the initiative here. Therefore the so-called New Social Movements must build up an alternative inter-nationality that will stand behind the state. Here again, we see a difference between claiming rights as an end and valuing the right to the insertion into responsibility to the ecobiome — to Nature. For the subaltern of the South, the issue is not conservation and re-cycling, it is ecological survival through claiming responsibility to Nature. The sacredness of animist space can prove a liberation theology, but not if it is museumized from above, only if we learn space as a name of absolute alterity, an alterity that is effaced as it is disclosed in the difference between Gross National Product and Gross Natural Product.[25]

(Incidentally, developing subsistence and small- and large-market farming is important for the constitution of the subject for academic freedom in another way as well. Without such a support system, a large part of the population is obliged to engage in migratory — rather than merely migrant — labor. I do not have to recount the soul-devastating effects of this. Let me say the obvious practical thing: if there is no class to teach for six months in the year, a literacy drive is hopeless.)

Am I suggesting that academic freedom, rather than an inalienable formal right, is what has come to be known as a New Social Movement, in postcoloniality? I am close to that. But does not such a suggestion transgress the very concept of a "freedom?" This is indeed the point I have been driving at all through this essay.

Academic "freedom," like all rational formal freedoms, can only be exercised by its own transgression, by being "bound" to content. Pure "freedom" is "guaranteed" by the exercise of the constitution of a possible subject, already the commitment to a content. We have experience of a society of largely unexercised guarantees, a society just by default.[26] A robustly just society is where the members, when acting self-consciously within rational and privative norms — never adequately possible — see freedoms not as ends but absolute means to protect their transgression, which is also their exercise. No justification of the *exercise* of academic freedom can be drawn from within academic freedom. It comes into being in its own binding. We cannot read Foucault without accounting for Najibullah.

We do not celebrate the public spectacle in *The New York Times* which, removed from the uncontested authority of the European narrative, cannot produce "a history of the present," as Foucault promised. Unlike Damiens, who illustrates the story, Najibullah can be read as desperately trying to negotiate its elements. He cannot stand as an illustration of the abstract movements of electronic capitalism. How had he understood Marx as he was caught in the crossfire between Moscow and Washington, so that the last resort seemed to be to translate a "political" text that takes from "fiction" its model? The postcolonial subject of academic freedom cannot afford merely to excoriate a governmentality whose benefits it quietly enjoys. We stand with the child as David in the name of a freedom in the future anterior, where translation of uncontested narratives is, as usual, necessary, impossible, and perhaps foredoomed.

Columbia University

Notes

[1] Michel Foucault, *Discipline and Punish: the Birth of the Prison*, trans. Alan Sheridan (New York: Pantheon, 1977); hereafter cited in text as DP, followed by page number.

[2] DP 314, n. 1. The consequences of applying something like this narrative to all the children of the world reveal themselves in the interested manipulation of "child labor" today and are discussed in my *Obtuse Angling* (forthcoming from Harvard UP).

[3] L. S. Stavrianos, *Global Rift: the Third World Comes of Age* (New York: Morrow, 1981); quoted in Jan Nederveen Pieterse, *Empire and Emancipation: Power and Liberation on a World Scale* (London: Pluto, 1990), 263.

[4] Peter Hopkirk, *The Great Game: The Struggle for Empire in Central Asia* (New York: Kodansha, 1994); hereafter cited in text as GG, with page references following.

[5] Rudyard Kipling, *Kim* (New York: Penguin, 1987); references to the Great Game begin on 195.

[6] Samir Amin, *Unequal Development:an Essay on the Social Formations of Peripheral Capitalism*, trans. Brian Pearce (New York: Monthly Review Press, 1976). This is the largely implicit presupposition of the entire book.

[7] *The United Nations and the Advancement of Women: 1945–1995* (New York: United Nations, 1995), 180.

[8] Nicola Armacost of Women's World Banking, at Conference on "Structural Reform, Governance and Sustainability: Issues in Law and Development," Columbia University School of Law, 7 March 1997.

[9] Spivak, "Ghostwriting," *Diacritics* 25 (summer 1995): 65–84. See also Djebar, *Les Blancs de l'Algérie* (Paris: Albin Michel, 1995).

[10] Melanie Klein, *Love, Guilt and Reparation* (New York: Macmillan, 1975), 191.

[11] Indeed, my childhood images of the Afghan, who lived fifteen hundred miles to the west, were altogether benign; from Tagore's short story "Kabuliwala," later made into a film by Satyajit Ray, and Syed Mujtaba Ali's *Deshe Bideshe*, an urbane account of Russo-Afghan diplomatic, intellectual, and cultural life in the fifties.

[12] Jacques Derrida, "Fors: the anglish Words of Nicolas Abraham and Maria Torok," *The Wolf Man's Magic Word: A Cryptonymy*, trans. Nicholas Rand (Minneapolis: U of Minnesota P, 1986), xi-xlviii.

[13] Julia Kristeva, "My Memory's Hyperbole," in *The Female Autograph: Theory and Practice of Autobiography from the Tenth to the Twentieth Century* ed. Domna C. Stanton (Chicago: U of Chicago P, 1987), 235. These words took on added violence at the time of first revision, in full deployment of "Operation Desert Storm."

[14] Derrida, *Of Spirit: Heidegger and the Question*, trans. Geoffrey Bennington and Rachel Bowlby (Chicago: U of Chicago P, 1989), 32.

[15] Farhad Mazhar, "The Corpse-Keeper of Revolt," in *Ebādatnāmā 2* (Dhākā: Prabartanā, 1989), 36. Translation mine.

[16] I can hear liberal and wise US readers recounting what a bad man he was and how bad the Soviet regime was et cetera. I can agree (or disagree) with all of that and still work with the figure who, at last ditch, was working on a translation as a remedy! A fellow-translator, and a figure: "Lenz" to my Celan (see Derrida, "Shibboleth," in *Acts of Literature* ed. Derek Attridge [New York: Routledge,1992], 370–413).

[17] Assia Djebar, *Fantasia: an Algerian Cavalcade*, trans. Dorothy S. Blair (New York: Quartet, 1985), 157; translation modified. This theme is continued in the depiction of the Algerian War of 1957–62 in a film named after the prison Barberousse. The women active in the War were so vocal in their objection, that the director Bouabdallah invited them to participate in a documentary where they recount their participation and their critique: *Barberousse mes soeurs*. I am grateful to Dr. Nadia Aït-Sahalia for showing me a private video of the film.

[18] This becomes all the more necessary today because of the cultural claims of writers such as Samuel P. Huntington and Richard Rorty. I have dealt with this phenomenon in greater detail in Chapter Four of *Obtuse Angling*.

[19] I borrow the construction "subject for" rather than "subject of" from Hélène Cixous, "The Laugh of the Medusa," in *New French Feminisms: An Anthology*, ed. Elaine Marks and Isabelle de Courtivron (New York: Schocken, 1981), 252–53. For a discussion of this see Spivak, "French Feminism Revisited," in Spivak, *Outside in the Teaching Machine* (New York: Routledge, 1993), 158–60. "Constitution of the subject for academic freedom" is not just a fancy way of talking about community involvement for the college teacher. It means investigating the details of rural literacy in the postcolonial state. I am thinking not only of Paolo Freire's well-known *Pedagogy of the Oppressed*, trans. Myra Bergman Ramos (New York: Continuum, 1981), but also of the "Freedom Schools" in the American South, Gonopathshala in Bangladesh, the schools run by the Shabar Kheriya Kalyan Samiti in Purulia District in West Bengal, India.

[20] For a description of this see Leerom Medovoi *et. al.*, "Can the Subaltern Vote?," *Socialist Review* 20.3 (July-Sept 1990): 133–49.

[21] I have developed this notion in "Social Security for Subordinated Groups," paper delivered at conference on "South Asia: Towards an Agenda for a Better Future," University of Cambridge, 18–19 June 1994. Upon that occasion, I was heartened to gain the support of Tariq Banuri (Sustainable Development Policy Institute, Pakistan) and Shapan Adnan (Shomabesh Institute, Bangladesh), both involved actively on that front.

[22] The extent of the system of preserving the public superiority of men is felt in such far-flung terrains as export-oriented foreign-capital computer factories in Ireland when men are regularly directed toward executive promotion and women toward production-line job renewal; and the famous glass ceiling for women who make it in corporate America. Foucault's point about the double conditioning of power — aggregative apparatuses or systems as well as the ability to know or *pouvoir/savoir* (here men and

women's sense of the world through internalized gendering) — teaches us that resistance, too, must inhabit both levels: anti-systemic feminist struggles as well as rural literacy (Michel Foucault, *History of Sexuality*, trans. Robert Hurley [New York: Vintage, 1980], 99). For a discussion of this, see Spivak, "More on Power/Knowledge," in *Outside in the Teaching Machine*. For the Irish example, see James Wickham and Peter Murray, *Women in the Irish Electronics Industry* (Dublin: Employment Equality Agency, n.d.). When these general feminist issues are entertained only systemically, it is not unreasonable to say that the more affluent arenas appropriate the progress.

[23] This is not a denigration of orality. Memory is the possibility of writing in the general sense, calling up an event in its seeming absence. In this sense, the great oral cultures have, paradoxically, developed the *principle* of writing in the psyche to a much greater extent than cultures which separate orality and literacy, make one dependent on the other, and construct phonocentrism on the basis of this polarization. It was for this reason that Derrida rebuked Claude Lévi-Strauss for his patronage, of a type often encountered in the Enlightened travelogue, of the Nambikwara as having been contaminated by the anthropologist's introduction of writing into their innocent orality: "The genealogical relation and social classification are the stitched seam of archèwriting [the principle of writing before the appearance of writing in the colloquial or narrow sense], condition of the (so-called oral) language, and of writing in the narrow sense" (Derrida, *Of Grammatology*, trans. Spivak [Baltimore: Johns Hopkins UP, 1976], 125). Writing in the narrow sense is a suture and supplement of orality, neither its opposite nor "the same thing," just as the computer is a supplement of intelligence, not "artificial" as opposed to "natural." The fact that access to writing in the narrow sense might destroy the special skills of writing-in-orality (though not, of course, the phenomenon itself) is a dilemma whose solution might be to museumize them and honor them *as special cultural skills*. It is certainly not to distance the rural girl-child from writing.

[24] It is only when, through collision with an alien discursive formation, subalternity brings itself into crisis and thus creates insurgency, that we can begin to track it. This is the lesson of the Subaltern Studies collective. I can understand the Sioux ghost dance religion of 1890–91 by this logic (James Mooney, *The Ghost-Dance Religion and the Sioux Outbreak of 1890* [(1896) Lincoln: U of Nebraska P, 1991]).

[25] In order not to be inaccessible to the general reader, I suggest in a footnote that, in the field of responsibility, economy and ecology can at best be each other's *différance*, in the way that I have described in "Supplementing Marxism." This *différance* is a disclosure in erasure of the call of the radically other, one of whose transcendental figurations is what we call Nature.

[26] See my discussion of Bruce Ackerman's interpretation of US constitutionality in the first part of Spivak, "Scattered Speculations on the Question of Culture Studies," in *Outside in the Teaching Machine*. Am I doing more than reminding ourselves that when someone like Frank Chikane rightly remarks about Black Consciousness, as I do here about academic freedom, that it is "a means to . . . the end . . . that we'd move into a non-racial type of society where there would be justice," the justice meant is a

task rather than an event (Raymond Suttner and Jeremy Cronin, *Thirty Years of the Freedom Charter* [Johannesburg: Ravan Press, 1986], 236)?

Lore Metzger and Ralph Freedman

IN MEMORIAM:
Lore Metzger 1925–1997

On January 31, 1997 at 10:45 in the morning, at her home, Lore Metzger left herself and her world, surrounded by her books, her paintings, her music. The last we saw before she went was her beatific smile — the silent version of her vibrant laugh. Her physician, calling to express her sorrow at Lore's death, said that of all the patients she has had to see die, she had never known anyone "who died so much at peace with herself and her destiny."

This is Lore in death as she was in life: belligerent, even scrappy in her struggle for life and justice but serene in her great integrity, giving of herself; impatient with fake authority while accepting the only true authority she recognized: humanity. Her devotion to those needing help, especially women, was exemplary. She was a bearer of friendship.

As a young girl Lore was a refugee. Born in Frankfurt in 1925, she and her family fled from Nazi Germany to Switzerland and eventually to New York. She long since ceased to be one, but unlike many who had once been victims of injustice, the adult woman Lore Metzger devoted her emotional and intellectual energy to others less fortunate than herself— whatever their origin. And she did so while retaining her clear head and superb sense of irony.

Lore was a creative scholar, a much admired teacher. From her doctoral work on Goethe's *Faust* at Columbia in the nineteen-fifties and her decades of consultation in the editing of Coleridge's *Notebooks* as part of the massive project at the Princeton University Press, to her teaching and writing, culminating in her book *One Foot in Eden* on the English romantic pastoral, Lore established herself as an innovative scholar in English and European romanticism. In recent years she widened her sphere to interpretations and reinterpretations of texts in the light of their meaning to women and issues of particular concern to women, focusing, among her many topics, on the novel from Jane Austen to Margaret Atwood.

From a small college like Mount Holyoke to large universities like the University of Washington and Michigan State until settling at Emory in 1968 as the first female full professor, Lore consistently squared her service as an academic citizen with her intense devotion to those she taught. For her students, especially but by no means exclusively women, she was the quintessential role model.

"Lore remained a powerful example," one student said. She was "an inspiration and occasional worker of miracles for women struggling to become feminist scholars." "I know that my life as a graduate student at Emory was enriched and made so much more human, friendly, and enjoyable by Lore's presence, both professionally and personally," wrote another. "And I know that the same was true for my friends. Lore was especially inspiring for women students, and she helped show all of us a great deal about integrity and personal strength and compassion. Her students are scattered far and wide now, but that legacy lives on with each of us." "She has meant so much to me," wrote yet another former student, "and I realized just how deeply she has affected me when I knew that I wouldn't see her again.... Lore is the best teacher I could have had. To me, she is always a tough and smart and gentle woman I so greatly admire." "She touched many lives," wrote one of her young colleagues.

Teaching spilled over into action. Lore fought for the recognition of women, helping found the Emory University Women's Caucus in 1974 and in bringing Women's Studies to Emory a decade later. And she extended this commitment to professional organizations in her field like her recent service to the International Comparative Literature Association. Earlier she had functioned as president of the Emory chapter of the American Association of University Professors and fought for justice for colleagues at the University Senate and Faculty Council. From this activism as a teacher and citizen emerged Lore's new role which she carved out for herself after her retirement in 1992. She joined an Atlanta law firm specializing in anti-discrimination suits. Though ostensibly a part time volunteer, she immersed herself completely in this new occupation as a second career for the remaining four years of her life. This turn embraced other forms of activism as well. For at the same time Lore joined the Atlanta Pro-Choice Action Committee and conscientiously gave over early morning hours to escort patients at abortion clinics and most recently involved herself passionately in fund-raising for the protection of the mentally and physically disabled. She completed an evolution from literature to advocacy which had long been coming.

Lore's courageous death underscored this dual commitment. Towards the end, an extraordinary moment of clarity, of humor — of intellectual presence — defined this remarkable woman.

Already partly unconscious from lack of air the day before she died, she turned to my daughter-in-law who touched her foot regularly to recall her to consciousness. "This reminds me of the Third Voyage in Swift's *Gulliver's Travels*," she said, smiling at us as the inveterate teacher she was, "of those pompous philosophers in Laputa who can't attend to reality without being roused to action by the flappers."

She taught us about reality, about distance, about shaping and sharing a moment.

Lore was an artist of life, of knowledge, of friendship and love. She lives on.

Ralph Freedman

RALPH FREEDMAN:
Professional Life and Publications

Many of us who were mentored by Ralph Freedman think of him first as the perceptive and patient listener who resided in the attic rooms of East Pyne Building in the heart of Princeton's campus. Ralph was always there to encourage and suggest, to guide and nurture. Many of us contributing to this volume would not be in the professional positions we now occupy without Ralph Freedman's generous intellect and indomitable spirit. All of us, students and colleagues, have continued to profit from that personal and academic support during our professional lives. For his extraordinary kindness and relentless support, we are all deeply grateful.

Ralph Freedman began his intellectual career in the west, earning his Bachelor's degree in Philosophy from the University of Washington in 1948. In that same year, he published his first novel, *Divided*, which won the Lewis and Clark Northwest Award. His understanding of the novel from the inside out would later aid him in writing his pathbreaking volume, *The Lyrical Novel* (1963), which would influence so many of us, as well as students and scholars worldwide, in our own attempts to jump the generic boundaries of narrative and lyric. The novel-writing impulse remains with Ralph even today, and he anticipates completing his latest novel, "The Mark of the Tooth," this summer.

From the west coast, Ralph ventured east, to Brown University, to complete a Masters Degree in Philosophy in 1950 and on to Yale to complete his doctoral work in Comparative Literature in 1954.

Even before completing his Ph.D., Freedman became an instructor in Comparative Literature at the University of Iowa (1953–65). This must have been a time of intellectual excitement and ferment at Iowa with figures like René Wellek and Austin Warren producing groundbreaking work in *The Theory of Literature* and sparking an interest in literary theory that would last for several decades. As a young professor, Ralph Freedman would have been at home in this atmosphere. During these years at Iowa, his talents as a creative writer and his profound interest in literary theory culminated in *The Lyrical Novel*. While at Iowa Ralph also served as Associate Editor (1954–60) and Acting Editor (1957–58) of *The Western Review*. He rose to Chair Comparative Literature

(1962–65) before moving on to Princeton University's Comparative Literature Program, where he remained until 1988.

During eight of his 23 years at Princeton, Ralph served as the Director of Graduate Studies. In this capacity he made his many human contributions to the discipline of Comparative Literature by making sure that all of us did finally complete our graduate work and enter into the profession. He also continued to explore his interests in literary theory by serving as Senior Fellow at the School of Criticism and Theory (1975–88); as Resident Senior Fellow and Visiting Professor at the University of California at Irvine (1976–77), and as Visiting Professor at the School of Criticism and Theory at Northwestern University (in the summers of 1981 and 1985). He produced his acclaimed critical biography *Hermann Hesse: Pilgrim of Crisis* in 1979, edited a volume of essays, *Virginia Woolf: Revaluation and Continuity*, in 1980, and in 1987 produced a translation, *The Discovery of Slowness*, of Sten Nadolny's German novel.

In addition, Freedman conducted a National Endowment for the Humanities Summer Seminar on "Biography and Intention in Literature" in 1979 and lectured at the Beijing Foreign Studies University in 1987. After retiring from Princeton in 1988, Ralph went on to hold the position of Visiting Augustus B. Longstreet Professor of English and Comparative Literature and Director of Comparative Literature at Emory University from 1988–90. In Georgia, Ralph worked in a close and creative partnership with Lore Metzger, his colleague and companion, whose work and life we would also like to remember in this volume.

As this record of friendship and mentoring evidences, Ralph Freedman never tires of assisting students and colleagues in the discipline he loves. His critical production also remains unabated as demonstrated by his latest masterful critical biography *Life of a Poet: Rainer Maria Rilke* (1996).

Given this record of accomplishment, it is not surprising that Ralph Freedman has won the major fellowships offered in humanistic studies: a Guggenheim Fellowship (1980–81), a National Endowment for the Humanities Fellowship (1984), a fellowship from the American Council of Learned Societies (1971) and a Yaddo Writer's Fellowship in 1969.

It is hard to imagine a professional career more filled with accomplishments — both intellectual and human. Those of us who are the products of the generosity of Ralph Freedman thank him. We hope that this volume will pay him some small homage.

Kathleen L. Komar

The Publications

Books:

Divided (novel). New York: E. P. Dutton, 1948. Winner of Lewis and Clark Northwest Award.

The Lyrical Novel: Studies in Hermann Hesse, André Gide and Virginia Woolf. Princeton UP, 1963. Published in the UK (Oxford) as well as in Spanish and Korean.

Hermann Hesse: Pilgrim of Crisis: A Biography. New York: Pantheon, 1979. Forthcoming in paperback: Fromm International Publishing Company, 1997. Also published in the UK (Jonathan Cape), as well as in German (Suhrkamp) and Italian (Rizzoli). Currently a Suhrkamp Taschenbuch.

Virginia Woolf: Revaluation and Continuity. Ed. Essays by Several Hands. Berkeley: U of California P, 1980.

The Discovery of Slowness. New York: Viking/Penguin, 1987. Translation of Sten Nadolny, *Die Entdeckung der Langsamkeit.*

Life of a Poet: Rainer Maria Rilke. New York: Farrar, Straus and Giroux, 1996. Forthcoming in German (Insel Verlag) and French (Actes-Sud), 1997.

"Mark of the Tooth" (novel). In progress.

Articles:

"André Gide's *Les Nourritures terrestres*: A Novel of Lyrical Perspective," *Western Review* 18 (Summer 1954): 271–88.

"Imagination and Form: *La Porte étroite* and *La Symphonie pastorale*," *Accent* (Fall, 1957): 217–28.

"Poet and Mask: The Drama of *Les Fleurs du Mal*," *Texas Quarterly* 1 (February 1958): Supplement, 52–59.

"Romantic Imagination: Hermann Hesse as a Modern Novelist," *PMLA* 73 (June, 1958): 275–84.

"The New Realism: the Fancy of William Golding," *Perspective* (Fall-Winter, 1958). Reprinted in *William Golding's 'Lord of the Flies': A Source Book.* (New York: Odyssey Press, 1963), 43–53.

"Saul Bellow: The Illusion of Environment," *Wisconsin Studies in Contemporary Literature* 1 (Winter 1960): 50–65. Reprinted in *Saul Bellow and the Critics.* (New York: Gotham Library and New York UP, 1967), 51–68. Also reprinted in German translation in *Amerikanische Literatur des 20. Jahrhunderts.* Frankfurt: Fischer Taschenbuch, 1972.

"Kafka's Obscurity: The Illusion of Logic in Narrative," *Modern Fiction Studies* 8 (Spring, 1962): 61–74.

"Gods, Heroes, and Rilke," *Hereditas: Seven Essays on the Modern Experience of the Classical.* (Ed. Frederic Will; Austin: U of Texas P, 1964), 5–30.

"Modern Poetics: 1750–1900," *Encyclopedia of Poetry and Poetics* (Princeton: Princeton UP, 1965, 1974), 503–14.

"Wallace Stevens and Rainer Maria Rilke: Two Versions of a Poetic," *The Poet as Critic* (Ed. F. P. W. McDowell; Evanston: Northwestern UP, 1967), 60–80.

"Symbol as Terminus: Some Notes on Symbolist Narrative," *Comparative Literature Studies*, 4 (1967): 135–43.

"The Possibility of a Theory of the Novel," *The Disciplines of Criticism* (*Festschrift* in Honor of René Wellek; ed. Peter Demetz, Thomas Greene and Lowry Nelson; New Haven: Yale UP, 1968), 57–77.

"Refractory Visions: The Contours of Literary Expressionism," *Contemporary Literature* 10 (Winter 1969): 54–74.

"The Poet's Dilemma: The Narrative Worlds of Günter Grass," *Dimension. Contemporary German Arts and Letters* (Ed. A. Leslie Wilson, Günter Grass Symposium. Special Issue; Austin: U of Texas P, 1970), 46–59.

"Eyesight and Vision: Forms of the Imagination in Coleridge and Novalis," *The Rarer Action. Essays in Honor of Francis Fergusson* (Ed. Alan Cheuse and Richard Koffler; New Brunswick: Rutgers UP, 1970), 202–17.

"Paul Valéry: Protean Critic," *Modern French Criticism* (Ed. John Simon; Chicago: U of Chicago P, 1972), 1–40.

"Person and Persona: The Magic Mirrors of *Steppenwolf*," *Hesse: Twentieth Century Views* (Ed. Theodore Ziolkowski; New York: Prentice Hall, 1972), 153–79. Abbreviated German version in *Hermann Hesses 'Steppenwolf'* (Ed. Egon Schwarz; Königstein: Athenäum, 1980), 131–34.

"Intentionality and the Literary Object," *Contemporary Literature*, 17 (Summer, 1976): 439–52. Part of Symposium, *Directions for Criticism: Structuralism and its Alternatives.* (Ed. Murray Krieger and L. S. Dembo; Madison: U of Wisconsin P, 1977), 137–59.

"Hermann Hesse im Wandel der Krisen," *Hermann Hesse Heute* (Ed. Adrian Hsia; Bonn: Bouvier Verlag, 1980), 25–60. Lecture at the International Symposium in Honor of the Centenary of Hesse's birthday, Deutsches Literaturarchiv, Marbach, 1977.

"Rainer Maria Rilke and the 'Sister Arts,'" *Literary Theory and Criticism* (Festschrift in Honor of the 80th Birthday of René Wellek; Bern: Peter Lang, 1984), 821–47.

"Krisis und schöpferische Gestaltung: Zwei entscheidende Begegnungen Rilkes," *Rilke-Rezeptionen/Rilke Reconsidered*, (Ed. Sigrid Bauschinger and Susan Cocalis. Translation by Ursula Michels-Wenz; Tübingen/Basel: A. Francke Verlag, 1995) 49–62.

"Abschied von allen Halbheiten: Hermann Hesses schwerer Weg," Internationales Hermann-Hesse-Kolloquium, Calw, 1997. [To be published, Winter, 1997.]

Selected Reviews:

"Novel of Contention: *The Quiet American.*" Review of *The Quiet American* by Graham Greene. *Western Review* 21 (Autumn, 1956): 76–81.

"*'New Criticism' und die Entwicklung bürgerlicher Literaturwissenschaft* by Robert Weimann," Review-Article, *Philological Quarterly* 44 (July, 1965): 411–17.

"Hermann Hesse." Review of Mark Boulby, *Hermann Hesse: His Mind and Art. Contemporary Literature* 10 (Summer, 1969): 421–26.

"*The Glass Bead Game.*" Review of Hesse's *Glass Bead Game*, translated by Richard and Clara Winston. *New York Times Book Review* (January 4, 1970): 4, 20.

Index

Abrahams, Cecil, 185
ab-use of the Enlightenment, 4, 219–220, 223, 226, 228–229
academic freedom, 4, 223–231, 233
Achberger, Karen, 184
Ackerman, Bruce, 234
Adnan, Shapan, 233
Adorno, Theodor W., 3, 156
Aeschylos, 68, 70–71; works by: *Agamemnon*, 68–71; *Oresteia*, 69, 71
Agassiz, Jean Louis Rodolphe, 117
Ait-Sahalia, Nadia, 233
Albrecht, Monika, 183
Alexiou, Margaret, 79
Ali, Syed Mujtaba, 232
allegory/allegorical, 2, 70, 72, 94–98, 104, 106–108, 125, 146, 216; and the allegorical quest, 3, 132, 136, 142, 143
Allemann, Beda, 30, 32
Althusser, Louis, 187
Amin, Samir, 220, 232
Amnesty International, 188
Andreas-Salomé, Lou, 25, 53, 56, 62
Anouilh, Jean, 77
anti-semitism, 72, 123, 126
Armacost, Nicola, 232
Arnold, Matthew, 155
art, 2–3, 31, 51, 58, 69, 92, 94, 97, 106, 108–109, 149–150, 168, 170, 173, 202, 213, 217, 225, 245; and highbrow audience/culture, 149, 151–153, 161, 163; and lowbrow audience, 161, 163; and middlebrow (bourgeois) audience/culture, 149–153, 160–161; and public reception, 155–157, 160, 166
Ashbery, John, 90, works by: "Clepsydra," 90
Attridge, Derek, 233
Atwood, Margaret, 4, 186–217, 237, works by: *Bodily Harm*, 186, 205, 210, 217; *Conversations*, 217; *Dancing Girls*, 186; *Good Bones and Simple Murders*, 188, 192, 201–202; *The Handmaid's Tale*, 4, 188–189, 194–195, 201, 204–205; *Interlunar*, 217; *The Journals of Susanna Moodie*, 188–89; "The Loneliness of the Military Historian," 4, 186–190, 192, 201; "Marrying the Hangman," 186; *Morning in the Burned House*, 201; *Murder in the Dark: Short Fiction and Prose Poems*, 212; *Power Politics*, 188; *Procedures for Underground*, 188; *The Robber Bride*, 4, 187–188, 201, 204–205, 208, 210, 212, 214–215, 217; *Second Words: Selected Critical Prose*, 201;

Selected Poems II: Poems Selected and New 1976–1986, 189–191, 195, 199, 201, 217;
Surfacing, 191, 202, 210;
Survival: A Thematic Guide to Canadian Literature, 189, 191, 201;
True Stories, 188;
"Two Headed-Poems," 186
Augier, Emile, 3, 119–121, 127, 130; works by:
Le Mariage d'Olympe (Olympia's Marriage), 119–120
avant-garde, 116, 149, 152, 166, 168–170

Bachmann, Ingeborg, 3, 172–174, 177–180, 182–184; works by:
Der Fall Franza, 174;
Malina, 172–176, 179, 183–184
Bail, Gabriele, 184
Bakhtin, Mikhail, 192
Banuri, Tariq, 233
Barnes, Djuna, 172; works by:
Nightwood, 172
Barrymore, John, 165
Barthes, Roland, 168, 197, 203
Bartsch, Kurt, 184
Bate, W. Jackson, 110
Baudelaire, Charles, 2–3, 84, 87, 89, 102–104, 106, 110, 121–126, 128, 131; works by:
"Une Charogne" ("Carrion"), 124;
"La Chevelure" ("The Mane"), 124;
"Correspondances," 102–103, 105;
"Le Cygne" ("The Swan"), 124;
Les fleurs du mal (Flowers of Evil), 123, 131;

"L' Héautontimorouménos" ("The Self-Tormentor"), 87;
"Les Sept Vieillards" ("The Seven Oldsters"), 125;
"Les Sept Vieillards" ("The Seven Old Men"), 89;
"Spleen," 84;
Oeuvres complètes, 110, 131;
"Tristesses de la Lune" ("Sorrows of the Moon"), 104–105;
Tableaux parisiens (Parisian Scenes), 124
Beer, Gillian, 133, 145
Beguin, Albert, 110
Benjamin, Marina, 130
Benjamin, Walter, 149
Bennington, Geoffrey, 232
Benveniste, Emile, 54
Berman, Marshall, 170
bestsellers, 150, 155, 171; and cultural authority, 150
Betz, Maurice, 54, 62
biological determinism, 3, 115–117, 120, 122, 127; and women, 118
Björk, Lennart A., 145–146
Blair, Dorothy S., 233
Blake, Willliam 3, 88, 95; works by:
Jerusalem, 88
Boardman, John, 79
Borgerhoff, Joseph L., 130
Boumelha, Penny, 134, 145–147
Bourdieu, Pierre, 150–154, 157, 168, 170
Boussuges, Madeleine, 80
Bowlby, Rachel, 232
Bradbury, Malcolm, 167–168
Bratchell, D. F., 145
Brecht, Bertolt, 77, 159, 208
Brooks, Peter, 131

Browning, Robert, 150
Brownley, Martine Watson, 4, 186
Buchanan, Patrick, 149
Buddha, 52, 62, 177
Burger, Peter, 170
Butterfield, Herbert, 195–198, 202

Calvin, John, 117
Candide, 95
Castellani, Jean-Pierre, 80
Castro, Jan Garden, 202, 217
Cerf, Walter, 111
Cézanne, Paul, 2, 82–83, 85–87; works by:
  Boy in a Red Vest, 87
Chaillot, Nicole, 80
Chang, Grace, 202
Chikane, Frank, 234
Chodorow, Nancy, 183
Christianity/Christian, 86, 94, 122, 128, 130, 133, 135–137, 139–144, 147, 155, 223; and Victorian patriarchal morality, 134, 141, 143
Churchill, Winston, 188
city, 3, 55, 58–59, 65–66, 73–74, 89–90, 97, 117–120, 122–126, 128
Cixous, Hélène, 233
Clausen, Jeanette, 184
Cohn, Carol, 189, 202
Coleridge, Samuel Taylor, 3, 95–96, 100–101, 103, 110, 131, 211, 237, 244; works by:
  Biographia Literaria, 96, 101, 110; and Fancy, 3, 95, 100, 110; and Imagination, 95–97, 100–103, 110
Conolly, Arthur, 220
Coulson, Jessie, 62
creativity, 9–10, 17–18

crisis, 1, 55, 64, 77, 132–133, 138–139, 218, 230, 234, 242–243; and bourgeois family, 132; and religious authority, 133, 139
Critique, 153
Cronin, Jeremy, 235
Culler, Jonathan D., 170
culture, 2–3, 52, 65, 67, 69–72, 74–75, 81, 116–117, 122, 125–126, 130–131, 136, 145, 149–150, 164–166, 168–171, 177, 184, 195, 201, 204, 223, 225–226, 228, 230, 234; and highbrow culture, 149–154, 165–166, 169; and lowbrow culture, 153, 166; and middlebrow culture, 150–154, 166, 168–169
Cunningham, Gail, 134, 137–138, 147

dance, 9, 13–14, 17–21, 40, 44, 234
Darwin, Charles, 3, 122, 132–134, 136–138, 141, 143, 145–148; works by:
  The Descent of Man and Selection in Relation to Sex, 148
Davidson, Arnold E., 202–203
Davison, Carol Margaret, 181, 185
De Courtivron, Isabelle, 233
degeneracy 3, 115–120, 122, 125–131, 133, 135, 137, 140, 142, 146–147
Deleuze, Gilles, 218
DeLillo, Don, 204, 206, 217
De Man, Paul, 167–168
Denning, Michael, 151
Derrida, Jacques, 181, 232–234
Descartes, René, 180
determinism, 122, 128, 141, 147 (*see also* biological determinism)

Development, 4, 219, 223, 226, 229–230, 232–233; women's development, 183, 209
De Vogue, Melchior, 52–53; works by:
  Le roman russe, 53
dialogism, 119, 192–194, 199
Dickens, Charles, 3, 121–123, 125–127, 130, 155; works by:
  Bleak House, 3, 121–122, 125–126, 128, 130
Dickinson, Emily, 2, 88–89; works by:
  "As if I asked a common alms," 89;
  "Before I got my eye put out," 88
Di Leonardo, Micaela, 189, 202
Djebar, Assia, 218, 225, 232–233
Dole, George F., 110
Dostoyevsky, Fyodor, 2, 51–59, 61–62, 153; works by:
  The Diary of the Writer, 57;
  The Double, 55, 62;
  The Idiot, 58;
  Notes from the House of the Dead, 57;
  Notes from the Underground, 57;
  The Poor Folk, 52, 57;
  The Possessed, 58, 62;
  Winter Notes on Summer Impressions, 57
DuBois, Page, 65, 67, 78–79
Dumas (fils), Alexandre, 3, 119–121, 130; works by:
  La dame aux camélias (Camille), 119, 121, 130
Du Maurier, George, 3, 150, 154–157, 159, 162–163, 166, 168–171; and *Trilby*, 3, 150, 152, 154–159, 161–162, 165–167, 171; and Trilby-mania, 150, 154–159, 162, 164–166, 168–169

duty, 64–65, 141, 227; and family piety vs civic order 66 (*see also* Sophocles' *Antigone*)

Ebbatson, Roger, 145
Edmonds, Rosemary, 62
Elshtain, Jean Bethke, 202
Elwood, William R., 77
Embirikos, André, 72
emblem, 97–99 (*see also* symbol)
Engell, James, 110
Enloe, Cynthia, 189–190, 201–202
Euben, Peter, 78
evolution, 117–119, 122–123, 128, 133, 135, 145
Eyer, Diana, 190, 202

Fagles, Robert, 2, 24, 32–33
fairy tale, 176, 205, 207–209, 214, 217
family, 3, 9, 65–67, 79, 117–119, 121, 123, 132–142, 144, 146–147, 204, 212; and degeneration of family values, 133, 135, 137; and displacement of the father, 133, 136 and family theory, 132
fallen woman/prostitute, 118–120, 123, 127–128, 218
Fancy, 3, 95–98, 100, 110, 243 (*see also* Coleridge and Fancy)
Fanon, Frantz, 218
fascism, 2, 67, 72, 74, 116
father, 3, 65–66, 73–74, 78, 82, 126–127, 132–134, 136–144, 146, 175, 179, 188; and divine father, 133; (*see also* name-of-the-father)
Felman, Shosana, 181, 183
feminist, 4, 65, 67, 70, 78, 133, 137, 146, 184, 189–192, 202, 204–205, 215, 217, 223, 234, 238

femininity 10, 13, 22; and contagious degeneracy, 116, 118–119; and female heredity, 119, 121; and female sexuality, 116, 127, 134
Ferguson, Kathy, 193, 202
Fish, Stanley, 149
Fitzgerald, Robert, 24
Forcey, Linda Rennie, 202
Ford, George, 130
Foucault, Michel, 1, 4, 135, 146, 181, 212, 217–223, 225, 231–234; works by:
Discipline and Punish, 4, 218, 220;
History of Sexuality, 217, 234, 232;
The Order of Things, 146
Fraigneau, André, 72, 80
Freedberg, Sidney, 88, 92
Freedman Jonathan, 3, 149
Freedman Ralph, 1–5, 10, 13, 15, 22, 24, 32, 51, 132–133, 142–143, 145, 172–174, 178, 180, 182–183, 185, 239, 241–245; works by:
Divided, 1, 241;
Herman Hesse: Pilgrim of Crisis, 1, 242;
Life of a Poet: Rainer Maria Rilke, 1, 3–4, 22, 51, 242;
The Lyrical Novel, 145, 172, 178, 183, 241;
"The Mark of the Tooth," 1, 241;
Virginia Woolf: Revaluation and Continuity, 242
Freire, Paolo, 233
Freud, Sigmund, 130, 136; and the father's name, 136 (*see also* name-of-the-father); and
Oedipal complex, 136
Friedrichsmeyer, Sara, 184

Gajic, Goran, 77

Gandhi, Mohandas Karamchand, 220
Garson, Marjorie, 140, 147
gender, 1–4, 9–10, 17, 20, 65–67, 71, 128, 130, 138, 176, 182–183, 189–191, 193, 208–210, 212, 215, 222, 227–229, 234; and feminist allegory, 70–72
Gide, André, 51, 62, 145, 183, 243
Gilbert, Sandra, 183
Gildersleeve, Basil L., 110
Gilligan, Carol, 183
Gilman, Sander, 116, 130
Glenn, Evelyn Nakano, 202
Godunov, Boris, 56
Goertz, Hartmann, 62
Goethe, Johann Wolfgang, 237; works by
Faust, 237
Goldhammer, Arthur, 80, 130
Goldhill, Simon, 78
Goodmorning America, 153
Goody, Jack, 201
Gose, Elliot Jr., 145, 147
Göttsche, Dirk, 183
Gould, Stephen Jay, 115–116, 122, 130
government, 97, 118, 149, 166, 219, 222–223, 229, 231
grace, 2, 15, 20, 25, 38, 80, 83, 93, 127, 137
Graff, Gerald, 170
Greenslade, William, 117, 130
Grimm, Jacob and Wilhelm, 205, 208, 210, 217
Gubar, Susan, 183

Hadda, Janet, 183
Harding, M. Esther, 185

Hardy, Thomas, 3, 132–135, 137–140, 142–143, 145–147; works by:
Jude the Obsure, 132–135;
Tess of the d' Urbervilles, 3, 132–136, 145
Harper's, 157, 201
Harper's Magazine, 171
Harper's Monthly, 154, 156
Harris, Adrienne, 202
Harris, Neil, 170
Hasenclever, Walter, 77
Hawthorne, Nathaniel, 99; works by:
The Scarlet Letter, 98;
Head, Bessie, 3, 172–173, 177–185;
A Question of Power, 172–173, 177–180, 183
Heath, Stephen, 203
Hegel, G. W. F., 101
Hemmings, F. W. J., 62
Henkin, Leo J., 145
heredity, 115, 118–122, 126, 130; and hereditary determinism, 128
Hesse, Hermann, 1, 145, 172, 183, 242–245
Heywood, Christopher, 184
Higonnet, Margaret, 134, 146–147, 217
Himmelfarb, Gertrude, 146
history, 3–4, 55, 98, 115–116, 135–137, 186–190, 193–195, 198–199, 205–207, 211, 213–214, 217, 219–220, 222, 228–229, 231, 234
Hitler, Adoph, 67, 72, 115
Ho Chi Minh, 218
Hoffmann, Nina, 53
Hölderlin, Friedriech, 89; works by:
"Die Hälfte des Lebens" ("Half of Life"), 89
Holst-Warhaft, Gail, 78–79

Homer, 2, 24–25, 28–32; works by:
Odyssey, 1–2, 24, 32, 33–50;
Hopkirk, Peter, 220–221, 232
Horkheimer, Max, 3, 156
Horwitz, Howard, 203
Hough, Robert L., 110
Howard, Joan, 64, 77
Humphreys, S. C., 79
Huntington, Samuel P., 233
Hurley, Robert, 217, 234
Huxley, Thomas Henry, 117
Huyssen, Andreas, 170

Ibsen, Henrik, 52, 131–134, 136–137; works by:
A Doll House, 133, 140;
Ghosts, 131, 133;
Hedda Gabler, 134
imagery, 29, 67, 72–73, 75, 119–120, 123, 125, 132, 163, 174, 178–179, 188; of fire, 69; of sun, 67–68, 72, 75; of shadows, 68, 73; of water, 68, 73
Imagination, 3, 9, 52, 78, 91, 93, 95–98, 100–103, 105–106, 108–110, 115, 122–124, 126, 141, 145, 173–74, 181, 183, 192, 202, 226, 243–244
Ingersoll, Earl G., 188, 201, 217
irony, 123, 193, 237

Jacobsen, Jens Peter, 52, 147; works by:
Mogens, 147;
Niels Lyhne, 147
Jahn, Karen, 121–122, 130
Jaloux, Edmond, 53

James, Henry, 154–156, 170; works by:
: *The Ambassadors*, 171;
: *The Bostonians*, 170;
: *Daisy Miller*, 156;
: *Portrait of a Lady*, 156
Jameson, Fredric, 187–188, 201
Jean-Aubry, G., 110
Jebb, Richard, 78
Jelinek, Elfriede, 184
Jesus, 52, 62
Joan of Arc, 189
Johns, Jasper, 90; works by:
: *Land's End*, 90 ;
: *Out the Window*, 90;
: *Periscope*, 90;
: *Watchman*, 90
Johnson, Joyce, 184
Johnston, Judith L., 77
Jones, Ernest, 146
justice, 65–66, 73, 75, 76, 144, 234, 237–238; poetic justice, 30

Kakutani, Michiko, 168
Kant, Immanuel, 96, 101, 103, 109, 111, 117
Katz, Dori, 77
Katz, Marylin, 65, 78–79
Keats, John, 20, 23, 30, 89; works by:
: "Ode on a Grecian Urn," 20;
: "To Autumn," 89
Kessler-Harris, Alice, 77–78
Kierkegaard, Søren Aabye, 139
King, Katherine Callen, 2, 64
King, Martin Luther Jr., 76
King, Ynestra, 202

Kipling, Rudyard, 1, 220–221, 232; works by:
: *Kim*, 1, 220–221, 232
Klappert, Peter, 186, 201
Klein, Melanie, 222, 232
Knoop, Wera Ouckama, 2, 9, 13–21
Knox, Bernard, 32, 65, 78
Kolodny, Annette, 196, 203
Komar, Kathleen L., 3–5, 10, 22, 172, 242
Koschel, Christine, 183
Kovach, Thomas, 2, 24
Kramer, Hilton, 170
Kraut, Alan M., 130
Kristeva, Julia, 232
Kurtz, Donna C., 79

Lacan, Jacques, 3, 133, 136–137, 139, 142, 146–147, 184; works by:
: *The Four Fundamental Concepts of Psychoanalysis*, 147;
: *Ecrits*, 146
LaCapra, Dominick, 192–194, 202
Laqueur, Thomas, 116, 130
Lattimore, Richmond, 24
Le Dantec, Y. G., 110
Le Figaro, 153–154
Lederer, Mary, 185
Lefevre, Frederic, 62
Lehman, David, 167–169
Leishman, J. B., 63
Le Monde, 153
Lennox, Sara, 184
Lenson, David, 2–3, 94
Leonardo, 2, 81–83, 85–88, 92–93; works by:
: *St Anne Cartoon*, 81, 83, 93
Le Point, 153

Les Temps Modernes, 153
Leuwers, Daniel, 80
Levine, George, 133
Levine, Lawrence, 150, 161–162, 164, 170–171
Lévi-Strauss, Claude, 234
L'Express, 153
Lind, Jenny, 150
literacy, 1, 4, 220, 223–224, 226–230, 233–234; rural literacy, 227–230
Lombroso, Cesare, 130, 145
Loraux, Nicole, 79
love, 2, 12, 41–43, 49, 65–67, 74–76, 78, 80–81, 88–89, 92–93, 100, 119, 122, 135, 141, 143, 160, 176, 192, 201, 209, 211–212, 215, 232, 239; lovers, 15, 20, 42–43, 57, 65, 68, 119, 126–128, 201, 210, 215
Lydon, Mary, 78
lyrical novel, 1–3, 132, 143, 172–174, 178, 180–183, 185, 241, 243

MacAndrew, Andrew R., 62
MacDonald, Dwight, 151, 170
Macdonald, John D., 153
madness, 3, 126, 130, 145, 159–160, 162, 172–173, 180–183. 185; (*see also* women and madness)
Maisel, David, 130
Malak, Amin, 202
Mallarmé, Stéphane, 3, 106, 107–110; works by:
    "L'Après-midi d'un Faune," 108;
    Hérodiade, 108;
    Oeuvres complètes, 110
mania, 3, 149–150, 154–159, 162, 164–168, 171
Mapplethorpe, Robert, 149, 166, 167
Marks, Elaine, 233

Marquard, Jean, 184
Marshall, Brenda, 121–122, 130
Marx, Karl, 219–220, 231, 234
masculinity, 134, 179, 189–190
Matthiesen, F. O., 170
Maudsley, Henry, 133, 145
Mazhar, Farhad, 224, 233
McBrien, William, 78
McCombs, Judith, 199, 201
Medovoi, Leerom, 233
Melville, Herman, 99; works by:
    Moby Dick, 98
memory, 64, 81–82, 84–86, 96, 110, 142–143, 159, 165, 175, 183, 197, 199, 206–207, 214, 228, 232, 234
Metzger, Lore, 4–5, 204, 237–239, 242
Miller, Jacques-Alain, 147
Miller, Jean Baker, 183
Millgate, Michael, 135, 146
Milton, John, 85, 93; works by:
    Paradise Lost 85
Mitchell, Stephen, 13–14, 22
Mitterand, Henri, 131
Modersohn-Becker, Paula, 17
Mondor, Henri, 110
Monod, Sylvère, 130
Mooney, James, 234
Morgan, Rosemarie, 134, 141,147
Morton, Peter, R., 145–147
Moscussi, Ornella, 117, 130
Mozart, Wolfgang Amadeus, 153
Mueller, John, 171
Münster, Clemens, 183
Murdock, Kenneth, 170
Murnaghan, Sheila, 65, 78
Murray, Peter, 234

music, 2, 9, 13–14, 24–28, 30–32, 94, 152, 154–155, 157–158, 160, 163, 203, 237; and silence, 2, 30–31; and Rilke, 24–32
Mussolini, Benito, 67, 72

Nadolny, Sten, 242–243
Najibullah, 4, 218–221, 223–225, 229–231
naming, 135, 137, 142, 146; and the-name-of-the-father, 3, 133, 136–137, 139, 142, 146
Naturalism, 132
nature, 10–11, 15, 21–22, 65, 69, 86, 89, 99–104, 116, 121, 124, 139–140, 143, 147, 176, 178, 230, 234; and culture, 65
Nerval, Gérard de, 3, 99–100, 102–103, 110; works by:
  "Vers Dorés" ("Golden Verses"), 99
Newsweek, 153–154, 168
New Testament, 94
New Woman, 137, 143, 147
New World (Economic) Order, 220–221, 229–230
New York Review of Books, 153
The New York Times, 153, 169, 231 (*see also Sunday New York Times*)
The New York Times Book Review, 153, 167, 171
Nice, Richard, 170
Nordau, Max, 130
Nouvelles Littéraires, 53
Nouvel Observateur, 153
Novalis, (Friedrich von Hardenberg), 62, 172–174, 177–180, 244; works by:
  Heinrich von Ofterdingen, 174–177, 179–180

Ogungbesan, Kolawole, 178, 184
Ojo-Ade, Femi, 185
Olender, Maurice, 116, 130
Olivet, Fabre d', 30
O'Toole, Tess, 146–147
Otrepyev, Grisha, 55–56

Palmer, Carole L., 199, 201
Palmer, George Herbert, 24
Partisan Review, 153
patriarchy/patriarchal, 3, 66–67, 71, 79, 119, 132–138, 140–144, 180, 182, 184, 223, 227–229
Patrilogia, 94
Payne, E. F. J., 110
Pearce, Brian, 232
perspective, 2, 82–83, 197; gendered perspective (male or female), 1, 65, 138, 146, 202; historical perspective, 193, 198
Philosophies, 54
Pichois, Claude, 110, 131
Pick, Daniel, 116–117, 130
Pieterse, Jan Nederveen, 232
Pilgrim's Progress, 97
Pindar, 107, 110; works by:
  The Olympian and Pythian Odes, 107–108, 110
Plutarch, 189
Poe, Edgar Allan, 3, 95, 110; and Imagination, 3 (*see also* Imagination)
Politzer, Heinz, 30, 32
Pritchard, Allan, 122, 130
Proctor, Robert, 116, 130
Purcell, Edwin L., 156, 171
Pythagoras, 99–100

Radway, Janice, 151, 170

Ragussis, Michael, 135–137, 142, 146–147
Ramos, Myra Bergman, 233
Rand, Nicholas, 232
Ravenscroft, Arthur, 179, 184
Ray, Satyajit, 232
Reichenbächer, Helmut, 217
Rhodes, Cecil, 219, 223
Richards, I. A., 96–97, 110
Richer, Jean, 110
Rieu, E. V., 24
Rilke, Rainer Maria, 1–2, 9–24, 26–32, 51–63, 132, 172, 174, 176, 242–244; works by:
"An die Musik" ("To Music"), 30;
Die Aufzeichnungen des Malte Laurids Brigge (The Notebooks of Malte Laurids Brigge) 2, 25, 51–53, 61–62, 132,174;
The Book of Hours 15;
Briefwechsel, 32, 62;
Das Buch der Bilder (The Book of Images), 25;
"Der Duft" ("The Scent"), 30;
Duino Elegies, 12, 61, 63;
Der neuen Gedichte anderer Teil (New Poems: The Other Part) 24;
"Die Insel der Sirenen" ("The Isle of the Sirens") 2, 24, 27;
Neue Gedichte, 27, 30;
"Musik" ("Music"), 31;
"Orpheus. Eurydice. Hermes," 10–12, 17;
"Requiem for a Friend," 17;
Sämtliche Werke, 22–23;
Sonnette an Orpheus (Sonnets to Orpheus) 2, 9–17, 19–22, 31
Rimbaud, Arthur, 2, 82; works by:
"Mémoire" (Memory"), 82

Riviere, Joan, 193, 202
Rodin, Auguste, 28
Romanticism, 97, 173, 237
Rommel, Erwin, 188
Rorty, Richard, 233
Rouse, W. H. D., 24
Rubin, Joan Shelley, 151, 170
Ruddick, Sara, 190
Rushdie, Salman, 149, 221; works by: *Satanic Verses*, 149
Russett, Cynthia Eagle, 133, 145
Rutland, William, 133, 145
Ryan, Judith, 29, 32

Said, Edward, 206; works by: *Orientalism*, 206
Sartre, Jean Paul, 69; works by: *Les mouches*, 69
Savigneau, Josyane, 77, 80
Schmid-Bortenschlager, Sigrid, 184
Schnack, Ingeborg, 23, 62
Schopenhauer, Arthur, 106, 109–110
Schor, Naomi, 131
Schottelius, Saskia, 184
Schweik, Susan, 201
Segal, Charles, 12–13, 22, 65, 74, 78
Segal, Lynne, 202
sexuality, 10, 15–16,, 116–117, 124, 127, 130, 137, 141, 147, 217, 234
shadow and light, 68, 70, 73, 83, 85, 87–89, 93
Shaw, George Bernard, 131; works by: *Man and Superman*, 131
Shaw, Michael, 170
Sheridan, Alan, 146–147, 232
Shideler, Ross, 3, 5, 132
Showalter, Elaine, 116, 130, 133, 145
Shuja, Mirza, 221

silence, 2, 9, 13, 24, 29–31, 82, 109, 214, 217
Sizzo-Norris-Crouy, Countess Margot, 22
Skinner, Marylin, 32
Sophocles, 2, 64–68, 73–75, 78; works by:
  Antigone, 2, 64, 67, 73, 78;
  Oedipus Tyrannos, 68
Sousa, John Phillip, 161
Spencer, Herbert, 133
Spender, Stephen, 63
Spivak, Gayatri Chakravorty, 4, 218, 232–234
Stanton, Domna C., 232
Stavrianos, L. S., 232
Sternhell, Zeev, 116, 130
Stillman, Deanne, 77
Stillman, Linda K., 78
Stravinsky, Igor F., 149; works by:
  Rite of Spring, 149
Stock, Frederick, 161
Strindberg, August, 131, 133–134, 137, 140, 147; works by:
  Creditors, 140;
  The Father, 134;
  Getting Married, 140;
  Miss Julie, 131, 134, 140;
  The Son of a Servant, 147
Summerfield, Ellen, 183
The Sunday New York Times, 219
Suttner, Raymond, 235
Swedenborg, Emmanuel, 95, 101, 103–104, 110; works by:
  Heaven and Hell, 103, 110
Swift, Jonathan, 204, 238; works by:
  Gulliver's Travels, 95
Sword, Helen, 1–2, 9

Symbolism, 97, 244
symbols/symbolism, 1, 9–10, 13, 16, 19–20, 94, 97, 100–106, 108–109, 143, 175, 177, 179, 181, 244; and emblems, 97–100, 105

Tagore, Rabindranath, 232
Tavis, Anna, 2, 51
Tel Quel, 153
The Bookman, 155
Thomas, Theodore, 161
Time, 153–154
Times, 167–168, 221
Times Literary Supplement, 201
Tobias, Sheila, 202
Tolstoy, Leo, 2, 51–53, 57–62; works by:
  Anna Karenina, 59;
  "The Death of Ivan Illyich," 59;
  The Live Corpse, 59;
  Sevastopol Stories, 59;
  War and Peace, 59, 62
transference, 194, 196, 199
transformation, 1, 3–4, 9, 11–14, 18–21, 28–29, 101, 104, 106, 143–144, 156, 190, 221
Trilling, Lionel, 170
truth, 49, 68, 86, 90–92, 101, 128, 143, 147, 168, 178, 181–182, 193, 199, 205–206

United Nations, 219–220, 232
USA Today, 154

Valéry, Paul, 20; works by:
  "L'ame et la danse," 20
Van den Bruck, Moller, 52, 62
VanSpackeren, Kathryn, 202, 217

violence, 66, 74, 77, 79, 86, 121, 152, 190, 204–207, 209, 213, 215, 217, 221, 225, 227, 232
Virgin Mary, 95
Vlasopolos, Anca, 3, 115, 205, 217
Voltaire, François Marie Arouet de, (*see Candide*)
Volynski, A. L., 62
Von Ranke, Leopold, 195, 197, 202
Von Thurn und Taxis-Hohenlohe, Princess Marie, 30
Von Weidenbaum, Inge, 183

Waldinger, Ellen, 2, 81
Waldoff, Leon, 147
Warner, Charles Dudley, 157, 171
Warren, Austin, 241
Wassermann, Jacob, 52
Weigel, Sigrid, 183
Wellek, René, 241
Wellwarth, George, 167–168
Welnik, Josef, 62
White, Hayden, 193, 202
Wickham, James, 234
Wilde, Oscar, 150, 155, 165
Williams, William Carlos, 86, 91, 92; works by:
  "Between Walls," 91;
  "To Elsie," 92;
  Paterson, 86
Wilson, Sharon, 217
Wines, Roger, 202
Wolfe, Tom, 153
women, and consciousness, 172–174; and madness, 3, 172–173, 180–183; and (lyrical) self, 3, 173–175, 179–180, 182; and violence, 206–207, 210, 214; and war, 4, 190–191, 207

women writers, 3, 70, 172–173, 180–181, 183, 185
Woodcock, George, 186, 201
Woolf, Virginia, 132, 145, 151, 170, 172, 183, 226, 242–243
Wordsworth, William, 85, 89, 209, 217; works by:
  The Prelude, 89;
  "Tintern Abbey," 85;
  "Ode: Intimations of Immortality," 217

Yeats, William Butler, 28, 131
Yourcenar, Marguerite, 2, 64–75, 77–80; works by:
  "Antigone ou le choix" ("Antigone or the choice"), 2, 65, 67–68, 72–73, 75, 77, 80;
  "Apollo tragique," 2, 68, 70–73;
  Coup de grace, 80;
  En Pèlerin et en étranger (*As a Pilgrim and as a Stranger*), 79;
  Entretiens avec Matthieu Galey (*With Open Eyes: Conversations with Matthieu Galey*), 79–80;
  Essais et mémoires, 77, 79;
  Feux (*Fires*) 64–64, 68, 72, 77, 79–80;
  Mémoires d'Hadrien, 80;
  Les songes et les sorts (Dreams and Destinies), 72, 80;
  Le Voyage en Grèce, 79

Zedner, Lucia, 118, 130
Zeitlin, Froma, 65, 78
Zhong, Stephanie C., 183, 185
Zola, Emile, 3, 120, 126–128, 131–132, 137, 147; works by:
  Nana, 120, 126–127, 131